16.50

The Soviet Scholar-Bureaucrat

The Soviet
Scholar-Bureaucrat

M.N. Pokrovskii and the Society of
Marxist Historians

George M. Enteen

The Pennsylvania State University Press
University Park and London

With gratitude to my mother and father

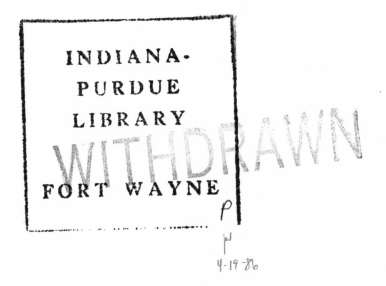

Library of Congress Cataloging in Publication Data

Enteen, George M.
  The Soviet scholar-bureaucrat.

  Includes bibliography and index.
  1. Pokrovskii, Mikhail Nikolaevich, 1868–1932.
  2. Historians—Russia—Biography. 3. Russia—
  Historiography. I. Title.
  DK38.7.P62E57   947'.007'2024   78-50002
  ISBN 0-271-00548-3

Contents

vi   *Contents*

Preface

One of the chief impediments to American studies of Russian history is the difficulty of evaluating the writings of Soviet historians. The elementary process of verifying facts often proves difficult, as does the more complex task of appraising their interpretations. Yet the current interest of Western historians in Soviet historiography attests to the need to remove this impediment. For American studies to remain rooted in pre-World War I interpretations is clearly inadequate: in no field of humanistic scholarship have interpretations and basic conceptions withstood the impact of subsequent events without major revision. Separating the wheat from the chaff in Soviet historical writing is an imperative undertaking.

One approach to this problem is historiographical study in its classical sense: the tracing of the development of the study of a specific historical event or movement, such as the *oprichnina* or the Decembrist uprising. By surveying the new sources, cataloguing the facts, and evaluating the relationships alleged to exist among them, one may determine the current status of a given problem. Another method is to attempt to reconstruct the major lines of evolution of the Soviet historical profession: using historical treatises and the activities of historians as source materials, one may chart the major tasks and problems of Soviet historians. This book employs the second method.

Any study of the early periods of Soviet historiography must center on the person of Mikhail Nikolaevich Pokrovskii. His life is so closely bound to the events of the 1920s and early 1930s that to exclude his biography would be to ignore a major part of the subject matter and to miss the point completely. By the same token, any attempt to study Pokrovskii would be empty if it did not set his career against the background of events taking place in the Soviet historical profession. This inquiry, then, is not historiography in the classical sense; it comes closer to what is called the sociology of ideas. It is a study of the evolution of a system of ideas and an attempt to take account of the forces conditioning the system. More precisely, it is an attempt to grasp the interaction between conscious ideology and the habits and practices of everyday life, between thought and circumstance.

My interest in Soviet historians was first aroused when I was an exchange student in Leningrad. It was less the writings of historians than their style in public discussion that brought on what I can only call a cultural shock. My provincialism had led me to expect only formal incantations or outright falsification, not the professional mastery of subject, the immense erudition and manifest love of the past that Soviet historians displayed. I had thought the restrictions of official vocabulary led Soviet historians to error, yet in Leningrad I observed that their assertions about history were very meaningful to them. If some of their questions were moot from my standpoint, I learned also that not all of my own were entirely empirical and without polemical content. To resolve the tension between my past and my present understanding of Soviet historiography, I began to study the renunciation of Pokrovskii in the 1930s. A survey of sources revealed the hopelessness of using the 1930s as a starting point. The main facts were assertions about Pokrovskii, yet these were obviously biased and in many instances false; in addition they were largely repudiated in the 1960s by their own authors. It became evident that I would have to make judgments of my own about Pokrovskii before I could evaluate statements about him. Of necessity, then, I studied the same subject matter as that treated by the Russian historians in their renunciation of Pokrovskii. In a sense I imitated Pokrovskii. I assumed that his ideas—his historical interpretations and his philosophical presuppositions about the historical process and the nature of historical knowledge—could be construed as a system, and that each component could be taken as a variable. Even in my preliminary reading of selected works, I was struck by the remarkable instability of Pokrovskii's views. Tracing the changes in Pokrovskii's views in quest for the underlying sentiment that would reconcile logical inconsistencies led me to understand that I could not confine my attention to the ideas themselves if I were to do more than construct a chronology. In other words, the system of ideas I assumed as present in Pokrovskii's intellectual legacy was not self-contained. Rather it was best considered as a variable in a larger system or as simply the expression of one of his roles in his society.

These conventional distinctions for a biographer created special difficulties for one working in Soviet history owing to limitations of source materials. I sensed that Pokrovskii's role in his family, his unconscious promptings, was a component in the larger system, but I myself could gain only faint images of this level of behavior, scarcely enough to convey anything to the reader or to demonstrate its impact on his ideas. Pokrovskii wrote an autobiography in the early 1920s, but this key work is consigned to archives where it awaits the attention of Soviet historians. Another important role of Pokrovskii's, with an obvious bearing on his scholarship, was his leadership of the historical sector, and his lead-ing role in the theoretical front. An assessment of Pokrovskii's ideas required constant reference to his administrative tasks, which in turn required reconstruction of the general milieu—if only in broad strokes. This plethora of facts—history, philosophy, organizations, passions—at times obscured Pokrovskii himself. After considerable study and pro-tracted conversations with Soviet historians, including a few of Pokrov-skii's students, I began to feel more at home in the milieu I was trying to reconstruct. Only then did I feel that I could accurately predict what I would find in the primary sources and appreciate the nuances in contem-porary Soviet writing about the earlier period. At this point I could construe Pokrovskii's ideas and the professional environment as expres-sions of his chief roles. I viewed each role as a component and the part of it that interested me as a variable in a system. The totality was Pokrovskii's behavior, if not Pokrovskii himself. I then realized that I was following the sage if not ancient advice of A.S. Lappo-Danilevskii, the eminent St. Petersburg Academician who was both a historian and a philosopher of history. With a traditional vocabulary, he defined the construct that I called a system. I was attempting to narrate the history of Russian thought "not merely in its leading principles but in its charac-teristic features, and not only in its general movement, but in its special development, which depends on local and temporal conditions of Rus-sian life." I viewed Russian thought and Soviet historiography in par-ticular as "part of a more complicated whole, namely consciousness," and sought to study it "under its relations to will and feeling."

My progress to this point confirmed an earlier suspicion that even by clarifying Pokrovskii's academic environment, I would not understand all the matters that puzzled me, for political events clearly helped shape the evolution of Pokrovskii's system. The premises shared by politicians and historians about the political consequences of scholarship foretold an intimate link between politics and scholarship. Yet even the politi-cians disagreed among themselves over details and implementation. Lenin, it is clear, opposed pluralism; non-Marxist theories could not legitimately compete with Marxism on equal terms in a dictatorship of the proletariat. There is little doubt, nevertheless, that he would have found distasteful the artificial uniformity and ritualization that existed under Stalin. Bukharin and Trotsky were closer to Lenin on this ques-tion, even if their views did not coincide with his fully. Their very ambiguity on this matter is part of their heritage. One cannot doubt, even if one cannot prove, that an outcome of the struggle for party leadership other than Stalin's triumph would have created different con-ditions for the writing of history. I nevertheless resisted the temptation to view scholarship as an epiphenomenon of political events, thus bringing party history into my narrative only briefly and mostly in the form of generalizations.

I shall forever be indebted to the many Soviet historians who shared their valuable time with me debating problems, some of which were of peripheral interest to them. Limitations of space do not permit my acknowledging all of them by name. I would like to express special gratitude to Academician I.I. Mints, who was Pokrovskii's assistant for a time at the Institute of Red Professors, and to M.E. Naidenov, of Moscow State University, and to his former graduate student V.A. Doroshenko. This study has benefited also from the advice and criticism of friends and colleagues in the United States. I would like to thank especially Ann Healy, Truman Cross, Stephen F. Cohen, Sheila Fitzpatrick, Elizabeth Valkenier, John M. Pickering, Carole Schwager, Thomas Magner, and S.V. Utechin, and above all Ronald B. Thompson, who supervised this work in its initial stage. I would like to acknowledge my debt also to the Library of Congress, the Fundamental Library of the Social Sciences (Moscow), the Hoover Institution, the International Research and Exchange Board (IREX), the Fulbright Program, the American Philosophical Society, and the Central Fund for Research of The Pennsylvania State University.

List of Abbreviations

Agitprop   Agitation and Propaganda Department of the Central Committee

GAIMK   State Academy of Material Culture

GUS   State Council of Scholars

IKP   Institute of Red Professors

Istpart   Commission for the Study of the October Revolution and the Russian Communist Party

KA   Communist Academy

RANION   Russian Association of Social Science Institutes

SMH   Society of Marxist Historians

Frequently cited sources are abbreviated as follows:

BH   *Brief History of Russia* (Pokrovskii, 1920–23)

BK   *Bor'ba klassov*

BKA   *Biulleten' kommunisticheskoi academii*

HR   *History of Russia from the Earliest Times to the Rise of Commercial Capitalism* (Pokrovskii, 1910–14)

HRM   *History of the Revolutionary Movement* (Pokrovskii, 1924b)

IM   *Istorik-marksist*

ISSSR   *Istoria SSSR*

ITsK   *Izvestiia TsK*

NBPM   *Na boevom postu marksizma*

NR	*Nauchnyi rabotnik*
OI	*Ocherki istorii istoricheskoi nauki v SSSR*
PM	*Problemy marksizma*
PR	*Proletarskaia revoliutsiia*
TP	*Trudy pervoi vsesoiuznoi konferentsii istorikov-marksistov*
VI	*Voprosy istorii*
VIKPSS	*Voprosy istorii KPSS*
VKA	*Vestnik kommunisticheskoi akademii*
VSA	*Vestnik sotsialisticheskoi akademii*

Introduction

Mikhail Nikolaevich Pokrovskii bridges three periods of twentieth-century Russian history. A contributor to prerevolutionary Russian culture, a guiding influence in early Soviet culture, and a symbol in Stalinist Russian culture—his name still arouses strong emotions and remains part of a complex generational conflict that promises to endure in Soviet life. Although it would be crude to say that when Stalin is up Pokrovskii is down, and vice versa, the suggestion is not wholly misleading. Pokrovskii's legacy is part of Stalin's legacy and will be an issue as long as Stalinism arouses controversy. Pokrovskii's life spans the great turning point in Soviet history—the collectivization of agriculture and the beginning of rapid industrialization. He witnessed and became endangered by Stalin's rise to power. He resembles an entire generation of revolutionaries, many of them leading figures in the 1920s, who suffered Stalin's wrath in the 1930s. Pokrovskii died in 1932, and the campaign of vituperation that followed was of unprecedented intensity against a scholar. Pokrovskii shared a fate of his former intellectual opponent Trotsky—his name defiled and his work proscribed. Pokrovskii resembled even more his old associate Bukharin: both had sought through judicious silence and timely dissembling to protect themselves and their associates and to keep faith with their most fundamental hopes.

The life of Pokrovskii also forms a bridge from the nineteenth to the twentieth century. As a young man he had chafed at the discipline of a revolutionary party; as an older man he became a transmission belt from the authority of the Bolshevik Central Committee. His life exemplifies the theme of a revolutionary turned administrator, a rebel who became not only a wielder of power but a symbol of it. In this sense, Pokrovskii was part of a worldwide phenomenon and shared a destiny with others of backgrounds and aspirations greatly different from his own. He represents numerous socialists who found themselves after World War I presiding over the destinies of others as cabinet ministers, trade-union officials, or Comintern functionaries. Pokrovskii resembles Maxim Gorky in this respect. The brilliant young rebel who had brought to life the uprooted and disinherited of Russia later became a chief codifier of socialist realism, a set prescription that greatly reduced the number of themes and forms that writers could legitimately employ. As a rebel turned administrator, Pokrovskii even resembles the American muckraker George Creel. During World War I, Creel, who had been an outspoken critic of political corruption, organized and headed the Committee on Public Information. He supervised the dissemination of a quantity of propaganda unprecedented before the Bolshevik Revolution. He mobilized the efforts of three thousand historians to put in pamphlet form the United States' reasons for entering the war. The former muckraker became a willing instrument of President Wilson.

Like many nineteenth-century theorists, Pokrovskii had assumed that socialism would be the consequence of prolonged capitalist development. The confinement of socialist revolution to Russia—the outcome of the Russian Revolution that brought the Bolsheviks to power even as it belied their earlier prognosis about world revolution—forced Pokrovskii to explain the rise of socialism in circumstances unforeseen in the Marxist classics. He is one of the intellectuals who, though possessing a deterministic outlook that saw men as subject to historical laws, helped to shape a new voluntaristic outlook that stressed the possibility of transforming human relationships in accord with conscious design through the agency of the state.

The investigator of early Soviet historiography again and again senses how important was the work of historians in Soviet life. Party officials and historians themselves demanded that the past be made useful. Industrialization, heroic leadership in World War II, enhanced status in the community of nations, even the passage of time—none of these could provide the vital links of identification and loyalty between the regime and the populace. Nor was there universal acceptance of roles delegated by virtue of images of the future. The church was of no avail, and the schools had achieved little impact. Thus even though there was so little Soviet history, so little experience marking the new path to the future, the burden of justification fell to the Marxist historians. Historians were, moreover, assigned the task of justification precisely when events seemed to belie expectations because the socialist revolution had been confined to a nation previously considered only completing a transition from feudalism to capitalism. The tensions of this circumstance are made apparent in Stalin's charge to historians to reconsider Lenin's legacy even when many prospective readers of historical works could remember the original forecast of world revolution. Nevertheless, the Marxist historians could ill afford to shirk this imposing burden, for party rule rested on promises about the future that claimed credibility by virtue of knowledge of the past.

Before 1917 Pokrovskii elaborated what he considered to be the Marxist-proletarian understanding of Russian history. By stressing the similarities between Russia and other European nations, he sought to show the "normality" of Russian autocracy: like any other state, Russia was the product of the interplay of class conflict. His system combated the national school of Russian historiography, a school that included most of Pokrovskii's predecessors and non-Marxist contemporaries, especially those who stressed the distinctiveness of Russian traditions and social evolution. They acknowledged a larger role for the state in unifying and shaping society than did Pokrovskii. In one way or another, and on virtually every page he wrote, Pokrovskii sought to prove that Russian autocracy was the instrument of merchant capital. Merchants and, equally important, serf-owning nobles who had been drawn into the market as producers and consumers used the state to fulfill their own needs. Russia was normal, according to Pokrovskii, in that merchant capital subordinated the state to its interests, and not the other way around.

From 1921 to 1928 Pokrovskii not only extended and disseminated his historical views, he performed as an "organizer of scholarship."[1] This phrase is difficult to define because there is no equivalent responsibility in American society. "Academic bureaucrat" suggests the closest equivalent—the scholar-administrator, possessed of both academic and entrepreneurial skills, who holds positions in private foundations, the government, and universities, and who thereby shapes science and educational policy at the state and university levels. Pokrovskii more than anyone else created the "historical front"—the phrase used to describe a hierarchical organization of scholars authorized to work out in full detail the Marxist understanding of the past and to show the falsity of rival theories. In the formative years of Soviet historiography, perhaps lasting as late as 1931, historians spoke in a variety of voices. The historical front was not monolithic but rather varied between pluralism and polarization, with blurred lines between camps as well as significant variations at each pole. Pokrovskii, related to both the Marxist scholars who manned the historical front and the non-Marxist scholars still in the field, was one of the few scholars Soviet officials deemed fit to lead in "using noncommunist hands in the building of communism."

Pokrovskii supervised a number of institutions discussed in this book. As deputy chairman of Narkompros, the Peoples' Commissariat of Education, and chairman of its State Council of Scholars (GUS), he was a major voice in policy making in higher education. He was also chairman of the Presidium of the Communist Academy (KA), a network of institutes that for a time sought to rival the older and better established Academy of Sciences. He supervised the education of historians and participated directly in the process as rector of the Institute of Red Professors (IKP) and as a member of the leadership of the Institute of History, one of the forebears of today's historical institutes of the Academy of Sciences. The Institute existed within several organizations before 1936; through much of the 1920s, it was a branch of the Russian Association of Social Science Research Institutes (RANION), which was a network of institutes where non-Marxists worked and taught under the supervision of Marxists. Pokrovskii led the Marxist historians most directly and the non-Marxists indirectly in his capacity as head of the Society of Marxist Historians (SMH). This offspring of Pokrovskii's scarcely outlived its creator; for a time it was almost his personal instrument on the historical front and the chief embodiment of the school of Pokrovskii.

Pokrovskii's justification of his policies, which can be termed his theory of cultural revolution, an enduring part of his legacy, is as important as the policies themselves. He shared the assumption prevalent among scholars and politicians that a close bond exists between scholarship and politics: historians should assist party authorities in effecting a cultural revolution by implementing a fundamental change in the popular outlook. They should help secularize, modernize, rationalize; that is, they should make scientific the traditional mentality of the Soviet peoples. An alteration of this sort was considered a prerequisite for building socialism. Pokrovskii devised a code of professional ethics for historians and for other scholars. He sought, within a framework of given assumptions about existence and consciousness, substructure and superstructure, to prescribe the most desirable relationships among scholars and between scholars and politicians.

Although Pokrovskii constantly reaffirmed the underlying theme of his system—the assertion of the class-dominated character of Russian autocracy—his interpretations of specific historical events were extremely unstable. So frequently did he change his mind that in my study of his writings the metaphor of a system gave way to the figure of a snake writhing as it shed its skin each season. In the last year of his life especially he performed a remarkable about face. In the face of criticism, he gave ground on issue after important issue. In general, he gave a more central place to the emerging concept of feudalism; in so doing, he increasingly limited and qualified his theory of merchant capital. It is questionable whether in the end anything remained to support his underlying theme.

Beginning in the second half of 1928, Pokrovskii changed his policies with respect to the organization of scholarship. For example, he played a major role in the liquidation of RANION's Institute of History. Then, to justify this policy, he modified his theory of cultural revolution. He abandoned the view that noncommunist hands were required for the building of communism. Thus ceasing to defend pluralism, he championed the quest for uniformity of scholarly opinion.

How is one to explain Pokrovskii's dramatic change? It is obviously connected with Stalin's triumph over Bukharin, his "revolution from above," which on the one hand transformed the Soviet socioeconomic order and on the other won him power and rendered him ever more secure. To avoid treating changes of ideas as a by-product of societal changes and to put the matter on a factual basis, it is necessary to provide links between these broad changes and the evolution of historical scholarship. One such link is what I refer to, for want of a better translation, as the theory of growing over (*teoriia pererastanie*)—a set of assumptions, hypotheses, and conclusions about Lenin's thought and about modern Russian history. This theory is the culmination of efforts of Soviet Marxist historians to accommodate the circumstance of an allegedly socialist revolution being confined to a nation just completing the transition from feudalism to capitalism. It seeks to demonstrate above all that this outcome was neither fortuitous nor a surprise. Lenin had foreseen it, the theory asserts, even before 1917, thereby anticipating the theory of socialism in one country. Moreover, the theory of growing over is an attempt to outline the economic and political processes that led to this outcome and to demonstrate thereby that Lenin's expectation was not a guess but a scientifically valid conclusion. Pokrovskii played an important role in elaborating the theory of growing over, probably not realizing at the outset that it contradicted in some instances and made superfluous in others his theory of merchant capital.

This modification of Pokrovskii's historical syntheses cannot be explained fully by reference to the theory of growing over, for the activities of historians were never matters of fact and inference entirely. Clash of personality, political difference, professional rivalry, and generational conflict were evident at each stage of Pokrovskii's work. In fact neither Pokrovskii's evolution nor the theory of growing over can be grasped without reconstruction of the major policies advanced with respect to scholarship and without delineation of the most important polemics engaged in by historians.

Pokrovskii's ideas were not highly esteemed by non-Marxist academic historians, and, despite his preeminence in the Marxist camp, some of his ideas were rejected in the early 1920s by Trotsky and by some party intellectuals who were far removed politically from Trotsky. In the second half of the 1920s, Pokrovskii's ideas were subjected to what might be considered normal academic criticism by his students. None of this prepared him for the fierce disputes that erupted in 1929. His critics, young and old, found a champion in Emelian Iaroslavskii, an old Bolshevik whose association with Stalin and Kaganovich gave considerable weight to his words. Fighting a rear-guard action, Pokrovskii altered his synthesis of Russian history, and he recast his theory of cultural revolution in such a fashion as to enlarge and exalt the emerging notion of *partiinost'* (party-mindedness). In describing Pokrovskii's struggle to preserve his authority, I have sought to make visible the mechanisms of change in Soviet historical scholarship. I hope that I have also provided suggestions that will interest students of Soviet politics.

The sources on Soviet historiography in the 1920s are not only more abundant and less opaque than those of the 1930s, they have been studied and enlarged upon by Soviet historians in recent years. The single most important source for this study is the published works of Pokrovskii. I have profited by the extensive and expert editing of his *Selected Works* (four volumes, 1965–67), whose appearance represents a great service to the Russian-reading public. It should be noted, however, that the republished texts of *Russkaia istoriia s drevneishikh vremen* (*Russian History since Ancient Times*) and *Russkaia istoriia v samom szhatom ocherke* (*Brief History of Russia*) are the ones that most closely approximate current Soviet interpretations. They reflect Pokrovskii's understanding of Russian history late in life, when he was trying to accommodate his synthesis to ideas then current. In brief, they are the least distinctively Pokrovskian.

A two-volume collection of Pokrovskii's writings, *Istoricheskaia nauka i bor'ba klassov* (*Historical Scholarship and Class Conflict*), published shortly after his death, has been reprinted in the United States.[2] Although these volumes reveal Pokrovskii's basic ideas about a variety of matters and show something of the evolution of his thought, a word of caution about them is also in order. They project Pokrovskii's favorite image of himself late in life—an unrelenting militant. They minimize the confusion he felt at certain moments, his vacillation, and even his temporizing in some matters of academic policy. I thought it unfortunate that these volumes were unavailable to me when I began to study Pokrovskii's writings. Now I think there are dangers in reading each major writing only in the context of other major writings. I would recommend to a future specialist that whenever possible, she or he read Pokrovskii's articles in the original journal or newspaper, that is, analyze them in the context of contemporary chronicles, reviews, and headlines. The great majority of Pokrovskii's writings and the most important ones can be found in the leading American libraries. I found a few other works in Soviet libraries; the most useful of these was a collection of Pokrovskii's letters published in 1933 by their recipient, Pavel Ossipovich Gorin, Pokrovskii's friend and aide. They and some archival extracts quoted in recent Soviet writings afforded me my only look behind the scenes.

Although numerous journals and books were consulted, a few journals that are available in the United States yielded much of the information: *Istorik-marksist* (*The Marxist Historian*), the chief publication of the Society of Marxist Historians and a remote predecessor of today's *Voprosy istorii; Bor'ba klassov* (*Class Struggle*), a popular historical journal published by the Society of Marxist Historians beginning in 1931; *Vestnik kommunisticheskoi akademii* (*Herald of the Communist Academy*), the most important single source for a variety of public discussions and for the history of the social sciences until 1936; *Proletarskaia revoliutsiia* (*Proletarian Revolution*), the chief publication on party history and the history of the Revolution, contains articles, discussions, reviews, memoirs, and correspondence. Also useful was *Nauchnyi rabotnik* (*Scientific Worker*), absorbed by *Front nauka i tekhniki* (*The Scientific and Technical Front*) in 1931, which helped me construct a chronology and informed me to some degree of events in fields other than historiography.

In Moscow I found two useful sources unavailable elsewhere, *Biulleten' kommunisticheskoi akademii* (*Bulletin of the Communist Academy*), published by the Information Department of the Presidium of the Academy and designed for internal communication,[3] and *Teoreticheskii front* (*Theoretical Front*), a newspaper, usually four pages, published about the activities of the Communist Academy.[4] These publications provided more detailed accounts than the general public chronicles. Since the information was of the same sort, they served to verify the accuracy of the chronicles. The editorials in *Teoreticheskii front* provided something of a check on my interpretations. The distinction between primary and secondary sources on historiography often becomes blurred; contemporary reflections on the state of the profession can be interpreted as both or either, as can latter-day ruminations set down by people who had participated in earlier events.

Historiography even before the Revolution was a major field for Russian historians; it held and holds a more prominent place in Russian than in American scholarship. This most likely reflects the familiar self-consciousness of Russian culture. In the 1920s historiography in part constituted a means for combating the influence of non-Marxist historians. In the late 1950s and 1960s it constituted a means of de-Stalinization. Although historiographical writing of the Stalinist period, especially the voluminous denunciations of Pokrovskii, are often resplendent with falsification and bad taste, some of it has redeeming value. For example, the most searching analysis of Pokrovskii's work was written by N.L. Rubinshtein (1941).* He has a talent for disentangling facts from conclusions and for ferreting out assumptions implicit in definitions; his work is

---

*Sources referred to by author and date in the text are given in full in the Bibliography.

a model of historiographical analysis. Even the writings of A.M. Pankratova, some of which are cited in later chapters, beneath their histrionics reveal challenging formulations about the significance of particular events in the evolution of Soviet historiography. More clearly than anyone else she posed the problem of determining the importance of Stalin's intervention in and party supervision of historical writing.

Soviet historiographical writings of the 1950s and 1960s are a source of unique value. My own work could not have been carried out without benefit of the polemical disputation that occurred after Stalin's death, for Soviet historians harvested an abundance of facts elucidating a variety of themes. The writings embody what to me are some of the best features of Soviet historiography: explicit concern with definition and discriminating use of models, that is, careful differentiation between mental constructs and documented events. In general, they display the elegance associated with formality and rigor. They also show scrupulous regard for facts, though it must be borne in mind that whole areas are removed from investigation, blurred, or misrepresented owing to political commands. The writings thereby enforce limitations that impel a foreign historian to retrace steps taken by Soviet scholars. Perhaps an attempt to identify these limitations will help clarify my assumptions.

In Soviet historiographical writings of the 1950s and 1960s, a single concern dominated the selection of facts and the formulation of themes. To what extent do past historical interpretations approximate or advance into present interpretations? How did each event and each idea contribute to the Leninist understanding of the past? How did the Leninist understanding of the past contribute to the building of socialism? In sum, how did we come to understand things as we do and come to be what we are? The assumption of Soviet historians that patterns of development other than the ones actually realized in the past did not exist is perhaps as sound as the contrary assumption. But the disinclination to see that the past, when it was present, contained a variety of perceptions of what the future would be is a shortcoming with definite consequences. Only in a rudimentary sense do Soviet historians, in the writings in question, treat matters as though tensions and contrasts between rival definitions of socialism were part of the substance of events. For example, the very way that competing historians posed the question of party supervision of scholarship bore implications about the nature of the socialism that was in the process of being built. The writings in question, then, fail to note that current opinions derive from existential circumstances as well as from the logic of ideas. They have the same conditional nature as do past opinions.

This perspective or approach is not confined to Marxist-Leninist writings; if it is very widespread in Soviet historical writings, it is, in some writings, subdued and overshadowed by other perspectives. But in writings on historiography it has crowded out most other perspectives. It betrays a measure of complacency and reveals a certain vested interest among historians; to a considerable degree, it is an outgrowth of political pressures. A principal danger of it is the undermining or destruction of the authenticity of the past. If an event is evaluated only with respect to its contribution to the present, the immediate consequences for participants—the marks left on individuals—are lost. The public as well as the historians are deprived of vicarious experience, and the past is made less usable. Though it justifies the present, it does not detach one from it. The future, as a result, is less rich in possibilities.

Perhaps it would be fairer for me simply to state that some of my assumptions and preferences differ from those of Soviet historians and cause me to seek some facts and pursue some themes that are of little interest to them. How my bias in favor of the existence of autonomous publics as a favorable condition of scholarship shapes my definition of the subject matter should become clear to the reader in the chapters that follow.

I have also drawn on the ideas of Western scholars, including Russian émigrés. An established body of commentary on the Soviet historical profession and a few works that can be considered historical exist. Historical scholarship has been the object of more study than any other academic discipline in the Soviet Union, though, at the same time, it has received far less attention than has the history of literature. Pavel Miliukov's 1937 observations on the posthumous fate of Pokrovskii are penetrating and still useful. The refined formulations of Frederic Lilge (1948) have been very helpful to me. Many of the essays in the 1962 volume edited by Cyril E. Black, especially those of Leo Yaresh, have proved to have enduring value. The writings of Paul Aron (1963) represent an elegant if somewhat premature synthesis on the evolution of Soviet historiography. I should point out, nevertheless, that work in this field as a whole is so fragmentary that it is impossible to devise even an elementary system of classification. No enduring controversies exist in the Western literature; no significant evolution or maturity of understanding has been gained. These remarks should be taken as a plea for more research in this field.

The advantages of a thorough historical understanding of Soviet historiography for the specialist in Soviet history are obvious. Only slightly less obvious are the advantages for specialists in the earlier periods of Russian history, who would be enabled to make better use of the findings of their Soviet counterparts. I hold the conviction that historiography is an ideal training ground for all specialists in Soviet affairs—political scientists, geographers, economists, and others. Too often the

Western specialist advocates a reverse application of Lenin's injunction to use only the facts when reading presentations by bourgeois professors: he tries to extract data while ignoring the conceptual apparatus of Soviet scholars. Historical understanding would help reveal the premises, working conditions, and political setting of Soviet social scientists. It would help the Western specialist identify the distinctive features of Soviet scholarship and comprehend the limits and bearing of Soviet assertions and concepts. If scholars, instead of just denying the conclusions of others, would rather refine their own conclusions in the light of contrary assertions, a genuine exchange of opinion could occur.

In the first two chapters I set forth the major facts of Pokrovskii's life and sketch the most salient features of his historical system in the form it took on the eve of the creation of the Society of Marxist Historians in 1925. In the following chapters I trace the changes in his system and account for them with primary reference to the activities of Marxist historians but with reference also to political conflicts.

1   Historian and Revolutionary

The most important events in the life of Mikhail Nikolaevich Pokrovskii coincide with major events in the history of the Russian Communist Party and the Soviet Union. The removal of Nikita Khrushchev from the Party Presidium in 1964 and the attendant call for "objectivity" about Stalin cast a new shadow over Pokrovskii's legacy. In 1956, Khrushchev's de-Stalinization speech at the Twentieth Party Congress paved the way for a reassessment of Pokrovskii and his return to the pantheon of revolutionary heroes. The year of Pokrovskii's death, 1932, marked the completion of the first five-year plan; in 1934, the effort to eradicate Pokrovskii's views was initiated. "The Teaching of Civic History in the Schools of the USSR,"[1] the decree that signaled the attack, also set into motion a major ideological and cultural reorientation. The attack on Pokrovskii grew in harshness and scope until in 1936 he was denounced publicly; by 1940 two special volumes (*Protiv*, 1939, 1940)—one of them entitled *Against the Anti-Marxist Conceptions of M.N. Pokrovskii*—sought to dislodge Pokrovskii's interpretation of Russian history while setting forth the Stalinist reinterpretation. The year of the left turn in the worldwide communist movement, 1928, also witnessed the celebration of Pokrovskii's sixtieth birthday. A grand public occasion, it armed Pokrovskii with the authority he needed to implement the party's tasks on the historical front. The Bolshevik Revolution in 1917 had created the possibility for Pokrovskii to act as the arm of the party in the field of historical scholarship. And it was the Revolution of 1905 that had simultaneously forged the mettle of Bolshevism and completed Pokrovskii's conversion to Marxism.

Youth and Education

Pokrovskii described the years before 1905 as his time of "democratic illusions and economic materialism" (1924d:210). He was born in Moscow near the close of the decade of reform, August 17, 1868. As his name suggests, he was descended from a clerical family. Though his father and grandfather had been state officials, and the latter had advanced sufficiently to become a permanent member of the estate of nobility,[2] his earlier forefathers had been priests or deacons. "I became interested in history at the age of seven," Pokrovskii recalled. "The first serious books I read were historical." Pokrovskii seems to have acquired a critical attitude toward the authorities, perhaps even a touch of radicalism, at home. His father's attitude toward church and state "was very realistic, to say the least." As a child he "forever heard all sorts of talks about the abuses of the administration, about the unenlightened lives of the higher officials and the Tsarist family, etc." Thus "not for a single instant" was he "ever a monarchist" (Sokolov, 1970:45–46).

Pokrovskii attended the same gymnasium as had his father, one noted for its training in classical languages. After being examined in a dozen subjects, including, Greek, Latin, French, and German, he was awarded a gold medal.[3] At the age of nineteen, he enrolled in the Historico-Philological Faculty of Imperial Moscow University. Pokrovskii had the good fortune of studying under V.O. Kliuchevskii, perhaps Russia's greatest historian, and P.G. Vinogradov, the eminent medievalist who later taught jurisprudence at Oxford University.

Some of Pokrovskii's fellow students were also marked for distinction. He attended classes with the future historians P.N. Miliukov, who was to become one of the main leaders of Russia's Constitutional Democratic (Kadet) Party, A.A. Kizevetter, also a future Kadet, N.A. Rozhkov, who was to be a Marxist historian, associating himself first with the Bolsheviks and then later with the Mensheviks, and D.M. Petrushevskii, a specialist in European medieval history who was destined to play the role of antagonist to Pokrovskii in the 1920s.

Pokrovskii received his diploma in 1891 and was thereupon invited to engage in advanced study with a view toward pursuing an academic career. He continued his study of European and Russian history, with most of his attention going to the latter subject. For some still unknown reason Pokrovskii later lost the confidence of his teacher. A dispute with Kliuchevskii during the master's examination, for which Pokrovskii had spent three years preparing, terminated his formal study. He never wrote a dissertation, nor did he prepare trial lectures or become a university lecturer (*privat dotsent*).[4] Sure of his calling, however, he lived by his wits—teaching in pedagogical institutes and secondary schools, giving private instruction,[5] and participating in what roughly corresponds to university extension courses for the underprivileged[6]—while continuing to train himself as a historian.

Pokrovskii began to write scholarly works while he was still associated with Moscow University. He reviewed books on Russian and Western European history for the bibliographical section of the liberal-populist journal *Russkaia mysl.*[7] He contributed eight articles on European history to a series of anthologies prepared under the supervision of Vinogradov.[8] Pokrovskii's lengthy articles testify to the breadth of learning expected of nineteenth-century scholars. He expounded his views on Russian history in an anthology edited by V.N. Storozhev (1898). In these writings he stressed the similarities between Russian and European economic processes, social categories, and legal institutions; he affirmed the historical existence of a Russian species of feudalism. Another of his characteristic ideas—one that I consider the axis of his system—was expressed as early as 1903: even before he became a Marxist, he had formulated the thesis that he would later consider the essence of the proletarian interpretation of Russian history. He undertook a polemic against what he was to call the supraclass theory of the state. The notion that Russian autocracy was the initiator of social change rested on "partly metaphysical, partly practical, in any case non-scientific presupposition" (1903:225). The Russian state, like all others, was the creature and instrument of social classes rather than their creator.

Pokrovskii disliked itinerant lecturing. In 1900, he requested Miliukov's assistance in finding a regular academic position (Miliukov, 1937:370); in 1902, however, the government authorities forbade his lecturing in public.[9] By that time, he had acquired family responsibilities, having married Liuba Nikolaevna, the daughter of a Muscovite merchant who had employed Pokrovskii as her tutor (Serebriakov, 1963). It is not clear how he supported himself. It was probably at this time that he became acquainted with the Muscovite Social Democrats, for about a year or so later he began to contribute to *Pravda,* a Marxist journal greatly influenced by A.A. Bogdanov.[10]

If Pokrovskii's path of professional development was checkered, so also was his ideological development—his path to Marxism. Most of his Russian biographers with access to archives depict a straightforward development, constant growth toward a preset goal. It is possible that they have been unduly influenced by Pokrovskii's own remarks made when he was eager to stress the soundness of his credentials as a Marxist, and when as a public figure he wished to show the path to Marxism as natural for any moral and intelligent person. At any rate, Soviet historians have ignored or overlooked a contemporary source published in the West—the memoirs of Pokrovskii's classmate Kizevetter. This unfriendly critic indicates that he was surprised by Pokrovskii's becoming a Marxist. Pokrovskii's path was probably neither as direct as Soviet historians indicate nor as mysterious as Kizevetter implies.

As noted earlier, Pokrovskii testified to having acquired a critical or even oppositional attitude toward the Tsarist government at a tender age. While still at home, he added, he lost his religious faith (Sokolov,

1970:46). "Hatred of bourgeois liberalism," he recalled in public remarks in 1928, he had nourished even at gymnasium. Yet there is no basis to think that political differences led to his altercation with Kliuchevskii. Pokrovskii said of himself that he became a "historical idealist" in the early 1890s, then later in the same decade an "economic materialist" and a "bourgeois democrat" (*NBPM:*36–37). In his unpublished autobiography, apparently written shortly after the Revolution for party records, he referred to himself in the student years as a "completely academic person." "I knew of Marx only by hearsay," he wrote. "Nevertheless, even as a student I independently worked out an historical world outlook—frequently materialistic, but not dialectical, i.e., devoid of revolution and class conflict" (Sokolov, 1970:50; 1964:81). But he affirmed the apolitical character of his outlook in the years before he began lecturing: "I was a timid undergraduate, packed with books, a head swollen with knowledge which I grasped from an academic standpoint, without any social consciousness." From the middle of the 1890s "step by step, from a timid undergraduate . . . developed a person with definite views" (Sokolov, 1970:50–51). He seems to have imbibed the doctrine of legal Marxism. In the late 1890s, in his own words, he "began studying Marxism, in the first year undoubtedly inclining toward revisionism." Legal Marxism was not "revolutionary, [which] means [it] was not genuine Marxism" (Lutskii, 1965:341). The period of Pokrovskii's apprenticeship as a revolutionary was to trouble both him and later his detractors and supporters. He noted late in life: "He who has experienced legal Marxism usually carries traces of that experience for a long time, certain survivals, unhealthy survivals of that non-dialectical, albeit materialist explanation of history" (1933, 2:268).

Pokrovskii's political-ideological stand even at the close of the century is not clear; thus it is by no means certain that he should be considered a Marxist. In 1898, P.B. Struve, then a prominent legal Marxist, presented an address about serfdom to the Moscow Juridical Society. Both Marxists and their populist rivals flocked to the meeting; the clamor was such that the meeting could be brought to order only be ejecting some of the excited students. Pokrovskii described his participation in the discussion presenting himself as the standard-bearer of Marxism:

> Thanks to my inability and complete awkwardness, I was beaten. Oh, it was difficult then to go against the authority of Struve. . . . A few hundred students and coeds furiously applauded him for five minutes. But Struve's report, especially his concluding remarks, showed me just how light was the scholarly equipment of this "leader." This made defeat in the dispute even more bitter: But defeated armies, it's said, learn well. (Sokolov, 1970:51–52)

According to Kizevetter, however, when Struve had finished,

> a small, uncomely person asked for the floor and began in a
> squeaky voice to take issue with the speaker. He did not agree
> with the avant-garde ideas of the speaker; he affirmed the gener-
> ally accepted standpoint of earlier liberal historiography. And that
> person, arguing with the standard-bearer of Marxism, was—Mik-
> hail Pokrovskii.[11]

Only after the turn of the century, in fact after Pokrovskii had been
forbidden to lecture and when he had begun to associate with Social
Democrats, is it fully evident that he had acquired a special interest in
Karl Marx. He worked hand-in-hand with I.I. Skvortsov-Stepanov, a
future editor of *Izvestiia* and *Pravda,* and with A.A. Bogdanov. This
connection with Bogdanov, a philosopher-politician who was to emerge
as one of Lenin's principal rivals within the Bolshevik Party, influenced
Pokrovskii's entire life and even his posthumous fate. Bogdanov's theory of ideology and his program for proletarian culture influenced Pokrovskii's image of himself and his understanding of his responsibilities as
a proletarian historian. It was his troubled affiliation with Bogdanov that
subsequently jeopardized Pokrovskii's standing as an old Bolshevik.

Pokrovskii nevertheless retained some ties with academic circles. "I
never received *Iskra* [a Social-Democratic newspaper], perhaps it was
my own fault," he wrote. "I obtained *Osvobozhdenie* [a liberal journal]
regularly" (Sokolov, 1966:7). In contradiction to other recollections
about his early life, he wrote that even as late as 1904, "I was a typical
'academic' . . . so insensitive [that I] could even get along with bourgeois democrats; only bourgeois liberals had begun to sicken us"
(1924d:210). Kizevetter, seeking to cast doubt on the authenticity of
Pokrovskii's revolutionary pedigree, reports that in 1905 Pokrovskii participated in conferences that gave birth to the constitutional Democratic
Party. In discussions, Kizevetter states, Pokrovskii stood with the conservative faction; "literally on the eve of becoming a Bolshevik," he
moved in Kadet circles.[12]

The Revolutionary

In 1905, Pokrovskii was thirty-seven years of age. He was short and
slightly built, with a head made prominent by eyes magnified through the
thick lenses of his spectacles. His demeanor suggested a ready wit and
an aggressiveness rooted in a sense of justice violated. He seems to have
been a militant historian even before he became a revolutionary. It was
in 1905, he wrote, that for him "class struggle . . . became a living fact"
(1924d:210). In April he stepped over to the Marxist camp. He became a

Bolshevik by collaborating with a team of lecturers that included Skvort-sov-Stepanov, Rozhkov, and V.M. Friche, a Marxist literary critic ("Traurnyi," 1932:71). The group frequently met at Rozhkov's apartment, and it was here that Pokrovskii became acquainted with a revolutionary publicist whose career curiously paralleled his own and who was to emerge as his principal antagonist—Emelian Iaroslavskii.

Together with Rozhkov and Stepanov, Pokrovskii helped organize a union of teachers. He urged the teachers not to adopt a platform that would appeal to all political parties. At a teachers' congress held later in Finland, he introduced a Social-Democratic program. Pokrovskii led a withdrawal of Social-Democratic sympathizers from the congress following the adoption of a liberal program ("Traurnyi," 1932:90). In June, the Moscow Committee dispatched Pokrovskii to Geneva, where he met Lenin. Even though the Bolshevik leader invited Pokrovskii to collaborate in his Geneva-based newspaper, *Proletarii,* one senses a slight disappointment on Pokrovskii's part. Lenin's preoccupation with armed uprising seemed somehow fanciful. Returning to Moscow with a quantity of illegal literature, Pokrovskii continued his work as a publicist, speaking and writing against the future Kadets. Though he was to boast of victories over the liberals, he directed some critical observations at what he considered to be his own party's doctrinaire opposition to the liberal intelligentsia: in a polemic against V.D. Bonch-Bruevich, a more experienced Bolshevik publicist, Pokrovskii urged that the Bolsheviks gloss over or at least not magnify their differences with the liberals, which he believed would be a sounder strategy for persuading uncommitted teachers to join the Bolsheviks. To Lenin this reflected Pokrovskii's inexperience in politics. By October Pokrovskii had come around and was ending his speeches with the cry "Long live armed uprising" (Sokolov, 1968:8–9; 1970:56–57).

In the small circle of Muscovite Bolsheviks, a professor of astronomy, K.K. Shternberg, became an expert on explosives, and Pokrovskii, using the name Domov, established himself as an authority on military strategy ("Traurnyi," 1932:71–72). He had the honor of being supervisory editor of the final (ninth) issue of *Bor'ba,* which called workers, soldiers, and citizens to armed uprising. The very next day he found six barricades around his own street (Lutskii, 1965:343). The strikes and uprisings had an emotional impact on Pokrovskii, tempering his revolutionary commitments. Twenty-three years later he wrote, "I appeared before the workers as a propagandist, but in fact they taught me, because only in the struggle of the workers in 1905 did I actually see before myself the genuine mass movement, the genuine class conflict which hitherto I had only read about in books" (1933a, 2:299). During the fighting in Moscow his apartment became something of a field hospital and communications center. After the uprising's defeat Pokrovskii was arrested and his apartment searched. He was released after a few days owing to lack of evidence.[13]

After the Revolution of 1905, Pokrovskii remained active in revolutionary politics, and he renewed his scholarly pursuits. Though he held high posts and moved in leading party circles, his political activities had less long-term significance than his activities after October, when he was further removed from the centers of power. A month after the Moscow uprising, he was taken into the fighting organization of the Moscow Committee, and in 1906, he was brought into the Committee itself. The police subjected his living quarters to frequent search, and when in August a wave of arrests swept over the Moscow Bolsheviks, Pokrovskii abruptly left for the Caucasus. "I had to disappear from the horizon," he later wrote about his departure (Lutskii, 1965:344–45). Evidently the authorities changed their minds about the Bolshevik danger, for Pokrovskii returned in October to participate in the electoral campaign for the Second Duma, personally conducting numerous meetings. Bukharin affectionately recalls Pokrovskii as a

> brilliant warrior in the Duma electoral campaign; . . . our darling but venomous Mikhail Nikolaevich—that Bolshevik poison was evident everywhere. How he made life miserable for our Kadet opponents! How it cheered the hearts of us young Bolsheviks— each well aimed blow at such pillars of Kadetism as Kizevetter, Novgorodtsev, and Miliukov! It was not an inarticulate shout or a cry of revolutionary desperation: it was a thoughtful, brilliantly argued, refined, and for all that a stunning blow. [With his] close cropped head, and his squinting, somewhat weak-sighted eyes looking through plain-rimmed glasses, he looked just like "the mother of the holy guillotine." (Bukharin, 1928)

Pokrovskii read popular historical lecturers to workers under the guise of giving music lessons. "The police, not seeing any direct musical success from our work, closed the door" (1965–67, 4:215). In the spring of 1907 he was sent by the Moscow Committee to the Fifth Congress of the Russian Social-Democratic Workers' Party in London, where he was made a candidate member of the Central Committee. The Bolshevik faction elected him to the Bolshevik Center[14] and placed him on the editorial boards of the chief Bolshevik publications. The police, taking advantage of his absence, made a thorough search of his apartment in Moscow and ordered his arrest. Returning to Russia, he had to reside in the Moscow suburbs (*na dache*). In August he journeyed to Finland to attend the Helsinki Conference of Social Democrats in the fall; there he was able to maintain close contact with Lenin and Bogdanov.

Instead of closer collaboration, intense contact between Lenin and

Pokrovskii brought out their differences. Lenin had urged Pokrovskii to write a history of the recent revolution; he even drafted an outline for him that enumerated the major themes. Evidently Lenin's sketch presupposed a protracted political holding action by the Bolshevik party (Sokolov, 1966:12–13). Pokrovskii, sharing Bogdanov's characteristic leftism, favored immediate revolutionary initiatives; he expected mass upheaval to resume within three or four years, culminating in a socialist revolution. He expressed the view, more accurate than he would concede later, that "each social class makes its own revolution; therefore the proletariat can execute only a socialist revolution." His prognosis excluded the host of stipulations involved in Lenin's distinction between a bourgeois revolution and a proletarian revolution and his theories about the transition from one to another. Pokrovskii affirmed that "the Russian revolution could succeed only as a socialist revolution" (1925b:1–2). He noted, "We know too well now that the Duma does not create miracles, that the path to freedom is thorny and bloody for the Russian people as for all peoples" (1907:11). Lenin did not approve Pokrovskii's revision of the proposed outline; the project was dropped. Nevertheless, collaboration between the two continued until Lenin departed from Finland with Pokrovskii's assistance.[15]

By 1909 Pokrovskii had to abandon his residence in Finland. In the spring, he traveled twice secretly but safely to Moscow to meet with his publishers and future scholarly collaborators. He also succeeded in making a trip to Paris for an important meeting of the Bolshevik Central organization. The meeting in which the followers of A.A. Bogdanov were drummed out of the party was not to be held, it turned out, until the summer. Pokrovskii was unable to wait. Owing to his wife's illness, he had to return to Finland. But it was probably on this trip that he had his long and evidently stormy meeting with Lenin, wherein the two thrashed out their differences. In vain Lenin sought to convince Pokrovskii that revisionism could not flourish on Russian soil. But he failed to shake Pokrovskii's convictions or to convince him that, in Bogdanov and his associates, he was keeping bad company (Pokrovskii, 1929b:21).

Back in Finland, Pokrovskii was being sought by the police. They had no photograph of him, only a general description: "light red hair, below average height, heavy, clean-shaven, wears a pince-nez." Pokrovskii was warned of his danger by Vaine Takanen, a Finnish police official, who, it seems, regularly aided Russian political refugees. Pokrovskii took a step that was either extremely audacious—and placed total confidence in the inefficiency of the police—or was extremely naive. He wired the police in the district of his former residence in Moscow, requesting that they inform the authorities in Helsinki that "no obstacles existed to [his] leaving the country." On August 25 Pokrovskii "personally wrestled" with the office of the governor general of Finland for a passport. It was not issued, but, at the same time, Pokrovskii was not arrested even though a search circular dated August 22 had been issued for his arrest. The search circular was the response to his wire to Moscow. His arrest was scheduled for August 28. Just a day or two earlier, it seems, he boarded ship and fled. His library reached him in Paris in November; his wife and four-year-old son joined him a few months later (Gukovskii, 1968:130–31).

Just after he established himself in Paris, he spent two weeks in Capri, lecturing on Russian history at the Bogdanovite school organized under the auspices of Maxim Gorky. His lectures elaborated the basic plan for his *History of Russia since Ancient Times*, and at this time he consolidated his ties with the Forwardists.

The Forwardists

Philosophical differences had led to estrangement between Lenin and Bogdanov; controversy arose later about party funds and armed expropriations. After Bogdanov had been expelled from the Bolshevik faction, he and his associates set up an opposition group known as Forward (*Vpered*).[16] The Forwardists represented a species of radicals who favored the most militant means of action. Bolshevism attracted them in 1905 because it seemed to be the most uncompromising revolutionary force in action. They broke with Lenin, or rather he broke with them over the feasibility of employing parliamentary institutions for revolutionary ends. The legend of the barricades, it seems, excited these men of letters more than did the image of the ballot box. The spontaneous creativity of the masses, to their minds, rendered superfluous the stratagems of politicians, yet most of them rejoined Lenin in 1917 when he again adopted a radical posture. Though differences remained, the former Forwardists were to play a prominent role in the history of Soviet culture (Utechin, 1958). In short, one possible interpretation of this period is that it was Lenin who had departed from the original variety of Bolshevism only to return to it in 1917 (Wolfe, 1955:520).

Pokrovskii later sought to minimize his differences with Lenin. Though conceding that he sided with the Forwardists as to the possibility of immediate revolutionary upheaval, he wrote that he stood as one with Lenin on the need to participate in the Third Duma. He denied ever having been an *otzovist* (one of those urging recall of the Bolshevik delegates to the Third Duma). He also denied ever having been a "Godbuilder," collaborating with or sympathetic to the efforts of Lunacharskii and Gorky to reconcile Marxism and religion. He recalled that Lenin had invited him to lecture at his party school in Longjumeau as evidence that theoretical differences were minor (1924e:286). An organizational question, Pokrovskii explained, was the primary cause of his break with Lenin—his suspicion that V.K. Taratuta, a member of the bureau of the Central Committee, was a provocateur.[17] Obviously, more than differences about organization matters caused the break. Pokrovskii was a Bogdanovite; if he did not share all the theoretical perspectives of the Forwardists, a group more heterogeneous than the Bolsheviks, he did share its outlook on spontaneous mass action. In addition, personal inclinations had a part. According to an Okhrana report, Pokrovskii had "considered himself unjustifiably insulted *by Lenin,* which he spoke about frequently."[18]

Soviet historians with access to archives dwell on Pokrovskii's remoteness from or proximity to Lenin. They thereby leave untold the details of their subject's relationship with Bogdanov—the prime mover of the Forward faction and one of the most influential thinkers in the formative period of Russian Marxism. The essence of Bodganov's understanding of Marxism was "finding obsolete elements and gaps in Marxian doctrine and trying to replace them and fill the gaps by modern ideas or by the products of one's own thought" (Utechin, 1964:213). Drawing on the ideas of the German philosophers Mach and Avenarius, Bogdanov moved away from dialectical materialism in the direction of logical positivism. He denied the universality of the dialectical process, a thesis which inevitably led him to go beyond the criticism of dialectical materialism to a reconstruction of the tenets of historical materialism. More than anything else Marx's theory of ideology dissatisfied him. His own view on the subject, which need not be expounded here, paralleled the work of others in the early twentieth century concerned with the origin and function of beliefs; it stressed the tentative, provisional character of ideas. Perhaps Pokrovskii caught the essence of Bogdanov's view in the phrase "Science itself moves and changes . . . there is no 'eternal' truth" (1920:12).

In Bogdanov's theory of history, the struggle of man against nature constituted the primary moving force, a view that stressed the importance of technology (Utechin, 1964:210). In the writing of history Bogdanov was highly original if rather schematic. He suggested, for instance, that feudalism could develop into a slave-owning order (1923:89). He emphasized the role of merchant capital in Russian history, a concept employed but not emphasized by Marx. Even this brief survey of Bogdanov's ideas reveals how greatly he influenced Pokrovskii. Merchant capital became a central theme in Pokrovskii's thinking, though he employed it in a distinctive and original manner. Bogdanov's emphasis on wholly economic factors reinforced what Pokrovskii had learned from legal Marxism. Although Lenin stressed arcane differences between dialectical materialism and logical positivism in Bogdanov's thought, it is difficult to see how and precisely in what way these matters influenced Pokrovskii, who was rather impatient with and even a bit hostile to the more recondite aspects of theory.

Bogdanov's cultural policy, however, influenced Pokrovskii's work. The Forwardists were anxious lest the middle class, through superior organizational ability, continue to dominate the workers. This shared feeling was part of the essence of the group. The bourgeoisie, they felt, might even control proletarian institutions, and they shared the conviction that the proletariat must create an independent outlook and in so doing transform itself into a collective body capable of creating socialism. In 1915, looking back on the heyday of the faction, an editorial in its journal noted:

> The idea of proletarian culture became the distinguishing trait of Forwardism. And we propagandized the idea within the party with all our strength, even more so when we observed elements of bourgeois thought and conflict in the international Social Democratic parties as a whole; opportunism had deep roots and serious significance in all the European parties. Hoping to overcome this within the workers' movement and fearing that it might lower the proletariat to subservience to the bourgeoisie, as we observe now, we moved into the foreground the idea of scientific-socialist education.[19]

Pokrovskii never worked out anything that could even be likened to a "theory" of proletarian culture, and one cannot assume that he simply adopted Bogdanov's. In fact he considered expressions such as proletarian scholarship to be indiscrete and unsuccessful. In 1910, as he approached the time of his break with the faction, he noted that the ideas stated in such terms were revisionist (*Bol'shaia*, 13:388–89). It is nevertheless undeniable that Pokrovskii held the conviction that the Russian proletariat must have its own interpretation of the Russian past, which it must counterpoise to the bourgeois interpretation. Even late in life he would revert to this theme. Though this was a conventional Marxist notion, it had special force for Pokrovskii because of his association with the Forwardists. For the rest of his life he manifested an especially sentimental attitude toward the working class.

The Forwardists, according to Pokrovskii, intended to create a separate party of their own. "As soon as I saw this, I shook the dust from my feet, and by spring 1911, I no longer had any relations with Forward" (Sokolov, 1964:83). Most of his time thereafter was spent in the Bibliothèque Nationale. In 1906 Pokrovskii had stated his philosophy of history in a brochure entitled *Economic Materialism*, which was promptly removed from sale by the Tsarist censors. From 1907 to 1910 he contributed to a nine-volume *History of Russia in the Nineteenth Century*.[20] In 1910 he began publication of *History of Russia since Ancient Times*.[21]

The *History of Russia since Ancient Times* absorbed most of Pokrovskii's energy from 1909 to 1913. Honoraria from his publisher provided him with better material circumstances than most Russian political refugees could afford. He resided in Paris but spent the summer of 1910 on the Isle of Jersey. He spent some time at the Forwardist schools in Capri and Bologna and made a few trips to the British Museum. But his working conditions were difficult. He complained constantly of the absence of important materials in the Bibliothèque Nationale and even more so of the poor organization of its Slavic holdings. The work appeared in installments, compelling Pokrovskii to meet numerous deadlines. He found himself, in addition to engaging in research and writing, constantly reading proof, fretting over reviews, worrying about sales, supervising the work of his collaborators, and arguing with his publishers about the format and price of the work. He was ill at times and sometimes worked in such haste that he had to send to St. Petersburg his hand-written rough drafts. He was fortunate that his life as an émigré, his years of external disorder, coincided with a period of internal order and great creativity.[22]

The last volume appeared in 1915; it was delayed by interfering censors and a court action that had begun in 1913. Mir Press, a publishing house established after the Revolution of 1905 and devoted to publication of radical, especially Marxist works, hoped that a few changes and deletions would save the volume. In the end, the entire stock was destroyed, and the work had to be rewritten.

History of Russia since Ancient Times is Pokrovskii's most complete, original, and elegant work. No doubt he was deeply gratified by the letter he received from a political prisoner incarcerated in Riga; the portions of the book he and his comrades had read, according to the letter dated April 12, 1914, created the impression that the "long-abused Russian people had finally found themselves, had finally found their true historian." His pen "brings to life the ancient manuscripts," and his "fiery language allows the ancient chronicles to speak again." By "clearly and simply" describing the ancient culture, "the freedom loving and creative energy of the Russian people," he nurtures faith "in the shining future of Russia" (Sokolov, 1970:72).

Pokrovskii's wartime research in the Bibliothèque Nationale resulted in publication of *Outlines of the History of Russian Culture*.[23] If his *History of Russia since Ancient Times* had been a response to Kliuchevskii,[24] this book, viewing Russian culture from an economic perspective, was his reply to Miliukov. He published articles in various

Social-Democratic journals, those of Lenin, Trotsky, and Gorky, and also in the liberal journal *Golos minuvshchego.* Early in 1916 he resumed his correspondence with Lenin. He edited and together with Gorky was in large measure responsible for the publication of Lenin's *Imperialism: The Highest Stage of Capitalism.*[25] With the outbreak of World War I Pokrovskii adopted a defeatist position: "During the war, I again became a Bolshevik in fact, though I made my relationship to the party formal only after having returned to the homeland in September 1917."[26]

Moscow

Once in Moscow, Pokrovskii received a party card that affixed his entry date as 1905. The Moscow Soviet of Workers' Deputies made him a delegate to the Democratic Conference, an assembly initiated by Kerenskii with the intent of providing popular support for the Provisional Government. The Bolsheviks made Pokrovskii one of their candidates for the Constituent Assembly, which made him a frequent speaker at mass meetings. After the seizure of power, he became a member of the Moscow Military-Revolutionary Committee and its commissar for foreign affairs. The Moscow Soviet of Workers' and Soldiers' Deputies elected him its chairman in November, which involved him actively in the governing of the city. In 1918 he became chairman of the Moscow Regional Council of Peoples' Commissars, a short-lived and historically neglected body. Nevertheless, most of Pokrovskii's energies were devoted to his duties as an editor of the *Izvestia of the Moscow Soviet of Workers' Deputies* (later called *Izvestiia of the Moscow Military-Revolutionary Committee*).[27]

To Bukharin again we are indebted for reminiscences of Pokrovskii in revolution. He recalled his fellow Muscovite's "calm and courageous detachment." With bullets flying, he was preoccupied with analysis of their trajectory. He is "some sort of *mathematician of insurrection,* our scholarly professor" (Bukharin, 1928). A declamation in the juncture between the October Revolution in Petrograd and the subsequent Bolshevik seizure of power in Moscow marks a high point in Pokrovskii's activity in national politics. The Moscow Military-Revolutionary Committee had publicly committed itself to armed uprising after the seizure of the Winter Palace. It had called its followers to attention but had not yet set them into action when, at its meeting on October 26, it received a telephone call from Colonel K.I. Riabtsev of the Provisional Government. He demanded that the committee cease arming the Red Guards. Under the influence of Viktor Pavlovich Nogin, a Central Committee member and high-ranking Bolshevik in

Moscow, the committee hesitated. One of the secretaries, A.A. Dodo-nova, went to the nearby offices of *Izvestia* and persuaded its editors Skvortsov-Stepanov and Pokrovskii to enter the meeting. We are told that Pokrovskii's speech, studded with references to the Paris Commune, stressed the "need for decisive action." The impact of his words is impossible to assess, because the Committee's dilemma was resolved when Riabtsev's adjutant called and advised the committee that military action against it had already begun (*Moskovskii*, 1968:34–35).

Just a few days after establishing Bolshevik power in Moscow, the Military-Revolutionary Committee created a Commissariat of Foreign Affairs for the purpose of establishing relations with the foreign consuls in Moscow.[28] Pokrovskii was made its head, and N.M. Lukin was designated his deputy. Lukin, a professionally trained historian, was still known by his revolutionary pseudonym, Antonov. This appointment marked the beginning of a long and close association between Pokrovskii and Lukin. The Committee instructed Pokrovskii to set up a passport bureau and also to find offices for the Commissariat of Foreign Affairs.

Pokrovskii also served the Military-Revolutionary Committee by drafting, in collaboration with Skvortsov-Stepanov, its "Decree on the Press," which was adopted without changes. What is striking about the decree today is its near apology for the restraints imposed upon the opposition press just after the seizure of power. But the decree itself should be thought of as a Bolshevik instrument in the electoral campaign for the forthcoming Constituent Assembly. Freedom was proclaimed for all parties, without exception, for agitation in the elections. The Committee stipulated that only authors who called for uprising against the Soviet government would be turned over to revolutionary courts (*Moskovskii*, 1968:212).

Although the high posts held by Pokrovskii in the Soviet apparatus in themselves make him a significant figure in the Moscow insurrection, he was clearly not one of the indispensable few. He stood a few steps away from the centers of power in the unfolding drama—the Moscow Regional Bureau and the Moscow Committee. With full justification he could write, "I at my very modest post was also a participant in the Revolution" (Sokolov, 1970:81). He always spoke modestly about his role as revolutionary and once referred to himself as a "mere journalist" (1924a). Reminiscing at the time of his sixtieth birthday, he coyly admitted that when a proposal was made in the Presidium of the Moscow Soviet to arrest the local Kadet leadership, he opposed it. He apologized also for the fact that as chairman he had arrested only two people, one of them by mistake (*NBPU:*35).

Pokrovskii was a member of the commission that drafted the constitution for the Russian Soviet Federated Socialist Republic (RFSFR), and in May 1918 he became deputy commissar of education, a post he was to hold throughout the remainder of his life. His last great adventure in high politics took place in connection with the Treaty of Brest-Litovsk. He entered the negotiations affirming that "the proletarian revolution . . . must spread on an all-European scale, or it will fall in Russia" (1917). It was this assumption that determined his stand at Brest-Litovsk and in the intraparty conflict that surrounded the negotiations. Yet the specific grounds of his opposition to the treaty are not altogether clear.[29]

Pokrovskii, together with many other Muscovite Bolsheviks, formed the faction of Left Communists, and he contributed to its short-lived journal, *Kommunist*. He supported Bukharin to the degree that he seceded from the party after the peace was signed. A State Department cable, dated March 31, 1918, from Maddir Summers in Moscow to Robert Lansing reports the following interview with Pokrovskii:

> The president of Moscow states that Russia has made no treaties regarding boundaries Ukraine, that Russia does not consider itself in state of war Ukraine and that Soviets will immediately withdraw all troops from this section to avoid giving Germany excuse carrying on further military operations and occupying further territory Russia as soon as conditions western front admit in order to control grain supplies and prepare for world shortage foodstuffs. He expects Moscow to be occupied in May. Regarding new army, he considers resistance to Germans impossible and will give them excuse to advance. He thinks Government will be compelled move beyond Volga and there re-constitute forces.[30]

Pokrovskii very likely was transmitting a message that if the Allies failed to support the Bolsheviks, German power in the east would increase as a result.[31]

A cable of June 6, 1918, from American ambassador David R. Francis, which was a plea against recognition of the Bolshevik government, contains the following passage: "Pokrovskii called yesterday says Soviet Government admits 'we are a corpse but no one has the courage to bury us . . . . ' "[32] Perhaps the safest interpretation of this remark is that Francis distorted Pokrovskii's meaning by failing to provide the context and by adapting it to his own purpose. Otherwise Pokrovskii's remark is either a gross indiscretion or evidence of a dimension of intraparty conflict not hitherto perceived. It may be necessary to revise the view that by late spring the Left Communists had abandoned their program for guerrilla warfare. At any rate, this involvement with the Left Communists represents Pokrovskii's last political difference with Lenin.[33]

This brief sketch of Pokrovskii informs us, however inadequately, as to what made him a Bolshevik historian. We know next to nothing about his early family life or what might be called his unconscious dispositions. I could glean only dim impressions of the man from the few personal materials available. Bukharin's sympathetic reminiscences stress his stern commitment to revolution. Miliukov remembers him as hostile to other historians. He recalls the youngest member of Vinogradov's seminar as one "usually morosely silent, [who] always wore a look of someone just insulted and not properly appreciated" (1937:370). Kizevetter reflected on his classmate's destiny:

> Of slight build and with a squeaky voice, he was distinguished by immense erudition, fluency of speech, and the ability to heap sarcasm on his opponents. Though quiet and mild in appearance, he concealed in himself an unhealthy conceit. He did not manifest, like Rozhkov, a candid directness of mind. And if at present [1929] after extensive practice the pose of a straightforward Bolshevik has finally settled upon him, it is the result of strenuous effort. (Kizevetter, 1929: 284–85)

Pokrovskii's fellow Bolsheviks, especially his students, have fonder memories. They recall his solicitous attention to his infirm wife. Those who knew him *na dache*—in informal situations beyond the reach of professional roles—remember especially his simplicity and democratic charm. His students recall how generously he shared his time with them and his patience in exercising supervision. A.I. Gukovskii, a former student, recently wrote:

> Pokrovskii gave much attention to the participants in the seminar. First of all, he manifested a genuine, vivid interest in the papers, and this encouraged each and all. There was nothing of the mentor in him, and this created a good comradely atmosphere. He was jarred by being addressed "Professor" and was pleased by the good Russian word, "Tovarishch." . . . Even in his brief remarks at the seminar, one sensed a vast mastery of the literature, which was disclosed in full in his extended papers, articles and books. Pokrovskii was ready with apt comparisons, often drew historical parallels, sometimes unexpected, but always the kind one remembered, and which called forth the necessary associations. He loved winged words, appropriate folk sayings, and eschewed aphorisms in foreign languages or the classical Latin and Greek formulas that gave one's speech the appearance of learning and that were invariably heard in the lecture halls of the pre-revolutionary universities. However an unusual turn of phrase or uncommon stress sometimes reminded one of his solid grounding in the classics.

Gukovskii remembered also the other side of Pokrovskii's nature. Even though "usually so even-tempered," he

> was capable of unrestrained flare-ups. Those who knew him remember that in those outbursts of irritation, which, generally speaking, were very rare, his voice would break to a falsetto and his pen would produce bilious lines.[34]

The remarks of Miliukov and Kizevetter are not gratuitous: even some of the students who remained privately loyal to him throughout his denigration remembered clearly the other side of his nature—his harshness in debate and his ever-present inclination to vent sarcasm. Reading his works one senses both his democratic charm and his fearful anger.

The impressions fail to convey the specific motives that made Pokrovskii a revolutionary historian; no doubt he himself would have liked to think that intellectual honesty, love of justice, and sympathy for the downtrodden determined his path. Kizevetter and Miliukov hint that personal frustration made him long for the liquidation of the existing society. It affords little satisfaction to conclude that the truth lies somewhere in between. One can, however, at least suggest a link between emotional and intellectual dimensions of Pokrovskii's conversion. It is curious and revealing that he expressed his main premise—the idea that constituted his most important contribution to Russian historiography—even before he became a Marxist: his derision of the notion of a supraclass state. Marxism was the most apt, and probably the most forceful, underpinning for his assertion of the class character of Russian autocracy. As we shall see, Pokrovskii equated this assertion with Marxism and attributed the contrary thesis—the supraclass theory of the Russian state—to almost all non-Marxist historians. His understanding of Marxism supported him in a lifelong polemic against his teachers.

Once Pokrovskii took up his duties in the Commissariat of Education in May 1918, he became a member of the Communist establishment, with all its privileges and obligations. Some indication of the range of Pokrovskii's activities was presented in the Introduction. He kept up his production of books, articles, reviews, and prefaces after 1918 as well. During the Civil War he presented as lectures the first part of his influential *Brief History of Russia*.[35] It is a bold enunciation of his views that, in the absence of other textbooks, served a useful pedagogic purpose. But it is not a completely successful popular history; it exhibits a measure of vulgarization: only an apparent simplification is achieved, and there is considerable loss of refinement of meaning. Unfortunately, it is Pokrovskii's best known work. Even though Lenin praised him for his effort,[36] Pokrovskii himself considered it, from the standpoint of exposition, one of his worst books (1924d:212).

Pokrovskii was extremely active as an editor, both directly and as head of the newly formed Central Archives, and he was chief editor of its journal, *Red Archives*. He was a member of the board of Gosizdat (State Publishing House). He was for a brief time head of Istpart, a commission that functioned on a nationwide scale to collect materials on the Revolution. He was for a time one of the governing members of the Lenin Institute founded in 1924 by L. B. Kamenev. He was the principal founder of Workers' Faculties (*rabfaki*), schools specially organized for the purpose of preparing workers for entrance into institutions of higher learning. His most important duty in the scholarly network was his leadership of the Communist Academy, which was at first a forum and propaganda center that was later to claim for itself an eminence higher than the Academy of Sciences.[37]

Within the Commissariat of Education, Pokrovskii was chairman of the State Council of Scholars (GUS), a body that decided major issues in higher education. In 1921 he became chairman of the Commissariat's Academic Center, which supervised GUS and the Chief Administration of Scientific Institutions, within which were found the Chief Committee of the Arts, Chief Archives, and Chief Museums. "He thus stood at the head of all the scholarly institutions in the country" (Komarev, 1932:21).

Pokrovskii was now a pillar of order and a central figure in implementing the policy of building communism with the hands of noncommunists. He continued to collaborate with Lunacharskii, his superior in the Commissariat of Education, and with V. P. Polionskii, another former Forwardist, in the publication of the literary journal *Pechat i revoliutsiia* (*The Press and Revolution*). But he had begun to dissociate himself from his Bogdanovite past. In 1920, together with Bukharin, and at the direction of Lenin, he helped pass a resolution against Proletcult, an ostensibly Bogdanovite literary movement, at a conference on literature. As a result, Proletcult was brought into the Commissariat of Education.[38]

Pokrovskii was something of an adornment in the powerless but symbolically important representative institutions. He was elected to the All-Russian and then All-Union Congresses of Soviets and then to their Central Executive Committee, where most likely he functioned as an expert consultant and occasionally attended sessions of the Council of Peoples' Commissars. He also participated in the work of party congresses and the Comintern. In the trial of the Socialist Revolutionaries in 1922, an event that almost completely destroyed that party and served to discredit Bolshevism with European socialists, Pokrovskii was the "public accuser" and sought to dignify the proceedings with a long historical article.[39] What was probably his most important political act he carried out as a historian—his public dispute with Trotsky that began in 1922.

Pokrovskii's great status had unpleasant aspects. It seems that not all the Russian Marxist historians shared the prevailing enthusiasm for him. In 1923 he published a work on the revolutionary movement full of careless formulations and inept figures of speech that provoked immediate criticism and would embarrass him subsequently.[40] Another unpleasant feature of Pokrovskii's life was party discipline. He chafed slightly: "I, like many old Party intellectuals, reacted querulously and with dissatisfaction to external discipline," he wrote. "But I should say that recently I've begun to notice that without it some things are unrealizable and in the given instance this external discipline will aid us" (*VKA*, 1923, 6:420).

Moreover, his health had begun to fail under the stress of overwork. Like most leading Bolsheviks, he was burdened with many posts. He complained that the Central Committee itself had assigned him twelve positions, even though it had twice decreed that he should be released from administrative work for the sake of his scholarship (*VKA*, 1925, 12:382). In 1922 he received the following letter from the Central Committee, signed by one of its secretaries, V. V. Kuibyshev:

> Comrade Pokrovskii: By resolution of the Secretariat of the CC RKP(b), April 28, and the decision of the consulting physicians, April 26, you are to maintain the following schedule and regard this as a matter of Party discipline: to be outside Moscow in a *dacha*, twice a week, to confine your working hours to four or five hours a day, to cut down administrative work, to lie down for two hours a day after dinner. (Sokolov, 1963:37)

Despite his infirmity, Pokrovskii was active and popular in party circles. Such was the thirst for knowledge and the enthusiasm for historical investigation that when Pokrovskii lectured at what is now the Leninist Komsomol Theater, the house "was always packed to overflowing" (Sidorov, 1964:120). Party discipline brought compensations.

2 Pokrovskii's Synthesis of Russian History

The Science of History

Pokrovskii was not a philosopher of history, but he was highly self-conscious and constantly reiterated the importance of philosophy of history or of what he called methodology—possible understandings of the nature of the historical process and the character of historical knowledge. Though his statements were neither rigorous nor formal, and certainly not without ambiguity, they are reflected in his historical findings. His views were in flux in the early 1920s; it is necessary, therefore, to show their evolution.

Pokrovskii's first principle is historical determinism. People, like all other natural objects, are subject to laws. Society, like nature, is as it must be. The various human activities—writing literature and producing goods, for example—"do not depend on our will, but develop according to certain laws, as immutable as the law which determines the rotation of the earth around the sun" (1924f:12). This is a statement of historical determinism, which Pokrovskii equated with scientific understanding. Once this notion is accepted, "it is possible to contend only about one thing: is the theory of economic explanation the best from a scientific standpoint?" The economic explanation must be judged by the same standard as any other theory. Which of them "with the fewest distortions grasps the greatest number of facts?" This is an empirical standard, verifiable "only by special researches." The theory that meets the test most successfully, in his opinion, is economic determinism. "Up to this time such verification has pronounced in favor of this position" (1924f:12).

The next principle is historical materialism, which is a refinement of the postulates of historical determinism. It incorporates the concepts of class and class conflict. Marxism is

> more complicated than simple economic materialism: Marxism not only explains history by economic causes but depicts these causes in the precise form of class conflict. This is revolutionary historical materialism as distinguished from the peaceful, evolutionary economism of many bourgeois writers. (1920:40)

The views stated thus far would lead the reader to expect Pokrovskii to stress the completeness and efficacy of historical knowledge. To be sure, one would expect Pokrovskii to distinguish different sorts of historical knowledge and to correlate the variants with the social position of the investigator, but this should not vitiate the notion that society is knowable. It is subject to laws and one can take action because one knows the direction and outcome of action. Instead we find an unexpected emphasis. Pokrovskii stressed the tentative and conditional character of all historical knowledge. His most graphic illustration of this point occurred in a passage on ideology, which was to him an inherent component of historical knowledge:

> What is ideology? It is the reflection of reality in the minds of people through the prism of their interest. That is what ideology is, and in that sense, any historical work is, first of all, a specimen of a certain ideology. . . . All ideologies are composed of bits of reality; there are no completely fantastic ideologies; moreover, any ideology is a curved mirror giving by no means a genuine reflection of reality, but something that cannot even be compared to a reflection in a curved mirror. For in a curved mirror, you somehow recognize your face by some signs; there is a beard— there is no beard, there is a moustache—there is no moustache. But in matters of ideology, the distortion of reality can be so extreme that a brunette turns out to be a blond, a bearded person turns out to be as clean shaven as cherub, and so forth. (1923a:8–9)

Pokrovskii disavowed this figure of speech shortly after stating it. He thanked Bukharin for pointing out his error and added, "Marxism is not simply a reflection of reality through a prism" of working class interests, of false consciousness as it were. It is a "scientific theory, an objective historical theory," therefore, "to speak of a Marxist ideology is inexact." Unless we differentiate Marxism from ideologies, "we put our theory, which we consider scientific, and which in reality is objectively a scientific theory, on the same plane with fantasies of various eighteenth century thinkers such as Rousseau, utopian socialists, etc." (1924b: 82, 103–4). Pokrovskii's "error" represents more than a lapse of concentration on his part. It marks an attempt to come to grips with his Bogdanovite past and with current notions of proletarian culture. For Pokrovskii, Marxism was something more than a scientific method: "Not only social study (*obshchestvovedenie*) but an entire world outlook. . . . I do not wish to use words that will compel you to accuse me of God-building, but if one does not fear terminology, then one could say that Marxism is the religion of the free man, the liberated working man" (*Marksizm,* 1925:11, 14).

In 1926 he spontaneously reverted to the image of the curved mirror when delivering some impromptu remarks:

> It seems to me that it is best to acquire them [facts] directly from documents, and not from books where we have these documents in an already processed form, because any processing always distorts facts. I had to give an entire course of lectures on that matter at Zinoviev University [which included the passage about the curved mirror], which is probably known to some of you. There I demonstrated that historical ideology is the same as any other ideology and that to read a book imagining that in it facts are reflected as they are—is the same as reading Boehm-Bawerk and imagining that economic reality is reflected in it. (*Voprosy*, 1926:131)

Thus Pokrovskii's repudiation of the figure of a curved mirror by no means signifies that it is irrelevant for an understanding of his synthesis. The sentiment that prompted the controversial metaphor shaped his polemics and governed the creation of his synthesis.

Pokrovskii did not merely uphold the view that historical knowledge reflected class interest; he pushed this notion to its outer limits: the very source materials with which the historian is obliged to work are saturated with ideology. The claim by members of the bourgeoisie that their historical works are objective resembles their notion that parliaments represent all the people, he argued. Once admitting the validity of applying notions of class conflict to scholarship, they would be compelled to recognize the class character of parliaments, bourgeois literature, and bourgeois science. Doubtless Pokrovskii considered the very claim to objectivity to be a political act. The recognition of classes and their struggle is the "death sentence" for the bourgeoisie (1923a:11).

These statements require a little elaboration. Clearly Pokrovskii summoned all his eloquence to prove the conditional and limited character of historical knowledge, that is, that all historical writing reflects the class interest of the historian. The very title of the work in which these remarks are stated—*Bor'ba klassov i russkaia istoricheskaia literatura* (*Class Conflict and Russian Historical Literature*)—bears the same implication. Since these views subsequently enmeshed Pokrovskii in many difficulties, the circumstances under which they were formulated should be noted. *Bor'ba klassov i russkaia istoricheskaia literatura* first saw light as a series of lectures delivered in May 1923 to the students of the Communist University in Petrograd, an institute for the training of party cadres. His audience was composed of Marxists, thereby making proselytism pointless. It was against non-Marxist views *of Russian history* that Pokrovskii aimed his fire, seeking to eradicate what was after all the most widely held understanding of the Russian past at this time, even among Marxists. In short, circumstances cast Pokrovskii in the role of destroyer. Historical materialism was not his main concern, and it received its definition by implication from what was said about historical knowledge in general; it was guilty by association. Pokrovskii's stress on the tentative character of historical knowledge—a mood required for uprooting opposing views—could not but affect his own historical writings. When the occasion required the inculcation of new views, the establishment of a new orthodoxy, Pokrovskii's mood would be out of order.

The extreme formulation of his view—"history is politics retrojected into the past"—is a statement attributed to Pokrovskii by virtually all his Soviet critics before the 1960s, and by some Western critics. They suggest that it imparts the essence of his views of historical scholarship. However, as one prominent Soviet historian pointed out in 1962, the statement does not occur in Pokrovskii's writings.[1] Pokrovskii imputed this notion to his rivals: "The history written by these gentlemen [non-Marxist historians] is nothing other than politics retrojected into the past" (1928c:5–6). Thus, strictly speaking, to claim that Pokrovskii's statement represents his own views about historical knowledge is itself nothing other than politics retrojected into the past. Nevertheless, the statement is not wholly a distortion of Pokrovskii's views. The statement was cited on numerous occasions by Pokrovskii's followers while he was still alive. They would not have used it had Pokrovskii objected. It can be said then to represent, at least by implication, the most extreme formulation of Pokrovskii's views.[2]

Pokrovskii's understanding of the relationship between the economic base and the superstructure also presents a problem: how much weight should be given to economic phenomena in the study of social change? Before World War I, he placed the most urgent stress upon them. According to his own subsequent admission, in those early years he sought to explain almost all superstructural phenomena by tracing them to changes in the economy; for example, he traced the outbreak of the war to price fluctuations of the international grain market (1926b:9).

In the early years of Soviet power, he sought to eschew economic materialism in an effort to give prominence to other factors—mainly political activity. This trend became even more pronounced in later years. The following statement reveals the tenor of his thoughts in the early 1920s: "The process of history must not be thought of as something automatic, acting apart and independently from the will of the human beings that take part in the process and whose actions are its components" (*BH*, 2:239). Writing as he was after World War I for a communist audience, proving the significance of economic activity as a crucial factor was pointless. Pokrovskii sought rather to combat what he considered to be the vulgarization of economic determinism, that is, the rigid formulation of theories that denied noneconomic factors any role in historical development and any power to affect the economy. An example of the "colossal influence on the economy" exerted by "something from the ideological realm" is the telephone: like any other invention, it greatly accelerated business relations and negotiations. Political actions as well as inventions influenced the economy. The Battle of Waterloo destroyed the monopoly of French manufacture on the continent, and the Manifesto of 1861 assured the existence in the Russian countryside of a class of small-scale producers dependent on another class that rented land to it (1922a:40–41).

Despite the considerable weight attributed to the superstructure, the base still predominated:

> Would a telephone . . . have any use for a nomadic horde or band of Norman Vikings? Would it suit in any way an ancient Russian commune, where all the members . . . live in one hut? But the main thing is can one imagine the mass dissemination of telephones in a country lacking highly developed industry? . . . [Merely posing the question makes clear] the entire economic conditioning of influence from the "ideological realm." (1922a:41)

The influence of political acts also "can only be secondary." The defeat at Waterloo did not prevent the industrialization of France. And despite the attempt in the peasant reform to forestall the development of bourgeois relations in the Russian economy and the creation of a Russian proletariat, the peasant, in the final analysis, became enmeshed in a capitalist economy; a proletariat was formed and fulfilled its historic mission. "Not only is the appearance of phenomena in the 'ideological realm' conditioned economically (Waterloo would be inconceivable apart from Anglo-French economic competition), but their consequences go only so far as economic conditions permit" (1922a:42).

These statements inform us of the relative weight of superstructural and substructural elements, but their makeup and the character of their interaction—aside from the vague notion of "conditioning"— remain obscure. Additional statements by Pokrovskii addressed to this point do not clarify it. It is somewhat helpful to learn that Marxism "is more complicated than simple economic materialism: Marxism not only explains history by economic causes but also depicts these causes in the precise form of class conflict" (1920:4). But with what other social variables do economic classes interact? If such inventions as the telephone are superstructural, what is economics, and what are economic causes? Thus Pokrovskii's theory is open to the customary criticism raised in connection with most variations of the Marxist interpretation of history.

He has not delineated with sufficient clarity the economic base from the superstructure. His statements, though to the point, are vague and incomplete. In the late 1920s and early 1930s, in the course of a number of disputes, more elaborate and rigorous formulations of this problem were worked out, but not by Pokrovskii. Not being a pressing problem in the early 1920s, it received only offhand treatment from him. His imprecision on this score was the basis for the subsequent accusation that he distorted Marxist materialism in favor of economic materialism.[3]

Pokrovskii's understanding of historical knowledge bears the mark of a pervasive skepticism with regard to the possibility of discerning truth unaffected by the class interests of the investigator. With regard to the relative significance of substructural and superstructural elements in the historical process, Pokrovskii was clearly an economic determinist, but he eschewed and actually polemicized against the most extreme formulations of that position and sought to give some weight to superstructural elements. As concerns the character of interaction between base and superstructure, Pokrovskii's theoretical statements reveal no coherent position and, as a result, his notion of cause is indecipherable. This problem is important, and we shall return to it to clarify some of the pivotal issues of his interpretation of Russian history, which is summarized next.

The Course of Russian History

In treating the prehistory of the East Slavs, Pokrovskii affirmed the existence of communal institutions. His intention was to discredit the notion that private property is a timeless institution (Shapiro, 1962:580–82). The large family, in which all worked together and lived under one roof, Pokrovskii considered the basic social unit and an example of "genuine communism" (1910–14:9). The father of the clan, as the director of the economy, the upholder of military discipline, and the priest of the family cult, could dispose "of all the family members; he could slay or sell son or daughter as one might sell a pig or goat" (1910–14:10). Hardly an idyllic state of nature! Pokrovskii was unwilling to endorse the Morgan-Engels view that proclaimed the harmony and integrity of precivilized society.

The culture of Kievan Rus, the earliest stage of Russian civilization (862–1240), marked a "brilliant moment" in the Russian past, and numerous sources bear witness to its high level of material, political, and artistic culture. Despite the achievements of the ancient towns, they had little influence on social relations.[4] The towns represented a social order based on slavery, but this order never prevailed in the countryside. The "marauding merchants" pillaged the countryside but remained external to it. The communal family, evolving into the clan and then the tribe, finally yielded the feudal system. Pokrovskii found the genesis of feudal relations in the disintegration of communal property and the attendant social differentiation.[5] This development was not affected by slavery.

Feudalism predominated in Russia from the thirteenth to the sixteenth century, called the appanage period. Pokrovskii used the phrase "natural economy" to describe the feudal mode of production, though he had reservations about the phrase:

> Once upon a time the economic order in which men strove to get along by themselves, buying nothing and selling nothing, bore the name of "natural economy." The absence of limited circulation of money and the acquisition of goods in kind were taken as its specific characteristics. But the absence of money was only a derivative characteristic; the essential point was the absence of exchange as a constant daily phenomenon, without which it is impossible to imagine economic life as it is today. The cardinal point was the isolation of individual economics and, in application to large landholding, this period is called by modern scholars the period of isolated votchina, or pomestye, economy ("manoral," as it is also sometimes called, from the name of the English medieval votchina, the manor). (1910–14:18)

The producer was the peasant; the content of the class struggle was the expropriation of his produce by the warlords. The essential feature of feudalism "is that all the land with all its inhabitants is the possession of a small number of war-lords, who together with their armed retainers rule over the working masses" (*BH*, 1:51). Thus small-scale production was combined with large-scale landowning.

Feudalism may or may not entail serfdom, which is but one means of expropriating the surplus product of the peasants. It was absent in feudal Russia. The lords, though they compelled the peasants to forfeit their surplus produce, did not confine them to a manor. For the most part the peasants lived in scattered hamlets and constantly colonized fresh territories (*BH*, 1:51–52).

"The basic political sign of feudalism is the identity of landownership with power over people who live on the land of a given landowner" (1924f:174). This system does not require the existence of a state, and indeed Pokrovskii does not consider a state to have existed in Russia before the sixteenth century. Although he recognizes the existence of political organizations prior to the reign of Ivan IV, he considers them "associations" (1924f:166). The matter is largely semantic; Pokrovskii is inveighing against those non-Marxist historians who, in his opinion, sought to deify the state. He intended, following Bakunin, not so much to belittle the political abilities of the Russian people as to demean the dignity of the state itself, by depicting it as something transient and closely associated with the capitalist order. The state lives and dies with capitalism.

Incessant warfare accounts for the characteristic instability of feudalism. In the long run, a few succeed in imposing their wills on others, subduing many vassals and thereby enhancing their own power. This provides a generalized account of the rise of Muscovy. "By degrees a *feudal monarchy* grew out of the feudal chaos" (*BH*, 1:23). Not only relations among the warlords but economic changes as well account for the power of the Grand Prince. A more productive economy, permitting a more highly differentiated social structure, culminated in the birth of a number of medieval towns. Gradually, the Principality of Muscovy became an economic unit (*BH*, 1:56–57).

But the rise of Muscovy as told in *Russian History since Ancient Times* is more than statements deduced from a model of feudalism and has a broader frame of reference than the greed of princes, boyars, and churchmen. Pokrovskii suggests the existence of an elaborate network of political institutions that embraced the area from the Baltic to the steppe. Muscovy's pedominance is seen as the unintended consequence of this circumstance, not anyone's goal, nor the result of anyone's ideology.[6]

Pokrovskii found the decline of feudalism more difficult to describe than its origins. Elements of feudalism remained at least until the eighteenth century, but evidently these were vestiges of an overthrown social order, for after the eighteenth century, merchant capital, with its attendant economic, social, and political relations, predominated. Hence it is only in connection with the rise of merchant capitalism that the demise of feudalism can be understood. Merchant capitalism is one of Pokrovskii's most controversial concepts and the one most closely associated with his name; his employment of it is the key to his views, not only on the decline of feudalism but on the destruction of autocracy as well.[7]

The rudiments of merchant capital were present as early as the Kievan period (1924f:67). While still in embryonic form, it played a considerable role in the unification of Muscovy. But it was under Ivan the Terrible, especially after the founding of the *oprichnina* in 1565, that it prevailed. Pokrovskii discussed at length the increase of trade in the sixteenth century (1922c:144–51), which in his view led to the acquisition of considerable political power by the merchant class, or at least its wealthiest part—the *gosti*. Social relations in the countryside also underwent transformation. The self-sufficiency of the manor—the mark of natural economy—broke down as a result of the growth of trade. The lords sought to dispose of the peasants' goods in return for cash, which alone could procure the luxuries sold by the merchant (*HR:*112–13).

The merchants allied themselves with the squires (*pomeshchiki*) in a death struggle against the older feudal classes—the large landowners (*boyars*) and the church. Merchant capitalism—the two younger classes—triumphed in the revolution of 1565. Pokrovskii considered the *oprichnina* to be a temporary dictatorship that foreshadowed the more lasting one of autocracy. Russia was not under a dictatorship in the sense that it was possessed by an all-powerful state. Rather, owing to a local circumstance—the late arrival in Russia of merchant capitalism—especially severe and oppressive measures had to be adopted to meet international competition:

> This was a new country, possessed by the development of merchant capitalism . . . she had to win for herself a place in the sun from her older, more deeply entrenched rivals. To do this Russian merchant capital had to forge the country by iron discipline and to develop a genuine dictatorship. The embodiment of this dictatorship of merchant capital was, of course, Muscovite autocracy. (1922c:151)

The Tsars "not only served the interests of merchant capital, but became as it were identified with it" (*BH*, 1:84). Representing both types of social classes upon which the order rested, the Tsars exemplified the two main aspects of merchant capitalism. First, they were active merchants. Like the other members of this class, they favored serfdom, seeing in it a form of exploitation necessary for the existence of trade. By compelling the peasants to produce a surplus, this system provided goods for exchange. Second, the Tsars were landowners; like all members of this class, they considered serfdom a prerequisite to their availing themselves of the wares of the merchants. Serfdom, then, had its roots in the breakdown of the feudal natural economy and the rise of exchange relations. It represents intensified exploitation of the peasants—the use of compulsion to force them to produce a marketable surplus. The chief point is that autocracy did not arise from the necessity for the state to defend all classes of society from incursions from the steppe, which was an idea Pokrovskii attributed to his teachers. It derived, in his mind, from the economic interests of the merchants and landowners. For some hundreds of years, these two groups constituted a single economic interest and favored the same political order (1924c:252).

The distinctive mark of merchant capital was that it did not transform the mode of production: "Merchant capital, which exploits the independent small-scale producer, without interfering in production, and without creating production, and without limiting it, relies on the aid of non-economic compulsion" (1924b:15).[8] The peasants, as serfs, continued the small-scale production characteristic of the natural econ-omy. Merchant capital, though it represented a species of capitalism, locked the peasants in feudal relations. For their own part, the peas-ants strove for private landholdings—for their own (*muzhik*) form of capitalism (1924c:252).

Pokrovskii, we see, employed the concept of merchant capital to dem-onstrate that the Tsar and the state did not embody autonomous power: they were subservient to the dominant social classes. The state had no interests of its own and was wholly subordinated to the merchants and gentry. Obviously, this thesis is laden with political content. *Who* con-trols the state is a function of the stage of development of a given society. That some class possesses and uses the state in its own interests was one of the chief lessons Pokrovskii garnered from Marx. This point is the pivot of Pokrovskii's historical construct. His major works, in a sense all his works, reiterate and illustrate this thesis and thereby consti-tute a sustained assault against a contrary thesis, one that Pokrovskii described as the supraclass theory of the state. This is the notion that autocracy created the Russian social classes and itself fashioned the economy and social structure so as to defend the nation, and that the state was more innovative and powerful than particular social classes and embodied the general interest of society:

> Against this theory one must fight by the most decisive means, no less energetically than we fight against religious prejudice. I would even say—it is not as important to prove that Jesus Christ had no historical existence as that in Russia there never did exist a supra-class state. (1922c:146)

With this awareness of the political burden of Pokrovskii's system, clearer understanding of its substance is possible.

The intense social conflicts of the sixteenth century, plus the rapa-cious exploitation of the land by the early capitalists, resulted in the breakdown of the state. The attempts to bind the peasants to the land, the decimation of the *boyar* ranks by the *oprichnina*, the setbacks of the Livonian War—itself a reflection of the conflict between feudalism and merchant capitalism—led directly to the Time of Troubles. And its out-come, the election of the Romanovs in 1613, again represented "a vic-tory of the landowning gentry and merchant capital." But the temporary breakdown of the state had been so extensive that it had long-term consequences. Merchant capitalism of the seventeenth century resur-rected elements of feudalism. Those lords who had come to possess immense landholdings and numerous serfs had also acquired great au-thority over those dependent on them, a direct outcome of the break-down of the state. These landlords were sovereign on their own estates.

Collecting taxes and administering justice, they were the embodiment of the state in the eyes of the lower classes. The state, though its instruments of coercion were manifold, did not have extensive power, for the private power of the landlord predominated at the lower levels of society. The process of enserfment was completed under the auspices of merchant capital in the seventeenth century. Moreover, merchant capital required foreign markets as well as serfs, hence the resumption of expansion east and west in the course of the seventeenth century. Thus two of the cardinal institutions of Russia—serfdom and empire—were created by merchant capital (*HR,* 1:82–85, 90–91, 100).

The *oprichnina*—the first political order created by merchant capital— was merely a temporary dictatorship. Autocracy—the political order emerging in the seventeenth century—was a more fully institutionalized arrangement. The political order created by merchant capital rested on a social foundation containing elements of feudalism. Taken as a whole, this social formation represented a species of capitalism.[9]

Autocracy "consisted of a strong central government which controlled a bureaucracy admirably organized after the mode of a merchant's counting house" (*HR,* 1:99). The main prop of the state, besides the bureaucracy, was the standing army. With these two instruments at their disposal the Romanovs could expand the empire while maintaining serfdom. Finally, the church became an instrument of the state. The chief characteristics of the autocracy then are the following: it was capitalist and secular and was based on serfdom, bureaucracy, and a standing army.[10] These essentials existed in the seventeenth century "but only in a chaotic and formless condition." It was "during the Great Northern War that the machinery of the Romanov state took final shape" (*HR,* 1:99, 100). The Empire acquired its window on the West; serfdom and its attendant fiscal system were consolidated; the table of ranks imparted some semblance of order to the bureaucracy; Petrine military reforms made standard such matters as recruitment and logistics; and the state dominated the church.

Pokrovskii polemicized against what he considered to be the traditional view that the Westernization of Russia was a "military-financial necessity. Russia should become Europe because she will not otherwise be able to compete with European powers." He found the key to the Petrine reforms "in the conditions of European trade in the seventeenth century." The European powers, especially the Netherlands, needed Russia as a market.[11] From the political standpoint, the Petrine period marked the heyday of merchant capitalism. It attained its greatest prosperity, however, in the second half of the nineteenth century, when it was close to its demise. Political decline was apparent in the eighteenth century when the state, in order to suppress the Pugachev Rebellion, became a military dictatorship. The Rebellion itself and the changes it produced were signs of a deeper disorder. The entire social order in the late eighteenth century suffered a protracted crisis—a crisis so complex and profound that it only began to be resolved in the Emancipation of 1861. This crisis grew out of "the fundamental contradiction between the interests of merchant and industrial capital." It is necessary to backtrack to a series of events in the early eighteenth century, described by Pokrovskii as the "birth of industrial capital," to gain perspective on this crisis and the abolition of serfdom. Just as the rudiments of merchant capitalism came into being within the feudal order, those of industrial capitalism were born within merchant capitalism, precisely at the time of the Northern War (1700–1721). In organizing production, the industrialist centralizes production in the largest possible units, where he provides the workers with the necessary tools and machines and pays the worker a wage. Herein lies the fundamental contradiction: free workers, the prerequisite of a flourishing industrial order, were in short supply in Russia owing to the prevalence of serfdom (*HR*, 1:105).

The mounting crisis, stemming from this contradiction, can be traced only with difficulty. Industrial capitalism seems almost to disappear from view in the course of the eighteenth century, only to reappear in 1825 with the Decembrist Uprising. Within Russia, the Russian merchants themselves were overshadowed by their British and Dutch rivals. Pokrovskii's practice of citing fluctuation of grain prices on the London market is really a shorthand method of depicting the changing fortunes of the two antagonists. But the real state of affairs is obscure; the Emancipation does not resolve the contradiction:

> Merchant capital continued to grow, and only attained its greatest prosperity in the second half of the nineteenth century. . . . Even as late as the early twentieth century one of the most influential bourgeois parties, the "Octobrists," represented in the main the commercial capital of the old-fashioned merchants, while the interests of the industrial capitalists were championed by the "Cadets" and the "Progressives." The victories industrial capital was able to score were due to its alliance with merchant capital. The "liberation" of the peasants in 1861 (when they were liberated from a good part of their land, as well as from serfdom) could only be carried out because it was also in the interests of merchant capital and the complete disappearance of Tsarism was for a long time held up because merchant capital still needed it. It therefore survived till the Revolution of March 1917. The final political victory of industrial capitalism preceded the proletarian revolution by only eight months. (*HR*, 1:105–6)

Thus industrial capitalism passed through numerous vicissitudes, such as the Revolution of 1905, before its short-lived triumph over merchant capital in March 1917. And although industrial capitalism had been transformed into modern imperialism, it remained under the control of the old order.

The triumph of industrial capitalism resulted from the efforts of the working class, which had fought the chief battles in 1905 and delivered the coup de grace to merchant capitalism and then to industrial capitalism itself in 1917. The story thus has a remarkable ending, for it is the working class, born in the 1880s within industrial capitalism, that emerged victorious, resolving the contradiction between industrial and merchant capitalism by relegating them to a common grave.

Pokrovskii himself was dissatisfied with this historical construct and was generally tolerant of criticism—so long as it did not tarnish the picture of a class-dominated state and its attendant notion of merchant capitalism, and so long as it did not suggest that Russian development was unique and somehow exempted from passing through the same basic stages as other societies. The subsequent history of Pokrovskii's synthesis is in part an attempt to make a socialist revolution plausible in the context of the conflict between merchant and industrial capital. The following picture emerges: industrial capital, having attained economic predominance in the twentieth century, sought control of the state. But so simple a transformation was precluded by the existence of a powerful working class with its own revolutionary goals. When the industrial bourgeoisie discovered this in 1905, it withdrew from the revolutionary ranks. The workers, however, found an ally in the peasants, who were engaged in their age-old struggle against merchant capital and the feudal system. The workers proved capable of leading the peasants, since the peasants were backward as well as radical. Under these circumstances, the revolution ultimately turned toward socialism.[12]

Pivotal Issues

Historiography, a field of scholarship readily adaptable to partisan conflict, was a favorite subject of Pokrovskii during the 1920s. At the height of the NEP, when non-Marxist historians stepped up their work, historiography was a means of containing the influence of these "noncommunist hands being used to build communism." The theme of Pokrovskii's criticism of non-Marxists is identical with that of his own construct: his denial of the supraclass theory of the state.

The majority of Russian historians, including the most creative and influential ones, wrote in the interest of industrial capitalism, argued Pokrovskii. Merchant capitalism had its most forthright spokesman in N.M. Karamzin; it was also represented, though in somewhat oblique fashion, by the Slavophiles. The peasantry had only one historian—the relatively obscure A.P. Shchapov. Marxist historiography was initiated by Pokrovskii himself, for Plekhanov and Rozhkov represented merely the reflection of Marxism in bourgeois literature. They inhabited a sort of netherworld closer to Struve than to genuine Marxism. The most creative tradition culminated in Kliuchevskii and was continued by Miliukov. It derived on the one hand from S.M. Soloviev, who brought to prominence the role of the steppe—the idea that an original and distinctive political apparatus, itself capable of molding the social structure, arose in Russia in response to aggression from nomadic hordes; on the other hand was B.N. Chicherin, whose preoccupation with legal categories likewise implied a state endowed with creative powers.[13]

What links this creative tradition of Marxist historiography to industrial capitalism? In Pokrovskii's analysis, there are numerous connections, some that operate universally, wherever capitalism exists, and others that are instances of these universal laws or trends peculiar to Russia. It is not that bourgeois historians distort factual evidence to embellish capitalism:

> It should not be imagined that the bourgeois character of the latter [historical works] manifests itself only in a few distortions of fact or in the suppression here and there of things that are not to the advantage of the bourgeoisie; that it is limited to tricks that can be easily shown up and on which it is easy to get in the habit of laying one's finger. No, *the bourgeoisie has a historical outlook of its own*, which permeates every work on history ever written by bourgeois historians. The latter were convinced of the rightness of their outlook and adhered to it with complete sincerity. (*HR*, 1:236)

The bourgeois outlook derives directly from the nature of industrial capitalism, and Hegel provided its classical formulation:

> Industrial capitalism, accompanied, on the one hand, by rapid growth of large-scale machine production, a growth no one could escape noticing, and on the other by industrial crises, was . . . calculated to impress people with the mutability of all things. The philosophy of Hegel, which arose at the beginning of the age of industrial capitalism, had for its starting-point the idea that *everything flows*, that everything is subject to unceasing change.[14]

Eternal flux is not the only concept inherent in capitalism. The notion of order is required to conceal "a veritable chaos of capitalist competition," despite the fact that this order is nothing but "the dictatorship of a capitalist minority over the masses of workers and peasants." This requirement resulted in the deification of the state:

> The State introduces order in the chaos of "civil society," separates the latter into "estates," assigning to each a definite occu-

pation, etc. Out of the chaos is born a disciplined whole, the individual losing his freedom *qua* individual, but recovering it as part of the State collective. The logical conclusion was that the final goal of the State was *bourgeois democracy*[15]

With regard to Russia, not only academics but the capitalists themselves shared this outlook:

> The bourgeoisie controlled the working class by means of the machinery of the State. It was with the aid of the *State* that they tried to create a proletariat by depriving the peasants of the land. . . . It was likewise with the aid of the State that the capitalists forced the proletariat to work for them. . . . In these circumstances it is quite natural that the bourgeoisie should regard the building of a *State machinery as the principal and essential part of the historical process,* the backbone of history as it were. (*HR,* 1:236–37)

Russian historians embodied these concepts in the supraclass theory of the state:

> It was up to them to prove that in Russia the State was not the creation of the ruling classes, nor an instrument for the oppression of the rest of the people, but that it stood for the interests of the people as a whole, without distinction of classes. The "scientific" theory arose out of the practical demand of the bourgeoisie. *Academic learning* was used as a *means to dominate the masses.* (*HR,* 1:244)

Pokrovskii contended that the supraclass theory of the state carried a scantily disguised political message for the workers: it urged them not to seize power, since power does not and should not belong to any class. The state should be converted from autocracy to constitutional monarchy. Workers and peasants should seek such concessions as the eight-hour day and land redemption. "But political power should remain 'non-class,' that is, bourgeois" (1922c:146).

This attempt to connect industrial capitalism to a specific body of historical writing yields a number of conclusions. First, the alleged connection between capitalism and the concepts of flux and order is a long-standing thesis, and Pokrovskii is original only in applying it to what he calls the supraclass theory of the state. It can be described as ingenious and illuminating or as dubious and unconvincing. These terms, reflecting taste, are in order, whereas words such as verified or refuted are not. Pokrovskii's assertion is nonempirical; there is no indication of what sort of evidence will either verify or refute it. Moreover, to characterize the supraclass theory as inherently bourgeois is to beg the question. To make the connection between the mode of production and historical conceptualization convincing, numerous intermediate steps would have to be depicted, such as presenting facts about the publication of historical works: What was the character and influence of the censorship in Tsarist Russia? For whom did the historian write his works, and by whom was he employed? Not only did Pokrovskii bypass such questions about the mediation of ideas; he did not uncover fresh facts relevant to them. It should be noted, however, that he wrote in the decade when the discipline that has come to be called the sociology of knowledge was just coming into being.

A sampling of Pokrovskii's views on imperial foreign policy suggests again a less than subtle treatment of the relationship between base and superstructure. His point of departure was the alleged fact that "the age of merchant capitalism" was one in which "trade routes played a determining part in history."[16] Russia's wars were neither acts of national self-defense nor wanton expansion for reasons of state, but rather the outcome of the economic needs of merchant capital. The Livonian war, for example, was not so much a war of Ivan IV as an "aggressive policy" of merchant capital, which was "master of the Asiatic and of the great Volga-Caspian waterway which connected Western Europe with Central Asia" and now sought "the conquest of the European end of the waterway, the Baltic seacoast."[17] Imperial foreign policy in the eighteenth century provides another illustration. Toward the close of the Seven Years' War grain became Russia's main export, and *"it was mainly owing to the export of grain that Russian merchant capital attained its highest development."* Merchant capital skillfully exploited the need for grain in the nations of industrial capital:

> The best soil for wheat is the black earth of the Southern steppes. But this was a great distance from the Baltic ports; so we find Russia pushing southward, in the direction of the Black Sea. Twice in the course of the second half of the eighteenth century, Russia went to war with Turkey, with the result that Russia annexed the Crimea and Odessa . . . and obtained from Turkey a free passage through the Straits that lead from the Black Sea into the Mediterranean.[18]

These constructs are good examples of economic materialism. Quite plainly there is a one-to-one relationship between economy and politics. The ruling group understood exactly where its economic interests lay and adopted policies to promote them. Pokrovskii does not prove his claims by reference to statements of individuals but rather deduces what their motives must have been in view of the consequences of a particular policy or war. He himself discerned what the "real economic interests" of a group must have been, while its own allegations are deemed to be mere ideology.[19]

Citing examples from Pokrovskii's historiographical work and his treatment of foreign policy has not yielded a clear-cut formula for relating the economic base and the superstructure. A third example will demonstrate how complex the matter is. In treating the history of the revolutionary movement, Pokrovskii raised the problem of the origins of the tactic of political assassination. He makes it clear that this was not merely an act of madness by revolutionaries goaded by their own desperation, but rather one tactic among other possible ones, chosen for discernible reasons. He refers to the characteristic populist belief in the importance of "critically thinking individuals": the self-conscious, disciplined individual can remake the world. He then discusses the Russo-Turkish War of 1877, asserting that it was caused partly by Alexander II's hopes of reconciling the bourgeoisie to the existing state order by the conquest of Constantinople and the Black Sea Straits. But the failure of the Tsar made the war in the eyes of the bourgeoisie a "humiliation." "Never had Alexander II's government been so unpopular as it now became." This disaffection opened new vistas for the revolutionary movement. Realization of its original program had been impeded by the war, but then the movement found "a soil favorable as could be wished, but a soil very different from what it had hoped for." They had hoped for a peasant uprising. The outbreak of the war militated against a mass uprising and revealed the folly of addressing revolutionary appeals to the peasants. The outcome of the war made possible a reorientation toward the bourgeoisie. These events "demanded a complete re-organization of the whole revolutionary front." The response of the revolutionaries was the policy of terror. Pokrovskii insists that this response, although unwise, was closely connected to their ideology:

> If revolutions are made by "critically thinking individuals," it was clear that the force of reaction, the force of the government also depended on individuals, though of a different kind. And if it was desirable to increase the number of "critically thinking individuals," it was equally desirable to diminish the number of reactionary individuals and to exterminate as many of them as possible. (*HR*, 1:194)

It should be noted that the events cited above are all superstructural. Pokrovskii carried out, in the course of his narrative, a rather painstaking and refined examination of the intersection of superstructural events. He implicitly formulated a hypothesis explaining how a particular configuration of political and ideological circumstances gave rise to an important policy.

These three examples of Pokrovskii's work as a practicing historian illustrate his use of a number of modes of causal analysis. The third example was chosen also to suggest that he was a better historian than one might have concluded from a review of his statements about the nature of the historical process and from a summary of his periodization of Russian history.

A consideration of some of the underlying themes of Pokrovskii's works should help round out this sketch of his synthesis of Russian history. The traditional rulers of Russia are persistently derogated. If the first princes of Muscovy were nondescript, the last Tsar was notable for his avarice: "His mouth watered as he thought of the milliards that would pour into his pockets from Korea, and he was moved to tears when he contemplated the picture of his future wealth." Peter seemed worthy of mention chiefly because he died of syphilis and was a homosexual as well. The later Tsars had no claim to being the natural rulers of Russia, for due to Catherine the Great's extramarital liaisons, her descendants were "thoroughbred Germans" (*HR*, 1:53, 119; 2:89, 262). Statements manifesting a similar attitude toward the church can be found in Pokrovskii's writings. "Land grabbing" was a preoccupation of the church, and it "was among the most ruthless exploiters of the peasantry." The church's immunity under the Mongols derived from the fact that it prayed for the Khan and thus elevated him in the eyes of the conquered (*HR*, 1:55, 92). Such statements are of little analytical significance, but they colored Pokrovskii's writings and acquired in time considerable political importance.

Pokrovskii believed that only a sustained endeavor could overthrow the prevailing interpretations of Russian history. Above all, he sought to prove that Russia was not unique, that she had evolved according to the same pattern as other European nations. The Russian state was normal too, being the creature and servant of economic interests. His career may be considered a lifelong polemic against the national school of Russian historiography. His first efforts as a Marxist scholar were undertaken in the wake of the 1905 Revolution, when he lectured to groups of workers at a meeting advertised as lectures on musical theory. These workers felt little respect for existing authorities, and any constructions implying a secondary role for political struggle would have been out of place. Similar circumstances existed at the party school in Bologna where he first presented as lectures his *Russian History from the Earliest Times*. And the *Brief History* he considered basic training for the young Red Army on its way to the front (1933, 2:300). In this work, the role of merchant capital was raised to its zenith, illustrating in boldest terms the subordination of the state to the interests of the ruling classes.

Pokrovskii also began a polemical battle with Trotsky in 1922. Though of considerable practical significance, this engagement was of minor scholarly importance, for it did not modify the character of Pokrovskii's system as much as it clarified and sharpened it, throwing its distinctive features into bolder relief. Pokrovskii contended, and it is generally accepted, that the premises of the theory of permanent revolution were rooted in the conclusions of prerevolutionary historiography. Miliukov himself agrees with Pokrovskii on this point (1937:375). Therefore, the same arguments—illustrating the class-dominated character of the state—sufficed for Pokrovskii's dispute with Trotsky as well as for Pokrovskii's dispute with the non-Marxists.

The strands of anarchism in Marxism are an undercurrent in Pokrovskii's work. Although not readily demonstrable, they can be discerned in the passages on the state cited in the section on historiography. Of course, it is the bourgeoisie or serfowner's state being denounced. A harsh or critical word with regard to the Soviet state is not to be found. Strictly speaking, it is the supraclass theory of the state against which the author inveighs, yet a careful consideration of these passages in light of the total synthesis suggests an underlying hostility toward the state. Such an undercurrent is not remarkable in the work of a revolutionary historian, especially one who feels himself part of a worldwide movement on the verge of universal triumph—a victory that is expected to result in the abolition of the state shortly thereafter. When this expectation failed and the Bolsheviks decided that socialism had to be constructed in one country and their universal goals deferred, it could not but jeopardize the standing of Pokrovskii's synthesis.

Although Pokrovskii's system was shaped largely by the spirit of the times and his personal values, since he found it difficult to define merchant capitalism, the basic concepts of his system were ambiguous. What are the most important meanings suggested by the expression? What meanings are excluded? It is clear that he is talking about a certain phase of capitalism, preindustrial capitalism, which he considered to be dominated by a drive for primary accumulation of capital. Although production is not carried on by machines, the mode of production differs from feudalism: profit is an acceptable goal; economic decisions are made with reference to the market; and people produce for the market, not for immediate use. Merchant capitalism is one way of referring to and generalizing about mercantilism. In Russian history this concept has the merit of calling attention to a provisional coalescence of landlord-merchant interests. Soviet writings indicate that the concept makes better sense applied to the Muscovy and early imperial period than applied to recent centuries. Nevertheless, it is frequently unclear what is being described, an economic tendency or system, an actual historical epoch, or a particular social group. In one context it seems to be a socioeconomic formation, existing at the same high level of abstraction as the notions of feudalism and capitalism. In another context, it refers to merchants, and then to landlords enmeshed in market relations. One moment it is a stimulating, refreshing suggestion, the next a glittering generality. Pokrovskii tries to show what the nature of groups and individuals must have been by virtue of social relationships deduced from his theory. What results is a series of *ad hoc* explanations resting on the conviction of social determinism.

Another underlying dimension or mood in Pokrovskii's writings can be called populism. It stems from his sense of his own mission as a historian. His charge was far different from the present disposition of historians to work out a personal understanding of the past. And though he viewed himself as a scientist elaborating an understanding of Russian history based on the highest methodology available to investigators of social phenomena, this was overshadowed by his view of himself as a proletarian historian. He conceived of his science as an instrument that would allow the downtrodden to liberate themselves from historical views that helped sustain their exploitation. Of the various dimensions of Marxism, Pokrovskii responded most urgently and personally to anarchism and populism. This response was most likely abetted by the fact that these same dimensions were prominent in the Russian revolutionary tradition.

We can carry one step further our understanding of the consequences of Pokrovskii's methodological informality. It has been suggested that three distortions or deviations are equally possible for any Marxist historical construct—exaggeration of the role of the superstructure, or of social classes, or of economic processes ("Aperçu," 1957:1). A judgment based on Pokrovskii's methodological writings would uphold the traditional conclusion that he is guilty of economic materialism, despite his awareness of the shortcomings of the perspective. His assertions about the Russian past yield a different judgment; it is the second deviation he is guilty of, sociologism:

> Social classes . . . are extracted from the complex historical totality and hypostasized in an ideological fashion as the demiurge of any given political situation. Class struggle becomes the immediate internal "truth" of any political event, and mass forces become the exclusive historical agents . . . sociologism . . . tends to lead to voluntarism. . . . Lenin's Marxism, by contrast, is defined by the notion of a complex totality, in which all the levels—economic, social, political, and ideological, are always operating, there is a permutation of the main locus of contradictions between them. (Krasso, 1967:72)

For Pokrovskii, there were two such demiurges, merchant capitalism and the proletariat. These points of reference should become clearer in the chapters that follow.

Pokrovskii's ambiguities were not evident in the 1920s, when a variety of interpretations of Marxism abounded. When a more rigorous set of definitions was to be worked out, this could only imply an uncertain future for his synthesis. But the immediate prospects were good.

3 Evolution of Pokrovskii's System: The Russian Revolution

"The October Revolution is the point of departure from which derive all tendencies of our social science," stated Pokrovskii. Interest in the preconditions of the Bolshevik victory, he predicted, would direct studies still further into the past, finally illuminating all of Russian history from a new perspective (1928c:18). Two forces helped shape Pokrovskii's interpretation of the Revolution—the most dynamic element in his system of views from 1924 to 1928. On the one hand, he confronted the emerging doctrine of socialism in one country. On the other, he met adverse criticism of his previous analysis by some of his colleagues. In defending himself and taming his critics, Pokrovskii amplified some of his notions, while giving ground on others. Still polemicizing, he sought to reinforce his position by utilizing the vast amount of source material then coming to light.

The October Revolution: Preliminary Explanation

Pokrovskii did not write much about the Russian Revolution. Some of his articles about it were collected in a single volume, *The October Revolution* (1929b), and his seminars inspired some writings by young historians. Although almost everything he wrote bore upon the Revolution and its preconditions, it was not his specialty. In fact, he shied away from writing about it. When it was proposed to him in 1918 that he write an article entitled "World Revolution and the Russian Revolutions" for an anniversary volume, he refused. His reply is preserved in Central Party Archives: "I am purely a historian and not a theoretician." Pokrovskii turned down other such invitations or suggestions and even failed to act upon an authorization by the Central Committee to write a *History of the October Revolution* (Chernykh, 1969:295–96, 299).

One reason for his reluctance is the discrepancy between the original expectations and the actual outcome of the Revolution. In 1917 Pokrovskii wrote, "Once a proletarian revolution begins in Russia it must develop on an all-European scale, or it will fall in Russia. A Russian proletarian-peasant republic cannot exist surrounded by imperialist powers. Europe will not permit such a miracle."[1] In fact, this discrepancy was a major context, if not a cause, of many policies and conflicts in historiography and in other spheres of activity as well. Pokrovskii's work on the Revolution may be considered a fund of contradictions or, as suggested here, as a presentation of two distinct interpretations of the Revolution.

In the early years of Soviet power, Pokrovskii stressed the international character of the Russian revolutionary movement. He depicted Russian Social Democracy as one segment of the Marxist movement, whose national peculiarities were no more significant than those of any other segment. "The workers' movement was suppressed by autocracy with the aid of foreign capital—thus there was noted immediately, even in 1906, the international character of the future Russian Revolution" (1929b:76). If world capitalism embraced Russia, and through its loans made possible the continued existence of autocracy, then the Russian proletariat was locked in the same battle as the Western workers. The wave of strikes that had swept across Europe in the prewar years was the prelude to worldwide revolution. "*World bolshevism was born five years before the beginning of the Russian revolution*" (1929b:76).

He suggested a single difference, a minor one at the time, between Russia and the West. Merchant capital and industrial capital renewed their old conflict during World War I. The Tsarist government—"the instrument of merchant capital"—wished to withdraw from the war even at the price of a separate peace. Industrial capital, however, found the war profitable and wished to fight on to victory. As a result, Russian capital did not present a united front to the workers in 1917. In contrast, the German workers had to carry out their revolution against a unified enemy (1929b:76).

By 1920, Pokrovskii publicly expressed the conviction that revolution in the West was not to be expected in the near future: "There's no need to create illusions for oneself, *we shall remain alone for a considerable length of time*" (1920a:4). The very fact that the revolution had begun in Russia called attention to the distinctive features of her history. In a report marking the Fourth Congress of the Comintern, Pokrovskii dwelt on these features instead of those shared by Russia and the rest of Europe, which had dominated his interest earlier: "Russian development is explained by the fact that Russia fell into the channel of capitalist development extremely late, and thanks to this retardation, our capitalism developed stormily and rapidly" (1922b:31). This extraordinarily rapid development of capitalism resulted in the continued presence of contradictions "long since outlived" in the West. The Russian workers had not even the most elementary rights, such as the right to unionize. With wages less than half those prevailing in the advanced countries of Europe and three to four times lower than in the United States, Russian workers lacked the "illusion" of improvement current elsewhere (1922b:29–30).

This gradually shifting emphasis from features universal in the working-class movement to the distinctive characteristics of the Russian proletariat had its origins in the Soviet political scene. Pokrovskii was at grips with the problem troubling all thoughtful Bolsheviks—the isolation of the revolution in backward Russia. Only in 1923, with the publication of *Outlines of the History of the Revolutionary Movement in the Nineteenth and Twentieth Centuries,* did Pokrovskii formulate a consistent interpretation of the Revolution. In this controversial work Pokrovskii sought to describe Russian development as a self-contained process. The coincidence of two social wars determined the revolutionary outcome— the peasants as a whole, *including the kulaks,* against the landlords, and the workers against the capitalists.

Autocracy won a "brilliant victory" in 1905 but was nevertheless dissatisfied with its own prospects unless it could reconcile the bourgeoisie to its existence. P.A. Stolypin, from 1906 to 1911 minister of the interior and the chairman of the Council of Ministers, faced the task of creating an "alliance between merchant and industrial capital." He sought to liquidate the village commune, expecting this to open a vast internal market to Russian industrialists. But the unintended consequences, according to Pokrovskii, became the major ones. He cited numerous statistics that showed rapid change in land tenure and increase in the number of the *kulaks,* who stood shoulder to shoulder with their fellow villagers against the landlord. The "colossal" growth of independent landowning was an *unintended* consequence of the Stolypin reform which represented a threat to autocracy—for along with the burgeoning *kulaks,* there grew a revolutionary frame of mind (1924b:138, 141–44, 152–53).

Up to this point Pokrovskii's account seems clear. Merchant capitalism "dug its own grave" when, seeking to accommodate the wishes of the industrial bourgeoisie, it enlarged the proletariat and the *kulaks* and thereby strenghtened the agents, whether direct or indirect, of the socialist revolution (1924b:112, 159). But even in the *Brief History* Pokrovskii noted that such a view "reckoned in terms too short and then visualized the movement of history in too simplified a way (*BH,* 1:288).

The immediate consequence of the Stolypin reform in 1909 was a spurt of industrial growth. Although domestic capital played a greater role in this expansion than hitherto, the internal market failed to expand at a similar rate. Russian industry had become overproductive and required access to foreign markets. Finally, 1913 was a year of hesitation for Russian industrialists, and the economic prospects of merchant capital also began to dim. After 1911, grain prices and exports declined. The closing of the Black Sea Straits during the Turko-Italian War aggravated conditions, and Russian capitalism as a whole faced a crisis which, as it deepened, revived imperialist dreams (1924b:159–64). World War I was a scheme by Russian merchant capital to escape the domestic impasse. Pokrovskii was among the first revisionist historians, shifting the blame for the outbreak of the war from Germany to the Entente. He considered Nicholas II the individual chiefly responsible (1924b:181).

This argument linked the socialist revolution, which issued directly from the war, to the 1905 Revolution and connected it even to the centuries-old conflict between merchant and industrial capitalism. The point where the circle closes is the Stolypin reform. It was the consequence of the 1905 Revolution and the cause of the economic crisis from which World War I issued. The Russian historical process thus is self-contained; none of the necessary preconditions of the Revolution need be sought on the international plane. The war—the battering ram which finally destroyed autocracy—was, of course, an international event, but its causes were to be found in the Stolypin reform. This closes the circle.

Pokrovskii's synthesis is unsatisfactory from a variety of standpoints. It is extremely abstract and schematic. The prominent role attributed to the *kulaks* and the perfunctory treatment of party leadership would displease some of his Marxist colleagues. An analysis of World War I that found the basic cause in an antiquated form of capitalism rather than in the most modern forms of imperialism exemplified by England, France, and Germany would displease others. Moreover, great importance is attached to the war. While the Stolypin reform enlarged the proletariat and exacerbated the discontent of those peasants who lost their land, *thereby* creating the forces able to remake Russian society, the war alone provided the possibility for these forces to operate. One might conclude from Pokrovskii's analysis that Russia stood on the threshold of a long period of capitalist development, if only war could have been avoided. Indeed, he suggested as much himself:

> Parallel with the growth in the countryside of layers hostile . . . to merchant capital and autocracy, in the city, among the high bourgeoisie, grew an opposition mood, and without subtlety many very experienced and good Marxists at this time adopted the illusion that Russia had embarked upon the Prussian path of development. We shall have, they said, the development of a more or less normal bourgeois constitution, pushed forward, of course, by the

workers' movement, but without any new crises, without new revolutionary advances. (1924b:162)

This is a significant admission: a not wholly untenable interpretation of the Stolypin era, though in the long run it was to prove invalid, was that the bourgeois revolution had been completed in a fashion that entrenched capitalism.

If between revolutions Russia had been evolving in the direction of a parliamentary system, the Menshevik and "liquidationist" analysis at the time might be judged correct. Pokrovskii's reticence is evident: "I shall not guess—to guess in history is the cheapest thing—I shall not guess what would have been if in foreign policy, [matters] had been as felicitous as in internal [policy]" (1924b:162). If Pokrovskii cannot sustain his argument that World War I issued inevitably from Russian internal developments, he, in effect, confirms the Menshevik prognosis of Russian development.[2]

As concerns revolutionary processes, Pokrovskii stressed class conflict and mass psychology: "For the proletariat and the autocracy to live together on one planet was impossible" (1926a:608). It was axiomatic for Pokrovskii that workers favor socialism. Driven by hunger, they could do no other than seize factories in order to restore the economy. The socialization of Russia was instinctive.[3] Had Lenin been present or had the other Bolshevik leaders not been thrown off balance by the March days, the October Revolution might not have been needed. A workers' government could have been formed in March (1924b:213). "The dictatorship of the proletariat was present '*de facto*' even on March 12, 1917. It required eight months more to establish itself '*de jure*.' "[4]

The dominant characteristic of the Revolution—the spontaneous action of the workers—is unambiguous;[5] the role of the leadership is less so. According to Pokrovskii, Lenin adhered to the traditional schema of Marx, Engels, Plekhanov, and Rosa Luxemburg, which foretold a bourgeois revolution in Russia that would push forward the socialist revolution in the West. Lenin, badly informed while in Switzerland, still did not foresee a socialist revolution in Russia and expected a bourgeois revolution. Only in Sweden did he apprehend the forces that were in and of themselves driving Russia toward socialism. The February Revolution

> was inevitably a socialist revolution completely and objectively. Lenin, I repeat, did not bring the socialist revolution in his head from abroad, but the genius-like brain of Lenin merely better and sooner than others grasped the situation and understood that under such circumstances [*de facto* power of the workers], nothing other than the transition of the entire economic process into the hands of the workers, *i.e.* a socialist revolution as we understand it, could take place; nothing else could be conceived. The

objective conditions of the moment dictated just this same socialist revolution. And Lenin had to do battle for the sake of the
revolution not with the masses . . . but with the intelligentsia.
(1929b:221–23)

Leadership in the Revolution was a transient ingredient that did not
predestine its outcome. Lenin merely helped to divest his countrymen of
their illusions and thereby hasten the inevitable.

Taming Critics

After Pokrovskii published the *History of the Revolutionary Movement*
in 1924, he found himself in a controversy that lasted until 1926. In just
these years, his organizational base was taking shape, which facilitated
his routing of his critics. Ironically, some of his critics used arguments
foreshadowing those who would be involved in his posthumous liquidation. In upholding his views, Pokrovskii himself adopted arguments that
belied his stated interpretation of World War I. Once this lynchpin was
removed from his interpretation of the Revolution, he was prodded into
recasting his entire theory.

Pokrovskii's chief opponent was A.N. Slepkov, a graduate of the IKP,
who enjoyed a brief but flourishing career as a publicist. The most
prominent of the young intellectuals that gathered around Bukharin, he
was an editor of *Bol'shevik,* the Central Committee's theoretical journal,
and of *Pravda.* Despite the sharpness of the polemic, Pokrovskii and his
former student maintained friendly personal relations.[6] S.G. Tomsinskii,
the second critic, was a Marxist historian who had been trained before
the Revolution. The third opponent was G. Maretskii, an associate of
Slepkov. He picked up the standard when the others fell silent. In a
respectful, even-toned article, he enlarged the scope of criticism by suggesting that not only were particular concepts and interpretations of
Pokrovskii out of order, but his entire mode of analysis was, in certain
respects, un-Marxist (Slepkov, 1926). Pokrovskii responded to Slepkov
and Tomsinskii,[7] but he ignored Maretskii.

Slepkov, on the one hand, praised Pokrovskii's application of the
concept of merchant capitalism for illuminating the origins of autocracy
and for stressing the fact that it had always had a class character. On the
other hand, he reproached Pokrovskii for inflexibility in applying the
concept. It is especially misleading, contended Slepkov, when applied to
recent times, for it fails to take account of the "social regeneration of
autocracy":

> In the second half of the nineteenth century, a social regeneration
> of the landlords and landlord autocracy took place. Under the

influence of world economic ties and the growth of grain exports, the landlords *capitalized* their economy, and the landlord state built railroads, which are *large capitalist* enterprises, and encouraged the development of industry connected with railroad builders. (1924a:115)

The landlords, having thus undergone *embourgeoisement,* supported policies favorable to the industrialists. This important process should have been disclosed in Pokrovskii's theory.

As concerns the peasantry, Slepkov accused Pokrovskii of being unhistorical in depicting it as unchanging in its composition and goals in the course of three hundred years. Razin and Pugachev took up arms for the sake of restoring the state of affairs that preceded serfdom, not in order to establish private property. By 1905, when many peasants were already enmeshed in market relations, they sought to establish a form of capitalism. By 1917, market relationships and class stratification had become so widespread among the Russian peasants that they no longer constituted a united front against the landlords. The rich and poor peasants, the *kulak* and the *bedniak,* were locked in the class conflict typical of capitalism (Slepkov, 1924a:118; 1925:70–71).

The "social regeneration of autocracy," as sketched by Slepkov, turns out to be more than a revision of a few points in Pokrovskii's analysis; rather it is a new way of analyzing twentieth-century Russian history. Once capitalist relations had come to embrace the countryside, Russia was a fairly typical instance of capitalism. The landlords and the *kulaks* were capitalists; the poor peasants were semiproletarians. The great mass of Russians were subject to capitalist exploitation, opposed to capitalism, and hence, by implication, ripe for socialism. This account of the revolution ignores the theory of merchant capitalism. The political significance of this interpretation comes to light in Slepkov's concluding remark where he urged that "our task consists not in 'slighting peasant capitalism,' but in fighting for socialist cooperation among the peasants." In other words, since the majority of the peasants were ripe for socialism, they constituted an ally for the proletariat in the building of socialism, and, consequently, Russia could achieve socialism without world revolution and within the framework of the NEP. Slepkov chided Pokrovskii with failing to take to heart Lenin's advice on rural cooperation (1925:71–72).

To agree that Pokrovskii was hostile to the peasants or to the NEP, to reduce his position to a political equivalent, would be incorrect. Rather he upheld his own views and quite brutally upbraided and misrepresented Slepkov's analysis of the peasantry because he feared that his entire theory of merchant capitalism, the edifice which he counterposed to the national school of historiography, would topple. He charged that if such views as Slepkov's were accepted, they would be "a stick in the wheel of the Bolshevik conception of the Russian historical process" (1925a:125).

Tomsinskii upheld the notion of the social regeneration of autocracy by arguing that Tsarist foreign policy represented an instance of modern imperialism and not the old-fashioned imperialism associated with merchant capital. Colonialism in Central Asia and the Far East, he argued, was more profitable for industrial than merchant capital (1926:255).

While inveighing against Slepkov's analysis, Pokrovskii discreetly abandoned his own contention that rural stratification prepared the way for revolution by strengthening the *kulaks*. He thus considerably modified his stand, but no clear hypothesis replaced this view; indeed, considerable confusion characterizes his treatment of this problem.[8] For the most part, Pokrovskii stressed the backward nature of the peasantry: he minimized the degree of class stratification among the peasants. He endorsed the view that the peasants were revolutionary by virtue of their backwardness. They were being "sucked dry" by autocracy with the result that "in 1905 the *entire* countryside rose up, from the wealthy to the village poor" (1925c). Although Russian industry was highly developed, nowhere else were the peasants more oppressed or made into a "lower race." This widespread discontent assured that the workers would not be isolated in the course of a revolution (1929b:92, 94).

Of greater long-term significance was Pokrovskii's response to Tomsinskii. It determined his stand in a debate on the nature of Russian imperialism which was then taking shape in the seminar rooms of the IKP and would remain a theme in Soviet historiography up to the present day (Tarnovskii, 1964). The issue, in simplest terms, was whether Russia had been the subject of imperialism characteristic of "the highest and final stage of capitalism" or the object of the imperialism of others, most notably Great Britain and France. The problem obviously bore implications concerning the backwardness or advanced character of Russian society. In the course of time, one's stand on this matter would be equated with one's commitment to the possibility of building socialism in one country. In this dispute Pokrovskii sided with his student N. N. Vanag, who argued that the interests of foreign capital predominated in Russia. While a number of considerations influenced Pokrovskii's judgment, a major one was the fact that this thesis tied in neatly with and reinforced the theory of merchant capital. If finance capital (which practiced modern forms of imperialism) existed in Russia, it was subordinate to merchant capital, whose interests governed the state.[9]

Pokrovskii's understanding of imperialism was a steppingstone to a new interpretation of the Revolution. This new interpretation incorporated Lenin's so-called law of uneven development of capitalism. The essence of the new perspective can be discerned in the following passage, which Pokrovskii quoted from one of his colleagues:

> The capitalist world became ripe for the proletarian revolution; *therefore*, the Russian proletarian revolution became possible. . . . It breaks through not where the economic development of society has gone farthest, but where the *development of social contradiction* had gone the farthest. (Kritsman, 1925)

The nations of the world constitute a single economic system, and the system as a whole is ripe for revolution. Thus a nation may be ripe for socialism even if it has not completed the transition from feudalism to capitalism.

The Theory of Growing Over: A Revised Understanding of the October Revolution

Stalin set forth his own distinctive understanding of the Russian past late in 1924, when he affirmed that Lenin had foreseen the possibility of building socialism in one country. Slepkov favorably reviewed Stalin's work in *Bol'shevik;* while urging its widespread adoption, he called attention to one shortcoming, the idea that Lenin had foreseen the isolation of the Revolution as early as 1905, that he had *never* held revolution in advanced countries to be prerequisite for the building of socialism in Russia (1924b:102–5).

While Pokrovskii had enjoyed Lenin's confidence and had been at odds with Trotsky almost from the outset of the New Economic Policy, he stood aloof from Stalin, failing to praise him even after others had begun to.[10] One senses here the disdain typical of old Bolsheviks. Bukharin was an old comrade-in-arms from the Moscow organization; Pokrovskii respected and praised his scholarship and even defended it early in 1928 (1928c:13–14), thereby jeopardizing his own authority. Stalin returned Pokrovskii's disdain with subdued hostility even in the 1920s. In a letter to the German communist Arkady Maslow, Stalin classed Pokrovskii among the prerevolutionary leaders who had fallen by the wayside after the conquest of power. The letter remained unpublished until 1947 (1954, 7:43). In another letter Stalin praised Pokrovskii. In 1927, two IKP students asked Stalin his opinion of Pokrovskii's schema. As concerns "the theory of the formation of the Russian 'autocratic system,' " Stalin replied, Pokrovskii was "fundamentally correct" even though his work contained "extreme interpretations and a bias toward a simplified economic explanation." Stalin later deleted this reference to Pokrovskii from his *Collected Works*.[11]

Pokrovskii was by the mid-1920s a disciplined party scholar, his personal likes notwithstanding. The needs of the party, and Stalin's interpretation of Lenin's writing as set forth late in 1924, served as Pokrovskii's point of departure for his second theory of the Revolution. If it was the internal needs of Pokrovskii's system that required him to recast his interpretation, it was external requirements from the political sphere that determined the substance of the new interpretation. In the fall of 1925, just two weeks after his seminar at the IKP began, Pokrovskii assembled his students to inform them that the Central Committee had requested that they change its theme. The committee urged the students to postpone their research on agrarian problems of feudalism and to undertake instead the study of the Russian Revolution. As a result, a two-volume history of the October Revolution was published on the eve of its tenth anniversary (Pokrovskii, 1927a). The students wrote the chapters, and Pokrovskii provided the introduction; in it he outlined a new method for studying the Revolution.

For the first time the goals of revolutionary leaders coincided with the objective historical path—the destruction of capitalism and the establishment of socialism. Thus the pattern of the Revolution was evident from the outset and was present in the sources. The writings of the Bolshevik leaders "first of all the works of Lenin," were not sources merely in the conventional sense of being a fund of facts and impressions. They embodied the basic pattern of events. The leaders needed a "lever, with the help of which they could exert influence on the march of events." In Marxism, they found such a lever that provided an objective account of history's movement. If the role of leadership was unique and original, so is the task of the historian. He must apply the basic pattern to the Revolution as a whole. More than just filling in facts, he must interpret the pattern for all aspects of the historical process, showing how and why in the flux of things those results prevailed which were in accord with the Marxist-Leninist analysis (1927a:III–IV).

Still in 1927, just as the struggle with Trotsky approached its climax, Pokrovskii sought to implement the new principles of studying the Revolution. He presented an authoritative paper to a group of colleagues who discussed it at length and revised it for publication (1927b). In it he contrasted Lenin's understanding of the Revolution to Trotsky's, attempting to prove once and for all that Lenin had not rearmed himself with a new theory when he returned to Petrograd in 1917.

Lenin began writing the history of the Revolution, according to Pokrovskii's new account, twelve years before the event. In 1905 he predicted that the complete victory of the Revolution would be the establishment of a revolutionary-democratic dictatorship, which would mark the beginning of the struggle for socialism. When Lenin returned to Russia in 1917, he was armed not with a new theory but rather with a more specific and detailed version of the original one. This theory of revolution, though skeletal, guided Lenin's actions, and his actions provided experience for theorizing. A more detailed plan was possible in 1916 owing to new circumstances, first of all the imperialist war, which "to an immense degree brought closer the socialist revolution throughout the entire world" (1927b:4, 10). The means for connecting the bourgeois republic and the socialist revolution were becoming evident to Lenin, who thus "was the first author since Marx of a genuine theory of permanent revolution." By February 1915 Lenin foresaw an impending struggle for socialism in Russia. The immediate task was still the bourgeois revolution, but when he asserted the need for the separate organization of the rural proletariat, he was preparing for the socialist overturn. By 1916 Lenin saw some of the major characteristics of the socialist revolution. Pokrovskii quoted Lenin's "Results of the Discussion of Self-Determination," which appeared on the eve of the Revolution:

> He who awaits a "pure" [entirely proletarian] social revolution, will never get to see it. . . . The socialist revolution in Europe *cannot be* anything other than an explosion of mass struggle on the part of all the oppressed and dissatisfied. Portions of the petty bourgeoisie and backward workers will inevitably participate in it . . . and will inevitably bring with themselves into the movement their prejudices, their reactionary fantasies, their weaknesses and errors. But *objectively* they will be attacking *capital,* and the conscious vanguard of the revolution, the advanced workers . . . can unite and direct [the struggle]. (1927b:5)

In 1916 Lenin's plan "raised only a small corner of the curtain over the future," and the bulk of the details were still unknown and awaited the unfolding of events. Lenin understood "the reality of chance and to what degree the concrete details of the picture . . . can change even from today to tomorrow." Only *"practical demands"* compelled him to articulate the plan in greater detail (1927b:5–6). In 1917, with a fresh impression of the news of the fall of the monarchy, Lenin noted that only the first step of the Revolution had been completed. In his third "Letter from Afar," he called for a new combination of forces to achieve the socialist revolution. Part of Lenin's prognosis had to be revised, because certain possibilities put forth in 1915 had not been realized. At that time Lenin foresaw the possibility of cooperation with the petty bourgeoisie at the decisive moment of the Revolution. But the Social Revolutionaries and Mensheviks chose to divide power with the counterrevolutionary upper bourgeoisie. Their support of the latter in the July Days ended all possibility of cooperation with the Bolsheviks. This was the element of the plan that had provided for the peaceful acquisition of power, and after July it had to be put to rest. From the moment that he called for an armed uprising "we had Lenin's final conception of the October Revolution" (1927b:10, 12, 13).

In sum, Lenin in 1905 formulated a theory of the socialist revolution. It was to follow the completion of the bourgeois stage of the revolution—the establishment of a revolutionary-democratic dictatorship of the workers and peasants. By what means and after how long a period of time was not stipulated. Lenin had set forth the task of the socialist revolution; the form it would take had to be worked out in connection with emerging events. How the revolutions were to be bridged was still uncertain; only possibilities could be articulated, but his hypothesis about imperialism implied that the two revolutions could be telescoped. Step-by-step, in response to specific problems and in connection with the changing circumstances, Lenin discarded some possibilities and implemented others. With the call for armed uprising, his program and his theory were completed. For Pokrovskii this theory, in its emerging form, shaped the history of the October Revolution because it embodied its basic pattern.

Pokrovskii's analysis involves some questionable interpretations of Lenin's writings. He left out of his account all passages that held revolution in advanced countries to be prerequisite for the *completion* of a socialist revolution in Russia. He is saying that if Lenin in 1917 adhered to the same theory he had in 1905, how could the term "rearmed" be applied? If the old Bolsheviks had adhered to Lenin's theory, how could they have been out of step with him in 1917? The doctrine is subtle in that it reintroduced the international significance of the Revolution in a new way. The moribund state of world capitalism, the fact that it had entered the stage of imperialism, was a necessary condition for the Revolution. It no longer hinged upon World War I, it was no longer necessary to demonstrate that the war derived from the Russian crisis.

If Pokrovskii's interpretation of Leninism is dubious, his remarks about Trotsky are scurrilous. The curious thing is that he attributed to Trotsky a caricature of his own previously held theory. He argued that the essence of Trotsky's interpretation was expressed in the phrase "Without a Tsar, a workers' Government"—the fall of autocracy would inevitably result in socialism.

All the same, this article is an ingenious, even brilliant sketch of the Revolution. It is rich in nuance and distinctions that suggest the interaction of a variety of processes, and it brings out the subtle influence of leadership. The sketch marks an important stage in the development of a new discipline, Leninology, and it charts the opening of what Soviet historians call the Leninist stage of Soviet historiography. Pokrovskii's methodological principles are the point of departure for all subsequent Soviet research on the Revolution. He opened a politically significant scholarly debate that would last until 1931, when Stalin signaled that it was over.

Pokrovskii's rise to eminence was marked by conflict. His ideas, far from being inflexible, were highly unstable. Although he strove to vindicate his theory of merchant capital in the face of criticism, in his final account of the Russian Revolution, he did not even mention it.

4 Battle Lines among Historians, 1925–1928

The policy of using noncommunist hands in the building of communism was almost as old as the Soviet government itself. When the Communist Party in the early 1920s accepted the outcome of the Russian Revolution—the confinement of a socialist regime to an underdeveloped country—it sought means to guide institutions in which its members and supporters were a minority. The authorities created a network of scholarly institutions staffed by Marxist scholars; these paralleled the traditional institutions staffed and led primarily by non-Marxist scholars. Pokrovskii not only helped to create and administer the new institutions and to influence the old ones, he also sought to justify and codify relationships among scholars and between scholars and political authorities. In so doing, he helped propound a theory of cultural revolution. The theory proved more enduring than many of the institutions themselves.

The disposition to control and utilize the non-Marxist intelligentsia was not merely a passing mood of Pokrovskii. And though it could not have prevailed had Lenin opposed it instead of forcefully supporting it, it represented something more than the policy of the party's leader. It was a priority built into the organization of a variety of cultural, economic, and state institutions. Their structure implicitly distinguished between Marxist and non-Marxist cadres. The ruling party distrusted its potential rivals; its sense of state, however, induced it to recognize that the tasks of reconstruction it posed for itself required their collaboration. This resulted in a tenuous form of pluralism—one that affirmed the necessity of outgroups but denied their need for autonomy.[1]

The Communist Party showed active concern with the writing of history. In May 1921 the Politburo, in a meeting chaired by Lenin, directed the People's Commissariat of Education to prepare history textbooks and brochures.[2] The Agitation and Propaganda Department of the Central Committee (Agitprop) regularly held conferences with party historians to evaluate personnel in the Communist Academy, the Institute of Red Professors, and other party institutions of higher education.[3] Late in 1922, party organizations throughout the country met to find measures for countering the influence of hostile ideologists. Lecture teams were organized and dispatched throughout the nation. In January the Organization Bureau of the Central Committee called upon historians to take part in the ongoing ideological campaign against "all forms and varieties of counter-revolutionary ideologies" (*Iz istorii,* 1967:193). Nothing in such matters was left to chance.

Origins of the Society of Marxist Historians

The Marxist institutions set up to advance scholarly pursuits were untried but sustained by a state that justified itself by reference to a historically based ideology. The chief center of Marxist scholarship was the Communist Academy, which had begun in 1918 as little more than a discussion group and reading room, and which grew by the early 1930s into an array of research institutes, graduate seminars, commissions, societies, and the like. Historical research was carried out in a number of the Communist Academy's sectors, the most important of which was the Society of Marxist Historians, initiated in 1925. It sought to guide all Marxist historiography in and out of the Communist Academy and to circumscribe non-Marxist scholarship.

The Commission for the Study of the October Revolution and the Russian Communist Party (Istpart) was a second important center of historical investigation. Founded in 1920 as an agency to collect materials on the history of the Communist Party and the October Revolution, it contained a nationwide network of branches and worked in close association with the Society of Old Bolsheviks. Its chief journal, *Proletarskaia revoliutsiia,* predecessor of *Voprosy istorii KPSS,* published an immense amount of primary source material and became an important vehicle for political and historical discussion. A similar enterprise was the Marx-Engels Institute. It collected massive amounts of material on Marxism and the European labor movement. Another institution with a similar mission was the Lenin Institute, founded in 1923 and directed by L.B. Kamenev. These three were the components of what is today the Institute of Marxism-Leninism.

Another important center of Marxist scholarship was the Institute of Red Professors, the capstone of an elaborate network of party schools. Founded in 1921, it was an advanced school, the equivalent of a graduate center for party intellectuals, attended mostly by young Bolshevik veterans of the Civil War. Some important publications and even major controversies grew out of the institute's seminars. Like the Communist Academy and the Society of Marxist Historians, it was headed by Pokrovskii. Just slightly less important was the Society of Political Convicts and Penal Exiles, which was composed of former members of the revolutionary movement, both Marxists and Populists. It published the scholarly journal *Katorga i Ssylka*.[4]

The Central Committee made a major investment in the Communist Academy in 1925; it created seven new branches in the first half of the year, including the Society of Marxist Historians (SMH).[5] The basis of this decision became evident at the general meeting of the Comacademy in June 1925, when V.P. Miliutin,[6] an old Bolshevik of working-class origins, a practicing economist who was a deputy chairman of the KA, spoke. Contemporary social problems are theoretical as well as practical, he argued, "and that deviation, that incorrect approach, which we observed in our ranks among some comrades, and which provoked such heated discussion testifies to the fact that the need for greater profundity of theory is rapidly increasing" (*VKA*, 1925, 11:364). He referred to achievements of "bourgeois and petty bourgeois" scholarship, which required, he felt, "evaluation from the standpoint of Marxist-Leninist ideology." In a later speech, Miliutin urged that future "reports be collective works, and the fruit of collective reworking by the sections" (*VKA*, 1925, 12:366). By having the reports express the opinions of sections of the Communist Academy rather than individuals, dissent was impeded. The new institutions were instruments to advance research; they served also to stifle opposition by bureaucratic regimentation. Although the SMH was created to train Marxist scholars and to combat non-Marxist theories, the mode of organization was fixed in large measure by conflict with Trotsky. The authoritarian procedures would inevitably cloud relations with the non-Marxists and set limits on the tolerance for which the period is known.

Although Pokrovskii referred to the society as his "offspring" (*detishche*), teachers in a party school, Communist University of Toilers of the East, had formally initiated its creation. Among them was A.V. Shestakov,[7] who had been a Social Democrat since 1898 and had recently completed work at the IKP. A five-man commission was organized to plan a meeting of prominent Marxist historians and to draft a statute for the society.[8] Besides Pokrovskii and Shestakov, members were G.S. Zaidel, who would become Pokrovskii's arm in Leningrad, a city deemed saturated with the old ways of thinking, Ts.S. Fridliand, a reformed Trotskyite whom Pokrovskii authorized to supervise writing on modern European history, and P.O. Gorin, a former student of Pokrovskii at Sverdlov University. Gorin became the academic secretary of the society and as such its principal administrator; he was Pokrovskii's chief lieutenant and a close friend.

In March a founding meeting was held, and the society was formally created in June, though its statute gained approval only in February 1926, after passing through the council, the Presidium of the KA, the

State Council of Scholars (GUS) within the Commissariat of Education, and Agitprop. According to the statute, leadership was vested in a council of fifteen members and five candidate members. It was to be elected by the annual meeting of the membership but subject to ratification by the presidium of the KA. The council elected a presidium—its chairman was Pokrovskii—and the editorial board of the society's journal, *Istorik-marksist*—its chairman also was Pokrovskii. A revision commission, rarely ever mentioned, was also set up. It did not guide the day-to-day work of the society but evidently verified fulfillment of assignments and supervised the selection of members.

The goals of the SMH, as expressed in the statute, included the "unification of all Marxists concerned with scholarly work in the field of history [for] struggle against perversion of history by bourgeois scholarship [through] critical illumination of current historical literature from the Marxist standpoint." It also had routine professional functions, assisting members to obtain historical literature, to gain access to archives, and to receive funds for travel. A pedagogical task consisted of "propaganda and popularization of the Marxist method and acquainting the broad masses with Marxist achievements in the field of history."

The SMH, a society as opposed to an institute, was constituted of dues-paying members, not of a professional staff. "A voluntary tribune of Marxist historians," said Gorin (*IM*, 1927, 4:272). In keeping with the tradition of Russian scholarly institutions, two forms of membership were designated. Active members had to have published at least one work of historical research or to teach an independent course in an institution of higher learning. Corresponding members "support the Society by personal participation in solving scientific problems and also communicate with the Society through correspondence, notices, etc." By 1928 the society counted 250 members, 123 active and 127 corresponding.[9] Originally it consisted of four sections: history of Russia and the Communist Party, history of the West, history of social formations (sociology and orientology), and methodology (pedagogy). Moscow was its center; even in the early 1930s members complained about the slight influence of the society in the provinces and in Leningrad. Pokrovskii was disappointed that only a small proportion, about twenty percent of the society's entire membership, consisted of fellow-travelers, non-Marxists sympathetic to the party (*IM*, 1927, 4:272).

At the society's first open meeting, June 1925, Pokrovskii expounded upon the organizational and intellectual tasks of the society. Young communist historians and "the ever-increasing cadres of bourgeois historians who are close to us, who 'accept' Marxism," should unite their scientific endeavors: "When they were in school this need was met by the history seminars of the Institute of Red Professors, but as soon as their instruction came to an end, scientific ties were broken; yesterday's participants in collective work became solitary individuals, that is to say, they deteriorated in the most evident and obvious way."[10]

Consolidation of forces should accompany improvement in historical understanding. Economic materialism, that "kink" and "professional deformity," must be overcome. Before the Revolution it had been progressive "to collect an enormous amount of economic, or, more particularly, of historical statistical material." It was prerequisite "for even an elementary scientific understanding of history" and swept aside "once and for all the saccharine legends . . . which divided all historical figures in the good and the bad."

> But it is completely improper to substitute them for history. We must never forget the words of Marx and Engels to this effect— both repeatedly insisted on the point—that, although history is made in a definite economic setting, on a definite economic base . . . history nevertheless is made by living human beings who need not be directly motivated by economic factors.[11]

Most senior Marxist historians became members of the society. Emelian Iaroslavskii, Pokrovskii's former comrade-in-arms and future rival, was a member of the council, as was Wilhelm G. Knorin, a Latvian-born old Bolshevik and a specialist in party history. He had the highest political standing among its members. A member of the Military-Revolutionary Committee in Minsk, he rose to membership in the Central Committee of the All-Union Communist Party and in the executive committee of the Comintern.[12] N.M. Lukin was the party's most prominent specialist in European history.[13] Like Pokrovskii, he had been trained in Moscow University's historico-philological faculty and had then taken the path to underground activity. In 1918 he, like Pokrovskii, joined the Left Communists. He was a member of the SMH Council and the Presidium of the KA; he later was elected to the Academy of Sciences and was the head of its Institute of History. After Pokrovskii's death, Lukin became the leader of the historical sector until the liquidation of Pokrovskii's school during the purges, when he suffered for his misfortune of being Bukharin's brother-in-law. The society increasingly became an arena for the young historians, most of whom had been members of Pokrovskii's seminar at the Institute of Red Professors. This group includes such well-known figures as A.M. Pankratova, I.I. Mints, S.M. Dubrovskii, A.L. Sidorov, and N.L. Rubinshtein.[14] N.N. Vanag, one of the most talented junior historians, is less well known because he failed to survive the purges. A.N.

Slepkov enjoyed a brief but distinguished career as a journalist upon graduation. He was closely associated with Bukharin.

The society regularly sponsored public meetings, where research findings were presented and criticized in lively discussions. Most reports were coordinated with public jubilees—anniversaries of important events such as the Decembrist Uprising and memorials for revolutionary heroes such as Bakunin and Chernyshevskii. The publication of the journal *Istorik-marksist* (*The Marxist Historian*) was also an important activity of the SMH. It differed from other Marxist historical journals of the period in that it did not usually publish source materials. It was deemed a journal of opinion. Scholarly articles and stenographic notes of some of the public discussions filled most of its pages, but it also contained book reviews and a lengthy chronicle of professional news. About half the articles treated Russian history, mostly the revolutionary movement. About a third treated European history; almost all of these were about the French Revolution. The editors sought articles about the United States, but admitted in 1927 that they were unable to find a Marxist historian with sufficient knowledge of American history. The journal published numerous articles, reports, and discussions about the teaching of history. By the time the third issue of *Istorik-marksist* appeared (1927), the number of subscribers had grown to almost fifteen hundred (*IM*, 1927, 4:276).

The tone of *Istorik-marksist* was militant, though in the early years it was criticized for being too descriptive and insufficiently critical of non-Marxist literature and lax in rooting out vestiges of economic materialism.[15] This accusation was just: despite the circumstance of the SMH's origins and the continuation of intraparty conflict, the tone of its journal was far more civil than it would be in the 1930s. An indication of the tolerance of the 1920s is the inclusion in the ranks of the SMH of A.E. Presniakov, the prominent Leningrad Academician, and the ex-Menshevik N.A. Rozhkov, who, though moving close to the Bolsheviks before his death in 1928, had been condemned to death by them during the Civil War, and who continued to base his research on his own interpretation of Marxism. Academician E.V. Tarle, whose standing was to become in itself something of a rough index of the range of toleration, at the time was occasionally invited to participate in the work of the Communist Academy and even to lecture at the Institute of Red Professors (Nosov, 1967:57).

Popularization of historical knowledge absorbed much of the energy of the society. A series of books on the medieval and modern history of both Russia and Europe appeared under the general editorship of Pokrovskii. In 1930 the society began to publish a second journal, *Bor'ba klassov* (*Class Conflict*), popular, illustrated, and very militant.

Non-Marxist and Semi-Marxist Historiography

The very title *Society of Marxist Historians* "drew a line of demarcation between bourgeois scholars and those who stood on Marxist positions." Such a society was necessary "to rally young forces . . . and to assist those historians who strove to move over to Marxist positions" (Sidorov, 1964:134–35). Russian and Western scholars agree that non-Marxist historiography preempted the field in the early years of Soviet power, until at least 1925.[16] This situation prevailed despite the fact that a few non-Marxist historians had been deported in 1922 along with other members of the intelligentsia and that often historians had "to purchase the right to publish."[17] The 1920s were a distinctively creative period for the older generation of Russian scholars, one in which highly technical document analysis was combined with bold hypotheses to recast the problem of serfdom. The application of the concept of feudalism to Russian history was continually broadened, and finally it was employed to describe the Kievan period. This theme, which was an undercurrent in the 1920s, emerged in 1932 when it received its classical formulation from B.D. Grekov, a national-minded historian who chose not to emigrate after the Civil War, and who is considered by many to have been the foremost Soviet historian.[18] It was taken over as their own by the Marxist historians and became the basis of the system of views that replaced Pokrovskii's. For the non-Marxist historians, this period was the final glow of the silver age of Russian culture.

The most important centers of non-Marxist scholarship were the Institute of History of RANION (Russian Association of Social Science Institutes) in Moscow and the Academy of Sciences of Leningrad (Platonov, 1927). The academy's history and philological department contained a number of research organizations including the Permanent Historico-Archeographic Commission,[19] the Russian-Byzantine Commission, and the Paleographic Museum. These bodies had resources enough only for archival work. The academy's research and training was carried out in GAIMK (State Academy of Material Culture). Although this institute was founded in 1919 on the base of the Academy of Sciences' Archeological Commission, it was formally independent of the academy. This arrangement was the result of a decision by Communist authorities (Vainshtein, 1968:42). In 1927 it was brought within the framework of RANION.[20] GAIMK was headed by N.Ia. Marr, a prominent philologist who was one of the most important of the old scholars to embrace Marxism. Grekov joined its staff in 1930, and its graduate program produced such scholars as V.V. Mavrodin and I.I. Smirnov.

RANION itself was an assembly of fourteen research and teaching institutes organized and headed until 1927 by Pokrovskii.[21] The staffs were predominantly non-Marxist, though containing a strong Communist admixture—the students were Marxists. Whereas the Institute of Red Professors was created to provide propagandists, instructors, and scholars for party assignment, RANION's institutes were created to provide Marxist instructors and scholars for the national education system.[22] No doubt both considerations of expense and political goals inclined the authorities to centralize graduate training, so that it could be supervised and its results verified. RANION's Institute of History, in Fridliand's words, "assembled within its walls all that remained of old bourgeois scholarship." For "all these old luminaries," there was established "maximum freedom for scientific activity." Even those who "on principle did not wish to work at the Institute of Red Professors were permitted to work in RANION" (1928b:30).

The Institute of History was created in 1921 by a decree of the Council of Commissars. Just a year later some members of the Commissariat of Education, concerned about the influence of non-Marxists, urged the abolition of it and similar institutions. Their arguments were rejected on the authority of Pokrovskii and V.P. Volgin, another academically trained Marxist historian, who had been a Menshevik. The institute was attached to the Social Science Faculty (FON) of Moscow University in 1922. After an organizational shake-up in 1923, the communists established a majority in the presidium of FON and in the collegia of its individual institutes. Two years later the Institute of History was transferred to RANION, which marked a turning point: it became a graduate center, and, at the same time a "communist nucleus" was achieved on various levels.[23] In 1927 a branch opened in Leningrad.

By 1929 the Institute of History had a staff of thirty-five members and twenty-five research workers; thirty-seven graduate students were enrolled (*Uchenie zapiski,* 1929, 4:218–19). Its director, D.M. Petrushevskii, was *ipso facto* a leader of the non-Marxist historians and destined thereby for controversy. He was a medievalist who, like Pokrovskii, had been a student of P.G. Vinogradov; unlike Pokrovskii, he had not become embroiled in party politics. The authorities considered him progressive; even one of his prerevolutionary works was considered close to Marxism, and his textbook, *Outlines of the History of Medieval State and Society,* was employed in Soviet schools. The authorities expected further evolution toward Marxism, as it was widely held that one close to Marxism would inevitably embrace it in a socialist society.

The structure of the institute reflected its semi-Marxist character: it contained sections for ancient, medieval, and modern history; these traditional designations existed beside new sections for the study of non-European societies and colonial politics, sociology, and a subsection on nineteenth- and twentieth-century Russian history—the era of the revolutionary movement and the Communist Party. The same hybrid character was reflected in the composition of the staff. The Marxist component included Pokrovskii, D.B. Riazanov, N.M. Lukin, G.S. Zaidel, and V. Nevskii, an old Bolshevik, trained as a chemist, who had played an important part in the October Revolution. In the early 1920s he headed the Leningrad Istpart; he was brought to Moscow in the mid-1920s as head of the Lenin Library and was a recognized authority on party history. N.N. Vanag and A.M. Pankratova were IKP graduates now beginning pedagogical careers. The non-Marxists included A.E. Presniakov, E.V. Tarle, M.M. Bogoslavskii, M.K. Liubavskii, and V.I. Picheta.

The institute represented an uneasy compromise that could from no point of view, except perhaps the students', be considered ideal. Though conceived to complement the IKP, it became a rival. To the degree that it informally constituted a voluntary tribune, it rivaled the SMH. Arrangements afforded the non-Marxists little independence and security, and for the regime they created anxiety. This found expression in a Marxist review of one of the institute's publications. Grudging admiration for achievements in document analysis, and other technical matters was accompanied by condemnation of the writers for "reactionary principles, the absence of conceptions, and weakness of sociological analysis" (Mamet & Shestakov, 1927:210–17). When Agitprop heard the report of RANION early in 1927, it approved the institute's work in general but lamented the low level of training in Marxism. Even though the Central Committee and the Commissariat of Education approved RANION's work, the opinion persisted that it was incapable of training Marxist cadres. Many of the hopes and fears associated with the policy of enlisting the support of the old intelligentsia, while denying it its customary autonomy, were centered on RANION's Institute of History.

Early in 1928, a minor pogrom took place. An article appeared in the newspaper *Evening Moscow* complaining about the "demarxification" of the Institute of History and the resurgence of the old scholarship. The article quoted a student wall poster: "In our institutes, at some meetings of various sections the name Marx and even more so *the name Lenin* is *subject, as in Tsarist Russia, to witticism*" ("V chem delo," 1928). If Marx's name was "taboo," it was fashionable to cite bourgeois authors like Sombart and Weber, whose plagiarisms and falsifications of Marxism were taken "as the latest 'discoveries' of science." A student delegation appeared at Pokrovskii's office demanding a remedy; expulsion of almost ten percent of the student body resulted.[24] Some of the Marxist professors were accused later of defending their colleagues by depicting the students' campaign as an ultraleft deviation, baiting of specialists. Fridliand derided them for "taking pride in being accepted in the midst" of non-Marxists as " 'tame' communists" (1928b:29–30).

The national and ideological assertiveness reflected in the student out-
burst is characteristic of the time and place, as is the evidence of generational conflict. Perhaps the event was merely a release of tension following the Fifteenth Congress of the Communist Party and accompanying
the food shortage and forcible grain collections. That the students' demands so closely anticipate Stalin's personnel policies later in the year,
however, leads one to suspect that the event was contrived. Perhaps it
was a tactical experiment by Stalin's followers, a move to state in their
own terms the issues that separated them from their rivals. At any rate,
as late as August RANION was mentioned in a Central Committee
resolution as an adjunct of party schools (*ITsK,* 10 Sept. 1928:9).

Pokrovskii: His Practice and His Theory

The formative years of the SMH, 1925–28, coincide with the ascendancy
of Pokrovskii; circumstances worked in his favor. His participation in
the criticism of Trotsky enhanced his popularity in party society and led
to the republication of several of his works. He wrote as prolifically as
ever and enjoyed a status that entitled him to have his speeches and
many statements recorded and published. In 1927, for example, aside
from the republication of two early works and a collection in book form
of his articles on the Decembrists, there are over sixty items in his
bibliography.[25] Former students of Pokrovskii at the IKP were now
occupying positions of authority. "The Society itself might be considered the organizational manifestation of the school of Pokrovskii"
(Naidenov, 1961:91).

Pokrovskii's most important posts were deputy commissar of educa-
tion, rector of the IKP, and chairman of the KA. Being chairman of the
KA involved him with its branches: in addition to being chairman of the
SMH, he also headed a KA section on The History of the Revolutionary
Movement, a special commission called The History of the Proletariat in
Russia, and a commission on The Documentation of the Imperialist
War.[26] In 1927, in accord with the Central Committee resolution, most
likely initiated by Pokrovskii himself, a new commission, headed by
Pokrovskii and made up of representatives of the KA, the Marx-Engels
Institute, and the Lenin Institute, began to function. Its task was to
coordinate the work of these and other institutions,[27] but it had no
visible result, and Pokrovskii complained frequently of his failure to
coordinate the efforts of the Marxist institutions.

Even though he was a leader of Istpart and an editor of its journal
Proletarskaia revoliutsiia as well as a member of the governing board of
the Lenin Institute,[28] Pokrovskii could not bring these bodies together
beneath the KA. David Borisovich Riazanov, the eminent Marxologist
and traditionally independent-minded Social Democrat, stoutly main-

tained the autonomy of the Marx-Engels Institute. He had been at one time close to the Mensheviks, at another a member of Trotsky's Inter-Districters. After the Revolution he had sided with the Workers' Opposition, a trade union-based faction within Bolshevism that had proved to be among Lenin's staunchest opponents. He was not only the head of the Marx-Engels Institute but a member of the KA presidium and a lecturer at a variety of educational institutions, including the Institute of Red Professors. The Society of Penal Convicts and Hard-Labor Exiles also stood aloof from Pokrovskii. It would openly oppose him in the 1930s, but insiders were aware of some members' diffidence even in the early years.[29] They found support even in the first council of the SMH in the person of S.I. Mitskevich ("Sergei," 1967), a former member of the revolutionary terrorist group *Narodnaia Volia* and an old Bolshevik. Though trained as physician, he founded the Museum of the Revolution, and he was a recognized authority on the history of the revolutionary movement, including party history. Not only the imperiousness of the KA, but the historical views of Pokrovskii himself offended them. As seen in the last chapter, the intelligentsia had only marginal significance in Pokrovskii's synthesis of Russian history. The history of ideas held a lesser place than social and economic history. When Pokrovskii did take up the intelligentsia's ideas in the *History of the Revolutionary Movement* he stressed their remoteness from Marxism. Their understanding of history, in his view, assumed the supraclass character of autocracy.[30]

All the same, it would be difficult to overestimate Pokrovskii's influence on early Marxist scholarship in the Soviet Union. Not surprisingly, the works of his students bore the imprint of his temperament and interests. One of the main achievements of Marxist scholarship, in Pokrovskii's view, was to prove and to document the hegemony of the proletariat in the countryside during the 1905 Revolution. Among the most active of his students in this field were Dubrovskii, Gorin, and Pankratova. Pokrovskii himself had a keen interest in the Decembrist movement, and in the 1920s an immense amount of source material was published and studied. The main specialist in this field was M.V. Nechkina. Two historians—S.G. Tomsinskii and G.K. Meerson—debated the character of the *Pugachevshchina* in these years; Pokrovskii considered this debate fruitful even though it jeopardized some of his notions and in the long run overthrew them. Pokrovskii also edited a number of volumes prepared in his seminars at the IKP, which reflected his interpretations of subjects of major importance—Russian historiography and the Russian Revolution. These works should be considered part of Pokrovskii's legacy.[31]

Pokrovskii was a vital link between the party leadership on the one hand and scholars and scholar-ideologists in the field on the other. An important responsibility of his was to advise the leadership about ideological trends and about the political complexion of personnel. He had an important voice in deciding which non-Marxist scholars were fit for building communism and which were not. His reputation, nurtured by friends and enemies among his contemporaries, is that of a Savonarola-like foe of those who failed to share his opinions. Many present-day Soviet historians reject this judgment; their writings at least show the difficulty of making any such categorical statement. Fragmentary evidence, recently selected by Soviet historians, shows Pokrovskii almost a protector of the non-Marxist intelligentsia—*in the early 1920s*. Pokrovskii had warm praise for the aesthetic refinement and personal charm of Alexander Benois. Benois was an artist, art historian, and set designer closely associated with Sergei Diaghilev, with the Imperial Ballet, and later with the Ballet Russe de Monte Carlo. In these early years Pokrovskii even praised S.F. Platonov, who had not only been employed by the royal family as a tutor but, as head of the Historical Department of the Academy of Sciences, was a leading figure among non-Marxist intellectuals and as such a rival of Pokrovskii. "He behaves in the highest degree loyally and correctly" wrote Pokrovskii, commending Platonov for his efforts in reorganizing the archives. Pokrovskii considered him a "man of outstanding intelligence," an "extraordinary historian of conservative convictions."[32] If the scope of Pokrovskii's tolerance is obscure, it is clear, at least, that it was broader than Lenin's. Pokrovskii went so far as to urge the employment of former Mensheviks in the Social Science Faculty of Moscow University.[33]

When a large number of scholars considered hostile by the regime were deported in 1922, most likely Pokrovskii participated in the discussions of this policy; even without direct evidence we may assume that he played a role in the implementation. As a result three leading historians were expelled: V.A. Miakotin, who resumed his research in Sofia, A.A. Kizevetter, who did the same in Prague, and S.P. Mel'gunov, who did outstanding research in Paris and whose office became something of a center of émigré intelligence activities.[34]

In his reflections on the policy of using noncommunists in the building of communism, Pokrovskii stressed the need for preserving non-Marxist scholarship insofar as it helped fulfill the task of cultural reconstruction that the party had set for the state. He also shared a widespread anxiety about the possible harmful consequence of non-Marxist modes of thought and therefore sought means to circumscribe the influence of non-Marxists. His activity as an organizer of scholarship thus aimed at finding means for employing non-Marxists while subordinating them to the goal of developing a Marxist-proletarian culture. Although Pokrovskii's admiration for what he called "bourgeois culture" was slender, he disparaged as "absolutely undialectical" and "un-Marxist" the notion of "proletarian culture" as a thing "torn out of, independent of . . . the bourgeois culture of the past." He urged "recognition of the old science as a stage, which was surpassed, but which has to be experienced, which each Marxist initiate must experience, if only in summary form" (1933d:13–15). The living representatives of the old in their own way serve Marxism: as teachers, they impart skills needed by Communists; as scholars, they provide "academic production [of] sufficiently high quality to be very useful as material for future Communist researchers."[35]

Pokrovskii was mindful of the continuity of culture, but most frequently he stressed discontinuity and opposition of outlook and interest between bourgeois and proletarian cultures. As early as 1920 he had emphasized the need for the "creation of cadres of teachers, mainly in the social sciences, who can counter bourgeois falsification of these sciences with strict objective teaching about social phenomena, governed by the Marxist method" (Sokolov, 1963:39). His was one of the voices in the party urging it to harness the ideological currents manifest during the early NEP; he warned against "drift" and shared a widespread anxiety about the residual influence non-Marxist men and ideas would exercise (VSA, 1923, 6:433).

Pokrovskii wanted a sharp line of demarcation between Marxist and non-Marxist ideas and persons, and he counseled intimate collaboration among Marxists: "We unconditionally require an association of Communist scientific institutions which would work in accord with a single plan under unified leadership" (Kommunisticheskaia revoliutsiia, 1927, 5:28). He opposed setting tasks that would tax the resources of the Communist Academy, such as the proposal that it supervise all research—Marxist and non-Marxist. He cautioned against what would come to be called "administrative means," that is, coercion and intimidation of non-Marxists. With only minor variations he upheld two demands until 1928—that for an authoritative Marxist center and that for avoiding a policy of dispensing altogether with non-Marxist scholarship. The activities of the non-Marxist were legitimate only to the degree that they served the interests of proletarian culture.

The discrepancies in Pokrovskii's position were reconciled by his will and by a hope. He held out the hope of winning over the bourgeois specialists to the banner of Marxism. This would not happen next year, or even the year after, he predicted in 1924, but it was, he believed, entirely possible by the time of the tenth anniversary of the Revolution (VKA, 1928, 11:401). Then late in March 1928, he suggested that five years hence there would be no need even to discuss non-Marxist scholarship. The inherent superiority of the Marxist method, already proved factually by the evolution of Soviet social science, would remove the problem. It is not just that Marxism "infects" scrupulous non-Marxists.

"The facts themselves" of the respective disciplines drive them "toward the Marxist standpoint." Sometimes a scholar, "not without surprise even for himself, [will suddenly] realize that he is a consistent historical materialist" (*VKA*, 1928, 26:26).

Pokrovskii's disposition to marshal the Marxist cadres and arm them for combat with non-Marxists reflected his hopes and his notion of what constituted the most favorable environment for a spontaneous evolution in the direction of Marxism. But what if such an evolution does not occur? How can one respond to the assertion that the continued influence of non-Marxist thought is not residual but a consequence of political initiatives by one's class enemies?

Pokrovskii's observations reveal many of his thoughts and feelings about cultural change in what he considered to be an era of proletarian revolution. On an intellectual level, Pokrovskii was predominantly instrumental—the old culture was one of the tools at the disposal of the proletariat and then of the party to organize the masses in conformity with the tasks of cultural revolution: to fashion them into conscious makers of their own history. On the level of feeling, Pokrovskii was not simply instrumental but respectful and antagonistic, appreciative and derogatory toward both the monuments and the living representatives of the old culture. He shared the dilemma of all adherents of democratic centralism who emerged from the underground to positions of power. They who had been rebels seeking autonomy to elaborate and propagate an anti-authoritarian idea then as incarnation of authority had to define their relations to those who now claimed autonomy. The very ambiguities in Pokrovskii's observations reveal some of the tensions of this situation. What is clear is Pokrovskii's sense of the mission of the proletarian state. It should provide facilities for and actively foster the development of the new culture. If expedient, it should employ representatives of the old culture for this purpose.

What is unclear is Pokrovskii's distinction between the realm of politics and the realm of culture. His discussion shifts from one plane to another without sufficient modulation, and the matter is not clarified by his assumption that culture is ultimately dependent upon forces and relations of production. One eye perceives a given non-Marxist historian as the embodiment of a tradition the state lays claim to as heir, while the other perceives him as an exploiter and potential wrecker. A given history book might in one eye be an autonomous product and in the other a hostile act and a claim to power. The resulting blurred vision might cause one to feel deceived. Administrative means—intimidation and coercion—might suddenly be perceived as honorable political devices that one would be derelict in forfeiting.

Still another ambiguity with respect to cultural policy lies in Pokrovskii's insufficient definition of Marxism. Marxism is at once a map of reality and an instrument for self-realization of the masses. But how can one be an autonomous historical actor if one cannot decide what set of premises or combinations of them provide the best map of reality? What can autonomy mean if it does not include making such a decision?

Pokrovskii expected the passage of time and continuous cultural construction to resolve the practical problems that these ambiguities reflect. In due course Marxism would root out modes of perception and feeling that derived from the neolithic revolution. Marxism as a map and as an instrument would reveal its superiority to any rational person. Hence there would be no need to find a standard for determining when the representatives of bourgeois culture had lost their usefulness. Any honest non-Marxist scholar would in time perceive the falsity of his own premises and seek better ones. If egotism or perversity inhibited him, it would not matter; he would be without a public.

The October Revolution had created the sum total of conditions necessary for cultural revolution. To be sure, ideological combat was a component of the Revolution, but the Marxists already held the commanding positions. No further convulsions were necessary, and certainly no revolutions. Pokrovskii truly expressed the spirit of the NEP.

5   Cooperation Ends

Relations between Marxist and non-Marxist historians were defined by political circumstances and conditioned by evolving political conflicts. Pluralism was no more secure than the mood of compromise and the policy of reconciliation that had engendered the NEP. Like the NEP, it was deeply rooted in Soviet historical experience, in the trauma of the Kronstadt uprising and in the ideological implications of the Peace of Brest-Litovsk; it was never, however, fully accepted in all quarters of the Communist Party. Stalin's rise to power, especially the strategy he employed against the Right Opposition, significantly affected historians. In the face of grain shortages in the winter of 1927–28, he began to introduce new slogans that stressed the urgency of class conflict. While the emerging Right Opposition, headed by Bukharin, branded Stalin's new line as a recrudescence of Trotskyism, Stalin alleged that the old policy furthered the interests of capitalist elements within the country (Popov, 1934, 2:369). The temporary stabilization of capitalism that had ushered in the NEP, he in effect argued, had given way to an era of renewed class conflict; the success of socialism had activated capitalist opponents within and without the country into an alliance against Soviet power. In the Shakhty trial in the spring 1928, the conviction of foreign and native bourgeois specialists on trumped-up charges of wrecking, Stalin produced an object lesson. He followed up with a purge of the state apparatus and the trade unions (Popov, 1934, 2:376) and pushed the new line through the Comintern as well.

Though the liquidation of the NEP in itself foretold changes in the writing and studying of history, a number of different arrangements could have grown out of the existing state of affairs. Stalin's tactics—his eliminating the Right as he proclaimed struggle against foreign and native capitalists—dissipated most possibilities and determined the final outcome. If the hands of bourgeois specialists were unfit for the building of socialism, the long-range prospects for a pluralistic organization of the historical front were dim. Inevitably the range of tolerated opinion would be narrowed. But the immediate consequence of the new line was disorder and rancor, something of a polarization within each camp. The leader of the historical front, Pokrovskii, vacillated, dragging his feet until the outcome of the party conflict became clear. Even after he got in step, he could not close ranks behind himself. A new alignment impeded Pokrovskii's leadership, and then his scholarship came under attack.

Emerging Conflict

The first All-Union Conference of Marxist-Leninist Research Institutions began on March 22, 1928, under the auspices of the Communist Academy.[1] It met just after the opening salvo had been fired in the struggle between Stalin and Bukharin for control of the party's scholarly institutions. Shortly after the student disturbance in RANION's Institute of History, described in Chapter 3, a struggle ensued for control of the party unit of the Institute of Red Professors. The secretary of the Moscow branch of the party, N.A. Uglanov, according to his Stalinist accusers, had in February used the IKP party cell to trumpet the Right Opposition's views on industrialization and grain collections. In March he tried but failed to uphold the institute's party bureau in the face of the resulting criticism from the rank and file of the party cell.[2] Stalin had won the skirmish.

The candid discussions of the All-Union Conference provide an account of Soviet social science early in 1928: "It is necessary for the thousandth and first time to say that the situation prevailing now is unsatisfactory. This is known to everyone" ("Pervaia," 1927:278). Each delegate seemed to have his own grievance. One stressed the weakness of Marxism in the provinces and urged the dispatch, on a permanent basis, of scholars from Moscow and Leningrad. Another, M.I. Iavorskyi, a leading Marxist historian from the Ukraine, agreed, noting the predominance of bourgeois and petty-bourgeois ideology in the Ukraine. Alluding to Great-Russian chauvinism, he complained about "pressure from the 'Russian bourgeois school,' which could be felt even in Marxist circles." Another speaker observed that Marxist scholarship had scarcely risen above the level of popularization ("Pervaia," 1928:254–55, 271–73, 284–85).

The most provocative speaker at the conference was D.B. Riazanov, the head of the Marx-Engels Institute, whose wit impelled the discussion and kept the other delegates on edge. He objected to Soviet money supporting non-Marxists. If a student had the choice of working for Marx at RANION for eighty rubles a month or receiving up to two hundred and fifty rubles from another institution to work against Marx, he would choose the latter. Even in RANION, he continued, students lose their Marxism in the second year of study ("Pervaia," 1928:253). Riazanov's remarks highlighted an additional factor of relations between

Marxists and non-Marxists—pecuniary advantage. The Marxists were dissatisfied with the physical conditions of their own institutions. Most sections of the Communist Academy were housed in one or two rooms, and most researchers had to carry on their work in the libraries of other institutions.[3] These material circumstances, combined with the prospect of better facilities and better-paying positions, excited discontent.

The most comprehensive complaint was uttered by a delegate from RANION, its deputy chairman, D.A. Magerovskii. After summarizing the early tribulations of RANION (see above, pp. 70–72), he stated that by 1925 a communist nucleus had been formed at various levels, and Marxist principles had begun to triumph. Whereas previously each graduate student had been assigned a single advisor, now most of the work was done in seminars with the result that, despite vestiges of individual work, collective effort predominated by 1928 ("Pervaia," 1928:257). But the Communist advance had begun to falter. Each year RANION encountered greater difficulty in maintaining Marxist supervision over the non-Marxists. Behind this paradox was the insufficient number of Marxist cadres. Only twenty-five percent of the staff was communist; in fact, those active were an even smaller percentage, and it was becoming increasingly difficult to hold them, for they were being siphoned off by government offices such as Gosplan (state agency for the planning of science) and the Communist Academy. "To continue in this fashion is impossible. The problem of supervising both research and teaching . . . is becoming one of our major problems," concluded Magerovskii.[4]

The Marxists, it seems, were locked on the horns of a dilemma. The success of the Soviet government, the expansion of the Soviet apparatus, undermined party control of education. The burgeoning demand for "red specialists" in a great host of institutions encumbered their task of supervising "bourgeois specialists" in the education system. Judging from Magerovskii's account, a crisis was mounting: simply to hold the line would enhance the authority of non-Marxist scholars.

Various proposals to meet the crisis were entertained. What was now almost a traditional plea by Pokrovskii to transform the Communist Academy into a planning organ for all Marxist institutions was heard. An old suggestion of Evgenii Preobrazhenskii, stemming from before his expulsion from the KA as a member of the Left Opposition, was echoed. It called for a system of all-union conferences of organizations doing research in the same area, the intent being to set forth a general line in the presence of the leading specialists. More ambitious proposals called for the creation of a gosplan or even an all-union commissariat for scientific planning. This latter proposal seemed to imply planning for all scientific institutions, including non-Marxist ones such as the Academy of

Sciences. Even Iavorskyi, despite his misgivings about Great-Russian chauvinism, endorsed the principle of all-union planning ("Pervaia," 1928:265, 268–69, 271–73, 282). Riazanov, in spite of his irate criticism of the status quo, employed his wit to puncture the various schemes. He opposed any change that would place the Marx-Engels Institute within a larger bureaucratic structure. Pokrovskii reiterated the need for Marxists to unite their forces under the KA, "otherwise we shall drown in the mass of people of another ideology . . . who, of course, in each separate institution would be a majority. Only in the Communist Academy itself shall we retain a majority." A gosplan with Marxists "as the organizing center" is a sound principle, if somewhat fanciful at the moment. The idea of an all-union commissariat for science is, however, the goal of people of "too bureaucratic a frame of mind."[5]

The outcome of the conference was a resolution calling for the "creation of a united center, which would combine in one plan the scientific work of the entire Union" ("Pervaia," 1928:293). Within a short time, a combination of the various expedients suggested was adopted.

Summer Interlude

Criticism of non-Marxist scholars abated in the summer when joint Marxist–non-Marxist delegations attended historical meetings in Berlin and Oslo. In the activities of the delegations, however, one can perceive a reflection of the conflict manifested at the Conference of Marxist-Leninist Research Institutions and further deterioration of the policy of using noncommunist hands in the building of communism. Upon invitation from the Society for the Study of Eastern Europe (*Deutsche Gesellschaft zum Studium Osteuropas*), a delegation of Soviet historians headed by Pokrovskii visited Berlin (July 7–14, 1928).[6] The week consisted of banquets and conferences that coincided with the display of Soviet publications housed in the Prussian Academy of Sciences. At the opening reception, attended by political and scholarly luminaries of the day, a message from the government in the name of the Reichskanzler was presented. The message emphasized "that Germany in the highest degree is interested in the publication of documents on the history of the World War." N.N. Krestinskii, plenipotentiary to the German Republic, gave an address on the theme "German Scholars in Russian Historiography." Pokrovskii in his opening remarks "rejected the assertion that in Russia only Marxists were allowed to carry out scholarly activities."[7]

At a subsequent meeting Pokrovskii read a paper on the "Origins of Autocracy." S.F. Platonov elucidated the findings of his study of the Russian North. Characteristically he stressed the importance of merchant capital in the development of the region. Protestations of tolerance persistently emanated from the Soviet delegation. Responding to a jibe by Edward Meyer, Pokrovskii is reported to have asserted that "the Marxist conception bears the imprint of achievements of historical scholarship, the authors of which are by no means Marxists." He continued, "The strength of Marxism lies precisely in the fact that scholars who are not Marxists but simply good historians, conscientiously studying the facts, arrived at conclusions, affirmed by Marxist theory" (*VKA*, 1929, 30:242–43).

Professor Halvdan Koht, president of the Norwegian Academy of Sciences and chairman of the Organization Committee of the Sixth International Congress of Historical Science, invited the Soviet delegation to Oslo.[8] According to Pokrovskii, Koht considered himself a Marxist. Pokrovskii was grateful for the invitation, but in his report to the presidium of the Communist Academy he complained about the unpreparedness of the Soviet delegation. Whereas the Polish contingent had fifty members, and the French one hundred, the Soviet delegation counted only eleven. Pokrovskii sought to have a member present at each session. Almost all the Soviet historians wrote papers, but in discussion, Pokrovskii complained, they were usually silent: "I spoke twice, but I must say—not forcefully, and others were silent altogether." The topics of some of the papers read by the Soviet Marxists aroused interest and attracted young people to the sessions. But the Russians spoke German so badly that they could not even understand each other; as a result, according to Pokrovskii, the meetings usually were adjourned without discussion (1929a:231–37).

To make matters worse, the non-Marxist members of the Soviet delegation conversed freely with others. It was a conversation between Professor B.L. Bogaevskii and M.I. Rostovtsev, the prominent historian of antiquity who had emigrated from Russia during the Civil War and was present in Oslo as a member of the American delegation, that dramatized the Soviet presence. When Pokrovskii was elected to the presidium of the congress, Rostovtsev registered a complaint with local reporters. As retold by Pokrovskii, Rostovtsev complained that Pokrovskii was "not a scholar at all, but a destroyer of Christian faith, a wrecker of higher education and higher schools in Russia, and that a Marxist cannot be a scholar, for Marxism is a dogma that contradicts freedom of research and that there can be no scholars in Russia, etc." Koht disavowed Rostovtsev's remarks in the name of the congress, and Pokrovskii held an interview that also made the front page. In his speech at the closing banquet, Rostovtsev chose not to resume the exchange, but Pokrovskii was infuriated and throughout the remainder of his life would allude to the Oslo Congress as a manifestation of class conflict on an international level. In reporting to the Communist Academy presidium,

however, Pokrovskii boasted that Rostovtsev had done the small Soviet
delegation a "great service": he made it the object of attention. "We
enjoyed a certain popularity."[9] The Soviet delegation attempted to organize an International Society of Marxist Historians and convoked a
special meeting for this purpose. Only two historians attended, however.

The reporting of the conferences reveals the momentum of change in
the fall of 1928. Mints described the Berlin week to the readers of *Istorik-marksist*: "Addresses by the non-party, non-Marxist part of the delegation delivered a severe blow to the prejudice that in the Soviet Union
bourgeois historical scholarship is annihilated and [that those] who think
differently are mechanically repressed." Noting that although Marxism
was the dominant trend, it did not suppress other points of view, he
reported the following conversation with a German professor:

> "Can it be that there are non-Marxists in the delegation?"
> Mints, "There are, even one, for example, who remained Rector
> of a University, though even the Kadets were more radical than
> he."
> "I, to be sure, thought that the non-Marxists had been driven out
> long ago. . . . "[10]
> Mints, "You're correct, if you have in mind professors of theol-
> ogy."
> "Well, that is probably because you don't have theology depart-
> ments." (*IM*, 1928, 9:88–89)

Shortly after the article appeared Mints wrote a letter to the editors of
Istorik-marksist: he disavowed these remarks and expressed regret that
his article tended to minimize the militant character of Marxism (*IM*,
1929, 11:276).

Campaign against Non-Marxist Historians

Marxist historians searched out enemies in various sectors of the historical front in 1928. Medievalist D.M. Petrushevskii, as chairman of
RANION's Institute of History, bore the weight of the spring campaign.
Academicians E.V. Tarle, a prominent specialist in modern European
history, and S.A. Zhebelev, a historian of antiquity, found themselves
that autumn in the path of a hurricane. One can perceive in the treatment of these three historians a tendency for the campaign to become
increasingly less scholarly and more public. The discussion of Petrushevskii centered on his most recent book, *Outlines of the Economic
History of Medieval Europe*,[11] which had gained notoriety through an
unfavorable review by Fridliand (1928a). Then the Society of Marxist
Historians sponsored reports and discussions on March 30 and April 6.

The discussions themselves, if not brutal, were ill-tempered and unfair, yet they touched upon important methodological problems and initiated a debate that, over a period of years, refashioned the theory of historical materialism ("Disput," 1928).

Critics charged that Petrushevskii's book was an example of bourgeois idealism. Petrushevskii, they alleged, had taken over the methods of Alphonse Dopsch, the Austrian medievalist, and had consequently assimilated the doctrines of Max Weber.[12] Most of the participants in the discussion seemed to be conversant with and apprehensive about Weber's theories. In view of the fact that Soviet scholars held German scholarship in high esteem, following it closely and reviewing it extensively, it is likely that Weber enjoyed a certain vogue. He may be considered an uninvited guest at the discussion of Petrushevskii. The discussants devoted a considerable amount of time to expounding the notion of "ideal type," with the purpose of unmasking Petrushevskii and demonstrating that he had employed the "bourgeois" concept. According to A.D. Udal'tsov, a professor at the Institute of History, the doctrines of Max Weber represented an attempt by the bourgeoisie to formulate a world-view and systematic methodology in the hope of offsetting "creeping empiricism." To Stanislav Krivtsov, a former Bogdanovite who had become a party propagandist, such constructs, which exist beyond time and space, represented a reformulation and application to social phenomena of Kantian ontology and ethics. Like the categorical imperative, an ideal type is a command from a world beyond the realm of phenomena. It was to Krivtsov a complex of values arrived at by "disciplined, trained fantasy." Weber's principles are closely related to Heinrich Rickert's teachings: a historian "does not evaluate phenomena, but the relations thereof to definite cultural values." The concern with values revealed the subjective aspect of the theory, in Krivtsov's view. If an objective basis for values cannot be established, then any law is valid, any standpoint as good as any other; the theory devolves into a pluralistic, multifactor explanation. Yet not quite *any* standpoint is valid. An ideal type cannot embody just any set of values, but only those "alleged to be generally accepted." Attempts to formulate what values are "generally accepted" reveal the "wholly subjective character" of the theory ("Disput," 1928:81–82, 95).

Krivtsov's implied conclusion was obvious to his listeners: the theory is subjective because there are no "generally accepted values." All values are historically existent and express the interests of particular social classes. In the case of Weber, the values are the traditional ones of bourgeois society.

E.A. Kosminskii and A.I. Neusykhin defended Petrushevskii, their teacher, at the Institute of History, contending that the discussion misrepresented the book. Kosminskii denied that the book was directed against Marxism and that it was a rehash of Dopsch. On the contrary, it drew on many authors and represented a highly original synthesis. Neusykhin argued that whereas Dopsch stressed the similarity between patrimonial and modern capitalism, it was precisely this analogy that Petrushevskii rejected ("Disput," 1928:91, 101). The defense managed only to provoke Fridliand. It reinforced his conviction that Petrushevskii's book was less a work of scholarship than a political demonstration. Concerning Petrushevskii, Fridliand said:

> I would not say that this revolution in the views of Professor Petrushevskii is only his individual revolution. I would say that this is the logical style of bourgeois methodology . . . during the entire post-war epoch. . . . It proves that many of our best professors cannot tear themselves from the grip of anti-Marxist schemata.

For the self-styled Marxists and fellow-travelers, he warned:

> I must note that the saddest thing in our discussion is that we are all bound to Marxism; this is suspicious. Our task is to unmask such people who call themselves Marxists. We consider the affirmation by comrade Neusykhin—that he [Neusykhin] is to any degree a Marxist—a misunderstanding. . . . They wish to depict us as barbarians desiring to attack science in the name of Marxism. No! We shall carry on an intense struggle against the barbarian attack on Marxism on the part of the fashionable Western-European schools of philosophy and their Russian pupils. We shall strive so that in the USSR the old custom of bringing to Russian soil the newest, most fashionable, latest word . . . as a new discovery, a new "interpretation of Marxism" will be forsaken. ("Disput," 1928:86, 90, 126, 127–28)

Despite the trial-like atmosphere of these gatherings of the Society of Marxist Historians, they signified an important event in Soviet intellectual history, for here was a direct confrontation between Soviet Marxism and twentieth-century Western social theory.[13] Although on the surface it appeared that Western theory was dismissed out of hand, in reality there was a genuine encounter. The challenge of Weber was one of the factors that compelled Soviet historians to review and recast the tenets of historical materialism, and the new theory was partly a polemic against Max Weber. Weber had posed some of the problems that the Soviet historians sought to resolve in accord with their own premises. The socioeconomic formation that emerged in discussions in the early 1930s was a rival concept of Weber's notion of an "ideal type."

Pokrovskii led the attack on Tarle's book *Europe in the Epoch of Imperialism* (1927), claiming it underestimated the importance of class struggle in the half century before World War I and for attributing its outbreak primarily to German policy ("ententophilism").[14] To Fridliand, the book was a perfect example of "mimicry of Marxism," because Tarle had declared and actually believed that "his entire book is based on the study of Lenin, on the studies of Communist Marxists of the epoch of imperialism." Moreover, Tarle was genuinely surprised by the treatment accorded him by the Society of Marxist Historians (Fridliand, 1928b:27). Tarle's book was censured in a number of reviews and at a number of meetings.[15]

Granted an opportunity to defend himself on the pages of *Istorik-marksist,* Tarle sought to show that his understanding of modern history was essentially Marxist. He found the outbreak of World War I to be rooted in economic processes and class conflict. The chief underlying cause of the war was the "fact that in the *working masses* the disposition to check the strivings of imperialistic plunderers by every means was not sufficiently developed" (Tarle, 1928:101). An editorial note in *Istorik-marksist* nevertheless dismissed his arguments as those of a class enemy (*IM,* 1928, 9:108–9).

Academician S.A. Zhebelev and ten other Soviet scholars accepted an invitation to contribute to a collection of articles sponsored and published by the *Seminarium Kondakovianum,* an organized group of Russian scholars residing in Prague. Two similar volumes had been published previously, and there had been no outcry. The third volume, dealing with archeology and Byzantine art, was no more political than the other two, but it provoked a harsh outcry, chiefly because its appearance coincided with an intense campaign to influence the election of new members to the Academy of Sciences. Soviet authorities were in the process of revamping and reforming the academy in accord with their own principles of scientific planning. A lesser but still significant reason for the outcry is the fact that M.I. Rostovtsev, antagonist of the Soviet delegation at Oslo, was also a contributor to the volume.

Zhebelev and his associates were attacked first in Leningrad. Then in Moscow, I.K. Luppol, a professional philosopher and commentator on trends in the scholarly community, denounced their work in a public speech in Moscow's House of Scholars. The presidium of the academy on November 22 resisted the call that it demand Zhebelev's resignation. Zhebelev nevertheless deemed it appropriate that he apologize publicly for remarks he had made in the introduction.[16]

Pokrovskii in Step

In the polemic against Petrushevskii, Pokrovskii had been slow in getting off the mark. Speaking near the end of the second session, he denounced Petrushevskii in superficial, if bilious, terms, although just before the discussions—but after Petrushevskii's book had already attracted unfavorable attention—Pokrovskii had obliquely defended him. Petrushevskii's book revealed that he had lost his sure touch as a scholar, Pokrovskii told a conference of Marxist scholars. But his students, "young historians, who have mastered Petrushevskii's technique, approach us ideologically, because they are full-blooded people" ("Pervaia," 1928:267). By stressing Petrushevskii's performance as a teacher, Pokrovskii affirmed his usefulness.

If his stance had been conservative in the spring, when the discussion had centered on Petrushevskii, it changed in the fall; Pokrovskii indeed set the pace against Tarle. After convicting Tarle of ententophilism and tracing Petrushevskii's pedigree to Rickert, Pokrovskii addressed himself to the problem of backsliding on the part of the non-Marxist historians such as Tarle. He noted, first, that the specialists in Russian history were guilty of no such regression. Presniakov, Grekov, and others, he maintained, had been moving persistently in the direction of Marxism. Even the Eurasians posed the problem of the Tartar invasion in Marxist terms, and Miliukov himself in recent works devoted greater attention to class conflicts. "The spontaneous influence of Marxism" created a situation diametrically opposed to that prevailing among historians of the West. Petrushevskii was a "Presniakov in reverse" (1928b:3–5). The explanation of the situation, Pokrovskii continued, could be found in the organization of the historical front:

> In *Russian* history, there is a definite organization, there is a central group which tends in one definite direction—always broadening the area of its activity. In *Western* history, we have isolated Marxist researchers, *not less . . . but more numerous* than in Russian [history]. But they are completely unorganized. They sit in their corners . . . satisfied that the October Revolution guaranteed them freedom of research and expression in their narrow specializations. This would be normal if a democratic revolution had taken place guaranteeing "freedom of the press" for (peaceful, academic) Marxism. But we have had a socialist revolution; the ideology of the working class has become the ruling ideology, and those who represent this ideology are obligated to carry out organizational work in all areas, just as the entire class carries out such work in all areas in the life of our country. (1928b:17)

This passage seems to suggest that shortcomings of the non-Marxists may be attributed to the organizational failures of the Marxist historians.[17] It may be that Pokrovskii was protesting, if not the appearance of non-Marxist interpretations of European history, at least the paucity of

Marxist criticism of them. But if the precise arrangements he desired were unclear at the moment, his evaluation of non-Marxist scholarship had become clear and direct. It served only harmful purposes.

In the spring, Pokrovskii had shown a conservative inclination: he had been seeking to uphold existing arrangements on the historical front. His eloquent denunciation of the old specialists was phrased to make light of them as a threatening force, and he had been reluctant to bind their work to a comprehensive academic plan. At the Conference of Marxist-Leninist Research Institutions in March, he had summed up his justification of the status quo:

> It is necessary for me to point out that the very rebirth of bourgeois social science in Russia and its possibility and in some respects its success could take place only owing to the support of Soviet power, which was not a caprice, but inevitable and necessary. . . . If there were not this phenomenon, then let there be no doubt, Marxist literature would have constituted a monopoly from the very outset. I say that this would be bad; it would be bad because . . . social science strengthens itself through conflict . . . and if this conflict . . . resulted in that state of affairs, which foreigners consider to be the case, *i.e.* if only communists could practice social science, that would be bad. Undoubtedly, these bourgeois currents, bourgeois tendencies . . . are necessary for us; they are, to a certain extent, useful to us. They are not as necessary for me, whose teeth are already falling out, as for our youth to sharpen their teeth on them.[18]

By autumn Pokrovskii had changed his mind: he endorsed the notion of a capitalist conspiracy—capitalist elements within the country, kulaks, nepmen, and bourgeois specialists had joined hands with capitalists beyond the borders. Together they had launched an offensive against Soviet power. Pokrovskii implied that historians themselves, through their highly political behavior at the Sixth International Congress in Oslo, had persuaded him of the reality of an anti-Soviet campaign. It may be that events closer to home—the Sixth Comintern Congress in Moscow and the battle within Bukharin's home base, the Moscow Party organization, in the summer and fall—induced his change of heart. The existence of a worldwide anti-Marxist crusade provided the theme for a major article Pokrovskii wrote for the revolutionary anniversary issue of *Pravda* in 1928, "Class Struggle and the Ideological Front."

> Those anti-Marxist actions here in the U.S.S.R., the struggle with which some comrades are inclined to view as superfluous, even as a luxury, embrace only a part of the ideological front. [Its] base is not even in that class conflict which is being played out within the limits of our Union. Of course, if there had not been such a

> struggle, the corresponding "tendencies" would not have been able to find here a suitable environment; that's true, but our local conditions scarcely suffice [to explain] the appearance of independent anti-Marxism. The battle proceeds along an international front, and our side is obligated to use the historians of the U.S.S.R. in support of our allies on a world-wide scale.

He concluded:

> You can be assured that if that non-Marxist specialist sees before himself, not soft porridge but a firmly united front, he will recall immediately that even his grandfather in 1800 was a Marxist. (1928a)

Pokrovskii's acceptance of Stalin's perspective of an active conspiracy of capitalist elements within and without the country suggests a desire on his part to renew his mandate from the party leadership. It should be noted, however, that his avowal was not just public. In a personal letter, written on September 19, he expressed the same thought: "Between them, Rostovtsev and Platonov, there is in essence no difference—only the formal one that one is an 'external' emigrant, the other 'internal,' which does not concern our ideological front. It concerns a completely different sphere of relations, that we are not called upon nor obligated to resolve" (Gorin, 1933). Nonetheless I doubt that Pokrovskii believed these words. We have, I think, the beginning of dissimulation on his part out of fear lest he jeopardize his authority and lessen the acceptance of his historical ideas.

6 The First All-Union Conference of Marxist Historians

Preparation for the Conference

In March 1928, the presidium of the KA, after hearing a report from the Society of Marxist Historians, allotted the organization its future tasks. The KA resolution, probably inspired by Pokrovskii, commended the SMH for its work to date; then it complained that "a whole rank of institutions which conduct research in the field of history do not participate in any way, or almost in no way, in the work of the Society. (The Marx-Engels Institute, the Lenin Institute, and especially the Institute of History of RANION)" (*IM*, 1928, 1:309). The resolution also noted that public discussions and popularization had in the past been the chief work of the SMH; little inquiry had been promoted owing to the society's isolation from research institutions. "The Presidium urgently recommends to the Society that it develop its activity further in this direction [research], drawing into its work as many forces as possible." The KA resolution conceded that serious research was beyond the reach of the SMH unless its material needs were met. Establishment of a professional staff within the society was among the recommendations of the resolution.

The call for a Conference of Marxist Historians to enhance the influence of the SMH and to further the trend toward its professional status had been heard as early as 1927, when a young historian, M.V. Nechkina, urged that further progress required such a conference in order to confront tasks of research and to plan collective works (*Obshchestvennye*, 1928:162). Such conferences offered a low-key method of planning by bringing specialists in a given field face-to-face, confronting them with a general line, and posing, from above, research tasks for the entire field. The *Work Plan* (1928–29) of the SMH included such a conference. Citing both the scholarly and political-organizational tasks, it stated:

> The basic goal of the Conference is the summing up of the results of the development of Marxist historical scholarship, indicating the basic problems for the further development of the scientific treatment of history, the analysis of contemporary anti- and

pseudo-Marxist currents in historical scholarship and the resolution of a number of basic, controversial problems in contemporary Marxist historical scholarship. (*Plan,* 1928:80)

On the eve of the conference, Fridliand stressed its political significance. It "should affirm the necessity of decisive and clear political perspectives in our historical work." It should not only treat separate questions but affirm the principle of planned work, and also pose the problem of struggle with pseudo-Marxists by a united front of Marxists. By being "merciless, like genuine Bolsheviks," we can urge the remaining historians to enter our ranks. The conference, then, should "identify enemies, . . . unmask the danger of pseudo-Marxism and decisively liquidate wavering in our own ranks" (1928b:32–33).

Preparation for the conference took the form of publicizing, throughout autumn 1928, criticisms of the non-Marxist historians and of censure of "tame communists," who allegedly favored laissez-faire in ideological matters. Mints' turnabout is an example.[1] Pokrovskii, under the urging of Fridliand and Gorin, overcame his own vacillation. His sixtieth birthday celebration was an event in the publicity campaign. He himself viewed the jubilee as a political event (*NBPU:* 34).

Pokrovskii's sixtieth birthday jubilee was a great personal triumph, for he stood at the apex of his career in the winter of 1928–29. Even then, however, he had detractors and opponents. His old associate from the Forward faction, Anatoli Lunacharskii, in an article celebrating the jubilee, alluded to "certain dwarfs and twisted people" who denied that Pokrovskii was an authentic Marxist (1928:10). But these people seemed to have gone underground for the time. Few scholars in their own lifetimes have ever received so much praise; perhaps none has ever been the object of such hearty public tribute. Articles about him dominated *Pravda* and *Izvestiia.* Two pages of *Pravda* were devoted to him on October 25, and scores of newspapers throughout the country published articles about him and greetings to him from local bodies.[2] Pokrovskii's students and colleagues wrote most of the articles, but a few were written by prominent party leaders, including Bukharin. A testimonial meeting at the Moscow Conservatory climaxed the celebration. Such luminaries as Lunacharskii, Krupskaia, and Riazanov acclaimed him. S.F. Ol'denburg, permanent secretary of the Academy of Sciences, toasted Pokrovskii on behalf of the academy; Iavorskyi did so on behalf of Ukrainian Marxist scholars. Awarding of the Order of Lenin to Pokrovskii was the high point of the evening.[3] Though this was a major celebration, others were held at the IKP, RANION, and various other institutions named in honor of Pokrovskii. Outside Moscow, similar sessions were held in Leningrad, Tiflis, Baku, Voronezh, Rostov-on-Don, Kharkov, and Kazan. The acclaim was comparable to that bestowed upon certain Renaissance artists.

The Communist Party nurtured and exploited Pokrovskii's popularity. He was repeatedly made a member of the All-Union Central Council of Trade Unions and participated in the congresses and plenary meetings of the Comintern. He had the honor of addressing the Fifteenth Congress as well as the Sixteenth Conference and Congress of the CPSU. After the latter, in 1930, he was appointed to the presidium of the Central Control Commission.

At the peak of his success, Pokrovskii's health had begun to fail. In 1927 a ruptured blood vessel had almost blinded him in one eye, reducing his workday to four hours for the time being (*IM*, 1927, 4:270). By 1928 his fatal illness, cancer of the bladder, had been diagnosed. He spent the summer under treatment in Germany (*Pamiaty*, 1932:18). His situation has some puzzling features. He had begun to express doubt about the effectiveness of his own historical works. Even in 1927, in a remark in his IKP seminar, Pokrovskii conceded that he had exaggerated the influence of merchant capital: "This can be explained historically by the fact that I had to fight against a theory that denied any significance to the internal and external markets. I leaned too far backwards," he stated. "It would be very good if my students would concern themselves with correcting my shortcomings."[4] In his birthday speech, he referred to himself as a "precursor" of Marxist historiography and said, "I am still not a genuine proletarian historian." Just two months later Pokrovskii spoke of certain dark corners of his own mind that required ventilation.[5] It is a curious coincidence that just when Pokrovskii had come to accept Stalin's premise about international conspiracy and non-Marxist elements in Soviet society, he began to express reservations about his own efforts at historical explanation.

The Conference

Pokrovskii's December 28 opening remarks to the six hundred or so assembled historians set the keynote for the First All-Union Conference of Marxist Historians.[6] He stressed the inadequacies of non-Marxist scholarship. Though his assertions were familiar, his tone was not: "If there were some naive people who had believed in historical scholarship isolated from politics, then I submit that now, after the Congress in Oslo, there cannot be any." If some few still exist, they "are pathological and must be cured" (TP, 1:13). In addition to reading papers, Pokrovskii entered frequently into the debates, somewhat in the manner of a seminar instructor. His imperiousness resulted in part from the fact that some of the participants forwarded notes to him with questions about reports just heard. They preferred his comments on the papers to those of the authors themselves.

Moving into the foreground of Pokrovskii's thought was his conception of the historical process itself, and he used the conference as a platform to inveigh against economic materialism. He sought now to formulate a fresh interpretation of Marxism. In his major address to the conference, "Leninism and Russian History," he defined materialism as Marxism minus dialectics, meaning Marxism minus revolution. A purely economic interpretation of history, he argued, is satisfactory to any bourgeois, even to a Tsarist censor. He referred to economic materialism as an illness; for historians who failed to take the cure, it resulted in political errors (*TP*, 1:302–3). Pokrovskii cited statements of Marx and Engels about the importance of the superstructure and the role of chance in social processes, but the best formulation of his own that he could arrive at was the following:

> Not only economic materialism, *i.e.* the economic interpretation of history, but economic materialism plus class conflict—and even this is not Marxism. Only he who recognizes the political conclusions of Marxism, recognizes the dictatorship of the proletariat, [only] he is a genuine Marxist. (*TP*, 1:305)

This formulation emphasized the militant character of Marxist research but said nothing about the nature of the historical process.

He applied this new doctrine to Russian history as follows:

> By means of a purely economic explanation, by appealing exclusively to the laws of economics, while ignoring everything else, it would not have been possible to foretell that which actually did occur—that we would break through to socialism through any laws—in spite of narrow economic laws.[7]

Thus with regard to Marxism, Pokrovskii abandoned the narrow interpretation he had employed in creating his own synthesis, but he was unable to formulate a new interpretation. He was not, however, a "brake" on the development of a new doctrine. On the contrary, he called attention to the need for one and challenged his colleagues to elaborate it. This remained Pokrovskii's position for the rest of his lifetime; none of his subsequent statements amplified those just cited. He was dissatisfied with economic materialism but unable to formulate a more flexible version of Marxist theory.

However trivial Pokrovskii's statements were from the theoretical standpoint, they bore important practical conclusions about the writing of history: the historian is to inform his craft with a political sense, not by distorting his facts, but through his choice of topic. With regard to the first point, Pokrovskii spoke only in guarded terms. In his opening address he stated:

> One cannot assert naked slogans. Here one steps forth with a definite scientific work, scientific in the sense that it has been

scientifically proven. We have no need to strive for this artificially, because Marxism itself is the only scientific explanation of history. (*TP*, 1:14)

As to choice of topics, Pokrovskii demanded that they be politically timely. Precisely what he meant by this was a matter of misunderstanding both in his own lifetime and subsequently,[8] and his own ambiguity was partly responsible. At the First Conference, G.S. Zaidel, a Leningrad historian, attributed to Pokrovskii the view that medieval history is not an urgent problem. In his final speech to the congress, Pokrovskii took pains to dispel Zaidel's allegation. "I never expressed myself in that way. I never said that." Only one who is "amorphous and colorless" will choose a topic devoid of political content, but it is not chronology alone that determines relevance. Soloviev, for his first work, chose a subject remote in time—the *Rurikovichi*. But instead of concerning himself with whether they were Varangians, he studied their relations to clan society, because that problem was germane to the dispute about Russia's distinctive historical destiny (*TP*, 1:46, 77–78). A note of ambiguity regarding canons of political relevance clung to Pokrovskii's position with his stipulation that, for Marxists, the urgent problems are the workers' movement and the contemporary period of revolutionary struggle. He concluded his observations as follows: "I consider it a duty to make this correction in order to clear up the misunderstanding that I am some sort of enemy of the study of medieval history. I am an enemy not of the study of medieval history, but an opponent of those people who hide themselves from the living reality around them in an academic shell" (*TP*, 1:78).

Pokrovskii's preoccupation with historical materialism is partly explained by the tenacity of economic materialism within the SMH. He stated that he had initiated the campaign against economic determinism at the founding of the society, but that the conference itself furnished proof that the struggle had not been completed. He cited the discussions on imperialism as an instance of what we might call reductionism, with the disputants citing economic statistics, such as the size of foreign bank accounts, where they had questionable relevance (*TP*, 1:302–4).

The conference was an occasion for the propagation of Pokrovskii's outlook and the enhancement of his authority, yet it marked the beginning of the voicing of a rival set of historical views and an incipient challenge to his authority. For a year or so before the conference particular points of Pokrovskii's schema had been subjected to criticism in his own entourage—students and graduates of the IKP. Right after the conference, at three separate sessions held in April, his entire interpretation of Russian history was discussed. Pokrovskii was sufficiently riled to charge his former student A. Lomakin with counterposing his (Pokrovskii's) schema to Lenin's (Lutskii, 1965:362). At the First Conference itself the criticism was muted and indirect; to most participants it probably was inaudible. Nevertheless, it was the first public expression of a campaign that would produce an unprecedented clamor. The immediate issues were imperialism and the "theory of growing over," the interpretation of the Russian Revolution that Pokrovskii had sketched in 1927.

These interlocking problems bore implications about the level of capitalist development required for a socialist revolution to occur. As Pokrovskii noted in the discussion of Vanag's report on imperialism in Russia:

> Comrades, the questions touched upon in the report of Com. Vanag have acquired great urgency and have provoked such polemics because this is the approach to a considerably more general question—did we have independent imperialism [of our own]? Did Russia conduct an independent imperialist policy? And in connection with this [how should we] comprehend the October Revolution? The essence of the matter is the participation of Russia in the War and in the October Revolution. [It is] by no means confined to the specialized problem that we now argue about. (*TP*, 1:372)

In both the Section on the History of the Peoples of the USSR and the Section on Western History, the problem of imperialism was expounded. As noted in Chapter 2, Pokrovskii had supported those who affirmed Russia's dependence upon the advanced capitalist countries. Russia herself had not completed the transition from merchant to industrial capitalism. The degree of Russian independence in the second decade of the twentieth century would not, he argued at the conference, be revealed by a description of the amount and disposition of foreign capital in Russian banks. The fact that called for explanation was Russia's drive for acquisition of the Black Sea Straits. This goal could not be considered an instance of modern imperialism, for it was the age-old policy of merchant capitalism. To describe it as imperialism would necessitate calling Nicholas I and even Catherine II imperialists. The modern imperialism that existed in the Russian Empire was active in Persia and the Far East. It was indifferent to the Straits, but too young and weak to set national policy (*TP*, 1:374–75).

It was not only the material interests of the Russian landlords that impelled Russia toward Constantinople. There was also the British goal of "smashing together the foreheads of Russia and Germany. If you take what some people refer to as the psychological factor—the entire tangle of diplomatic relations—you will see how the Straits were used as a bait [to hook] Russia" (*TP*, 1:375). This was the "red thread" of diplomacy from 1910 to the outbreak of World War I—Grey and Millerand, representing Russia's future allies in the Triple Entente, urged Russia to fight for the Straits, while Kaiser Wilhelm promised Nicholas the Straits in return for dropping the alliance with Britain. Pokrovskii did not contend that his analysis solved the problem, but merely that he had devised the proper approach.

In the conference discussion, S.G. Tomsinskii, who had already publicly argued with Pokrovskii, as noted previously, disputed Pokrovskii's and Vanag's interpretation of imperialism. He was supported by N.L. Rubinshtein, the IKP graduate who had earlier defended Pokrovskii in print, and by I.I. Mints (*TP*, 1:380–83, 365–67, 353–56). Mints, another graduate of the IKP, had been so close to Pokrovskii that he became his assistant in the Institute of Red Professors. These critics drew on writings of A.L. Sidorov, who was to emerge as the leading specialist in the field and who had worked out his basic ideas in Pokrovskii's seminar. In due course, Soviet historians published an immense number of sources and studies on this subject. In 1928 and 1929 they mainly concerned themselves with matters of definition, attempting to clarify and distinguish Lenin's understanding of imperialism from other Marxist theories, such as Rudolf Hilferding's. The underlying and unstated problem narrowed down to the evident discrepancy between Vanag's and Pokrovskii's position and the new program of the Comintern adopted the previous summer at its Sixth Conference. The program distinguished three types of society on the basis of their degree of ripeness for socialism. The first two categories—developed and semideveloped countries—were considered ripe for socialism. Underdeveloped societies—the definition of which was bound up with the matter of imperialism—were likely to achieve only a bourgeois-democratic revolution (Tarnovskii, 1964:20).

The theory of growing over had even broader significance than did the problem of imperialism. It too touched issues in the Comintern Program, and thereby affected foreign policy; it too treated important events in the past. In addition, it inevitably affected appraisals of the scientific validity of Marxism. Was the outcome of the Revolution in keeping with prior expectations? Had Lenin foreseen the confinement of socialism to a single underdeveloped nation? At issue was one of the most important claims of legitimacy of the rule of the Communist Party. K.A. Popov read a paper at the conference entitled "The Problem of the Growing Over from Bourgeois-Democratic to Socialist Revolution," in which he attempted to vindicate Pokrovskii's approach while refining and generalizing his findings. Among other things, he asked, what are the peculiarities of a bourgeois-democratic revolution that grows over into socialism in comparison with bourgeois-democratic revolutions of the conventional type? His answers, though a step toward the definitive formulation, were found to be unsatisfactory. The first major issue, Popov's treatment of the social war between peasants and landlords, provoked disagreement. Mints alleged that Popov exaggerated the degree of under-development in Russian agriculture. He argued that the spurt of capital-ist development after 1905 had fostered significant social stratification among the peasants and had consolidated the ties between workers and the rural proletariat (*TP*, 1:116, 135). The second major issue involved Lenin's understanding of the revolutionary process. Mints again chal-lenged Popov's formulation. Though Popov had not said that Lenin held two different theories in 1905 and 1917 (that he was rearmed by Trot-sky's theory of permanent revolution), he asserted that they were two different formulations of the problem. Mints commented that even this was incorrect. There were "two dialectical resolutions of one and the same problem in varying concrete circumstances" (*TP*, 1:134). A Lenin-grad historian, M. Mishin, charged that in some measure Popov upheld the view that Lenin foresaw a proletarian revolution in the West as a prerequisite to the victory of socialism in Russia. Popov responded heat-edly from the floor: "I just directly opposed that" (*TP*, 1:145).

These problems were not resolved by the conference and would be debated at length and with passion for the next two years. They lay at the heart of most Marxist historical discussions.

A.M. Pankratova read a paper, "The Problem of Studying the Work-ing Class in Russia," in which she outlined methods for collective studies of the Russian proletariat.[9] This became a timely, popular, and politically significant area of research in the subsequent decade. Non-Marxist historiography, especially in the national republics, was cen-sured. Unmasking of bourgeois and petty-bourgeois historiography was carried out by historians from the Ukraine, Belorussia, Georgia, Arme-nia, and Central Asia. It was in connection with these reports that the interlocking problems of local nationalism and Great-Russian chauvin-ism moved into the foreground. That these problems were pressing at this time is suggested by the fact that the name of the Section on the History of Russia was changed to the History of the Peoples of the USSR. Pokrovskii's tightrope walking on this same issue suggests its urgency. In the preface to the minutes of the conference, he wrote that " 'Russian history' is a counter-revolutionary term." During one discus-sion, he censured the veteran Georgian Bolshevik F.Y. Makharadze for "leaning too far backward" to avoid nationalism. "We Great-Russians were the worst plunderers."[10] This is what one would expect from a historian whose entire career was a sustained polemic against the na-tional school of Russian historiography. Yet in the course of an open controversy with the Ukrainian delegation he felt constrained to say: "This united front of historical counter-revolution, comrades, indicated the necessity on our part to set up a firm united front of Russia and the Ukraine, perhaps for a time even setting aside Ukrainian, Bielorussian, and Great Russian, as they say, traditions'' (*TP*, 1:456).

The dispute with the Ukrainians erupted in the discussion of a report by M.I. Iavorskyi. Gorin (himself a Belorussian) accused Iavorskyi of nationalism. Z. Gurevich, a Ukrainian, countered by accusing Nechkina of Great-Russian chauvinism in her treatment of the Decembrists. Pokrovskii played the role of conciliator, minimizing the differences among the disputants.[11]

One of the conference's main achievements was the transformation of the SMH into an All-Union Society. That such an outcome was not preordained was suggested in Pokrovskii's concluding remarks: "I should admit that prior to the Conference I favored a federation of separate national societies, but the overwhelming majority . . . came out for a united society; we have heard no national protest here."[12]

Subsequent boasts about the First Conference being a victory were not empty.[13] Disputation had clarified a number of urgent intellectual problems and charted a path toward the Marxist-Leninist interpretation of Russian history. Organizational consolidation paved the way for the propagation of the emerging ideas. A major step in the direction of centralization of opinion and facilities was a polemic in the wake of the conference between Gorin and M.I. Iavorskyi.[14] Iavorskyi's arrest as an Austrian spy was the outcome. As mentioned previously, Iavorskyi early in 1928 had endorsed the view that scholarship should be planned on an all-union level (see p. 82). Despite the fact, however, that he was a member of the presidium of the First All-Union Conference of Marxist Historians, he was Gorin's antagonist in the dispute on the national problem, and then Iavorskyi's works were adversely criticized in discussions held in the Ukraine itself. His arrest most probably grew out of events connected with the course of collectivization in the Ukraine, and with purges in a variety of Ukrainian national institutions. His vulnerable position vis-à-vis the Society of Marxist Historians merely made him a likely object for the ongoing purge.[15] Iavorskyi's arrest seemed to excite a shudder among non-Marxist and numerous Marxist historians. No doubt Gorin's voice registered a new ring of authority.

Stalin's Defeat of the Right Opposition

The struggle to set the general line of the party entered a new stage after the plenum of the Central Committee in July 1928.[16] Each side, on the one hand the followers of Stalin and on the other the group that came to be called the Right Opposition—Bukharin, Rykov, and Tomskii and their followers—sought to present the resolutions of the plenum as consistent with its own purposes. The battle raged in almost all institutions; the most important theaters were the Comintern, the Trade Unions, and the Moscow branch of the party, which probably was decisive, since its domination allowed it to control personnel assignments in the central institutions. In July the Moscow Committee was in the hands of the incipient Right Opposition.

The Right tended to stress the economic shortcomings of the moment. Its leaders opposed large-scale increases of capital investment in heavy industry. Not only did they refuse to countenance immediate collectivization of agriculture, they opposed any policy that might in their view further strain relations between the state and the middle peasants. They minimized the alleged danger to the party from the Right; sometimes they indeed denied its existence by suggesting it was a contrivance of the Trotskyites.

This was the line taken by A.I. Rykov when he addressed an assembly of over 3000 Moscow party members. The July plenum was, he argued, a sign of the stability of the NEP. This was the line pursued also in the summer and fall by N.A. Uglanov, secretary of the Moscow Committee. It was reflected in his report to the Fifth United Plenum of the Moscow Committee and Moscow Control Commission (Mk i mkk), held on September 11 and 12, and in the resolutions of the plenum. Conflict within the Moscow organization and between its committee and the central party institutions became evident after the Fifth United Plenum of the Mk i mkk. Opposition to its resolutions was expressed in a number of district (*raion*) party meetings. In October G.K. Ordzhonikidze, chairman of the Central Control Commission, the agency chiefly responsible for party discipline, was instrumental in preparing a text to be circulated among Moscow party members. It reiterated Stalin's understanding of the resolutions of the July plenum of the Central Committee and marked the beginning of the wresting of control of the Moscow Committee from the hands of the Right Opposition.

An extraordinary United Plenum of the Moscow Committee and Moscow Control Commission, attended by 325 party members, began on October 18. Uglanov's opening report was adversely criticized by a number of speakers. After Stalin himself addressed the meeting on the danger of the Right, Uglanov felt constrained to retreat from a number of his positions. But his remarks have not been taken by Soviet historians to represent full self-criticism. Some of Uglanov's associates, however—secretaries of district committees—admitted major political errors. Uglanov continued to affirm the correctness of his position in subsequent speeches; the result was his replacement by V.M. Molotov on November 27 as secretary of the Moscow Committee.

Bukharin seems to have entrusted the factional struggle in Moscow to

Uglanov. Unfortunately, available information does not bring us close enough to the situation to judge whether his participation in the extraordinary October plenum of the Mk i mkk might have changed its outcome. "Notes of an Economist," published in September, is an implied criticism of the general line as conceived by Stalin. His speech "Lenin's Political Testament," delivered and published in January 1929, was a more far-reaching criticism of policies adopted at the November plenum of the Central Committee and of impending policies. Only late in the hour—after his program had been roundly defeated in the November plenum—did Bukharin go onto the offensive. He and Tomskii refused to work at their party-assigned posts in *Pravda,* the Comintern, and the Trade-Union Council, thereby threatening an open break with Stalin and public rebuke of his policies. On January 30 Bukharin, and on February 9 Bukharin, Rykov, and Tomskii, spoke at a joint meeting of the Politburo and the presidium of the Central Control Commission. Their program failed to carry the day, and they were subject to recrimination within the party apparatus.

The outcome of these events was a resolution adopted in April at a combined plenum of the Central Committee and Central Control Commission censuring the three leaders of the Right Opposition. For this occasion, more than 300 leading party members were brought together for reports and discussion of the intraparty situation. Iaroslavskii, as secretary of the Central Control Commission, delivered the opening report. Stalin made a lengthy and urgent address about the danger from the Right. The resolution of censure was endorsed by the Sixteenth Party Conference, held in the same month, which officially adopted the first five-year plan. Iaroslavskii addressed the conference on the need for a purging of the party organizations, governmental institutions, and institutions of higher learning. The second half of 1929 and the first half of 1930—a period that overlapped the drive for full-scale collectivization—witnessed just such a purge. Bukharin, Rykov, and Tomskii resisted self-criticism, or at least fully abject self-criticism, until November 1929. By then Bukharin and Tomskii had lost their Politburo seats.

Some observers may have foreseen Stalin's triumph and the nature of his line of policy even at the end of 1927, just as the struggle began to take shape. After the Central Committee plenum of July 1928, such an outcome would have been easier to predict. Bukharin may have had a clear understanding or perhaps only a fateful premonition when in July he sought an alliance with two of the discredited leaders of the former Left Opposition—Kamenev and Zinoviev. By September Pokrovskii had endorsed the Stalinist perspective by affirming the existence of an alliance and conspiracy against Soviet power of capitalist elements within and without the country (Gorin, 1933:97).

7   The New Offensive on the Historical Front

The Liquidation of RANION

When had it become possible to foresee Stalin's triumph over Bukharin? That is to say, when did the actual outcome of the party conflict become the likely one in the minds of those close to the scene? Even though there might not have been a single event that persuaded the overwhelming majority, the question is useful from the standpoint of the history of historiography. Hindsight permits us to view Pokrovskii's change as an indicator of Bukharin's declining fortunes. The report that Stalin blanched when confronted in November by what were in effect resignations by Bukharin and Tomskii suggests that perhaps all was not lost for the Right. Had the correct tactical line been found, they could perhaps have won or at least forestalled Stalin's victory. It is more likely, however, that by then any outcome other than the actual one appeared improbable. The feverish political activity in the winter notwithstanding, the outcome was probably foreseen clearly in October. After the extraordinary October plenum of the Moscow Committee and Moscow Control Commission, when Stalin's speech was followed by Uglanov's moderate self-criticism, a major turnabout would have been required to produce a different result.

It was at this juncture, when the defeat of the Right was impending but had not yet been consummated by the resolution of the Sixteenth Conference, that the First All-Union Conference of Marxist Historians met. Criticism of Pokrovskii had by then become a slight trend or a subdued campaign. Pokrovskii's change of heart between the spring and autumn probably indicates that he sought to shore up his authority. His mandate, which had been issued by Lenin and accorded so well with Bukharin, now required renewal by Stalin. Pokrovskii devised an initiative that proved to be a major event in the history of Soviet historical scholarship: during the First All-Union Conference of Marxist Historians, he became persuaded of the wisdom of dismantling RANION's Institute of History and of transferring its functions to the Communist Academy. This ended the experiment of using noncommunist hands in the building of communism. Marxism claimed a monopoly now; Pokrovskii, acting as though bourgeois specialists were party to a worldwide anti-Soviet conspiracy, urged a policy that would deprive many leading non-Marxist historians of their livelihoods and of the instruments of their profession.

In the course of 1929, most of RANION's institutes effected drastic changes of personnel and then were transferred to the Communist Academy.[1] Non-Marxist historians displaced from the Institute of History were thrust into the cold where many of them were engulfed by the wave of arrests that swept over the old intelligentsia in the course of the rebuilding of the Academy of Sciences. The most fortunate, it seems, found employment in higher schools, in libraries, and in the State Academy of Material Culture in Leningrad.[2] Many of these scholars were restored to honored positions in the historical profession after Zhdanov ended the ongoing cultural revolution in 1934. They again contributed to the building of communism but henceforth, at least avowedly, as Marxists.

In closing down the Institute of History at the end of the spring semester, the authorities chose a path of no return: Pokrovskii committed himself to a course as consequential as his earlier resolve to permit the existence of non-Marxist scholarship. Nevertheless, the circumstances surrounding his decision are unclear to this day. Without access to archives, it is impossible to learn exactly where and when this decision was made, and some obscurities still surround Pokrovskii's role.

In some quarters of party society, the Institute of History had always been deemed an unwise experiment. Some of the personnel of the Commissariat of Education held the view that RANION could not facilitate the preparation of Marxist cadres (Ivanova, 1968:118). This opinion gained adherents when Stalin changed his attitude toward specialists in 1928. At the same time, there was increasing discussion of broadening the research assignment of the Society of Marxist Historians, and those closest to Pokrovskii, such as Gorin and Fridliand, supported this aspiration. We learn from Gorin's remarks at the opening plenum of the First Conference of Marxist Historians on December 28 that the fate of the Institute of History had not yet been decided.[3] Then at some point during the conference, a decision was made to transfer the institute to the Communist Academy. "The most important practical result of the Conference," Pokrovskii wrote, "although it is not registered officially in the resolutions, but organically derived from the work of the Conference, [was] the idea of the need for creating a *Marxist scientific research institute of history*."[4]

During the conference Pokrovskii was won over by the idea of doing away with RANION's Institute of History; after the conference, he persistently championed the proposal. In January he initiated in GUS discussion of the proposal of the Commissariat of Education.[5] The Organizational Bureau of the Central Committee added to its agenda for January co-reports from the Commissariat of Enlightenment and from the Culture-Propaganda Department (*ITsK*, 1928, 29:8). On February 16 Pokrovskii brought the matter before the presidium of the Communist Academy;[6] on that day Gorin addressed the bureau of the presidium about the creation of a new Institute of History. A commission set up to supervise the organizational work consisted of Pokrovskii, Gorin, and E.B. Pashukanis, a legal scholar who directed the KA Institute of Soviet Construction (jurisprudence) and who was a member of the KA presidium. The Party Central Committee decreed on March 8 that the Communist Academy should proceed with the organization of a new Institute of History and that RANION's Institute should merge with it and cease independent existence by November 1. On April 12 the Central Executive Committee of the All-Union Congress of Soviets ratified the decision. The July plenum of the Central Committee in effect endorsed the proposal by designating the Communist Academy the national center for the planning of science.[7] The new Institute of History opened in the fall; it was solidly Marxist, a branch of the Communist Academy, and directed by Pokrovskii.

If Pokrovskii's role in liquidation of RANION from the time of the First Conference of Marxist Historians (December 28, 1928–January 4, 1929) is sufficiently clear, how he arrived at this resolve is not. He had defended the Institute of History in the spring of 1928, after it had already come under attack. And despite the increasing harshness of his denunciations of non-Marxist scholarship in the fall, he did not repudiate the rights of the scholars in RANION. Even Pokrovskii's close associates with access to archives, who sought in commemorating his memory to show the persistence of his militance, were unable to cite statements before 1929 wherein he unequivocally favored closing the institute. It was during the discussions at GUS that Pokrovskii first made such a statement:

> We did not take over these institutions: they fell into a stupor, and the matter could go no further. In their spirit, in their outlook, these institutions remain the same as they were before. And recently, in connection with the activization of the intelligentsia, they acquire something of an aggressive character. . . . It is necessary to put an end to this, especially since we have passed that epoch when we needed only scholars who recognized Soviet power and, in quotation marks so to speak, only scholars of a Soviet type. All this is done with. Now we need communist textbooks, and scholars who participate in the building of socialism.[8]

Reviewing the decision itself, Pokrovskii conceded:

> Before the [first all-union] Conference, we faced the question of

founding an Institute of History in the walls of the Communist Academy. But there was vacillation; can we cope [with it?] Do we have enough strength and ability? After the Conference all doubts and vacillations disappeared. (1930b:10)

Since Pokrovskii admitted that prior to the First Conference he had doubted the wisdom of the modest proposal of creating an All-Union Society of Marxist Historians and favored instead a more modest federation of national chapters, and in view of his expression of "surprise" at the fact that "so late, only after eleven years" did it become evident that non-Marxist scholarship "in its approaches and methods is entirely unsuitable" (*IM*, 1929, 14:5), one may conclude that the "doubts and vacillations" included his own.

Pokrovskii implies that the grounds for his decision were wholly intellectual, that the First Conference of Marxist Historians compelled him to reappraise work on the historical front. "Thus the first thing that our Conference proved is the existence here of genuine Marxist historical scholarship," he wrote, "not in the form of popularization and general courses (in that form Marxist historical scholarship existed even before the Revolution), but in the form of research work" (*IM*, 1929, 11:6–7). The Marxists, in effect, had matured sufficiently to dispense with the aid of their opponents. But there are indications that Pokrovskii's decision was not made on these grounds; the critical elements more likely were Stalin's emerging predominance in connection with his denunciation of capitalist elements within and the appearance at the First Conference of a tendency to challenge Pokrovskii's views publicly and probably to derogate his leadership privately. His chief lieutenants, Gorin and Fridliand, committed to the new policy since early 1928, probably persuaded Pokrovskii to set about proving his usefulness to the Central Committee, lest he (and they with him) share the fate of the Right Opposition.

If the exigencies of the moment affected Pokrovskii's decision, it may also be that his entire life history, his polemical disposition and memories of his estranged relationship with his teachers and peers, affected his resolution.

In spring 1929 Pokrovskii used the Sixteenth Party Conference, the KA plenum, and the Second Conference of Marxist-Leninist Research Institutions as forums to trumpet twin themes: the culpability of the old intelligentsia and the need to expand and consolidate Marxist facilities. Despite occasional lapses, "we should, of course, be able to build communism with the hands of non-communists, but we communists should direct this process" (*VKA*, 1929, 32:212). Pokrovskii usually championed the cause of the red specialists, as in this characteristic rhetoric of the spring of 1929:

The moment had come when it was necessary to put an end to the peaceful cooperation which still existed in some scientific areas between Marxists and scholars far from Marxism or even hostile to Marxism. It was necessary to begin a decisive offensive on all fronts of the scientific world, creating our own Marxist science.[9]

Just a year later he would write the following:

Now we come to a new and still more grandiose feat. Old bourgeois Russia, thrown to the ground by October, but still floundering, still not giving up the hope of rising at some time, has become a rotting corpse. Its older brother in the West with horror begins to realize that the union of *Socialist* republics is not a word but a fact. (1930d:8)

Pokrovskii punctuated his conversion to the new policy with public attacks on individual historians. On the pages of *Pravda,* he upbraided P.F. Preobrazhenskii, S.B. Veselovskii, and N.M. Druzhinin for various forms of backsliding.[10] Pokrovskii placed himself in the foreground of the struggle against the non-Marxists as if to give the lie to any possible accusation that he had faltered in the campaign.

Pokrovskii's New Theory of Cultural Revolution

Very quickly after reaching his decision, Pokrovskii prepared a defense of it. He was not merely discharging his duty as an organizer of scholarship in so doing; one senses a personal need for justification. Indeed, his decision had been highly innovative and violated principles that had evolved since the Renaissance. He had, it seems, a bad conscience. The justification is one of the most enduring elements of Pokrovskii's legacy, affecting not only cultural policy but the very understanding of cultural revolution.

Pokrovskii did not ostensibly recommend the establishment of a Marxist monopoly in scholarship; rather, he urged the creation of conditions in which Marxism could compete without disadvantage.[11] He cast himself in the role of underdog. "It is time to adopt here that form [of ideology] which suits a country where the dictatorship of the proletariat governs, and [where] Leninism is the only acceptable ideology for the great majority." It has been said "more and more frequently" in recent years, "Marxism exists, but Marxist historians—where are they?" And when we created a "*voluntary* grouping of such historians, many people doubted whether a real base existed even for such a modest beginning." The First All-Union Conference of Marxist Historians showed that a "voluntary society in the realm of Marxist-Leninist historical scholarship . . . is clearly insufficient."

Pokrovskii proposed that age and experience were of little significance for historical research, and he praised the young Marxists for posing fresh problems, such as imperialism and Russian participation in World War I, that were outside the ken of the old scholarship. "No matter what the situation was, now a new generation is present. This must not be forgotten for a moment." Henceforth scholarship would consist of collective enterprises:

> Sometimes, in fact frequently, a director's baton will be required. And here we come to grips with the basic fact, about which the thought of the Conference almost constantly turned and from which at the Conference itself was drawn the most suitable practical conclusion. Our scientific research institutions in the area of history are fully in the hands of old people. The director's baton is held in the hands of the "worthies" themselves or those authorized by them, but for whom the sumptuous marble memorials in the cemetery of ideology have long been ready. We have still not a single scientific institution in the field of history, where our scientific youth, youth no longer students, but youth, creative youth, who are moving science forward—can feel themselves [to be] in their [own] ideological environment, can feel themselves at home and see around themselves in the capacity "of the older generation" no one but the elderly representatives of the ideology, for which they struggle, which permeates that very youth.

This vivid passage reveals first that Pokrovskii drastically revised his understanding of the history of ideas in the Soviet Union, which he had expressed in March 1928. He had stressed then the intellectual and organizational hegemony of Marxism. Now, while pointing up the intellectual competence of the young Marxists, he stresses their alleged subordination to the "worthies." The old scholarship presides; its representatives hold the dominant positions, and it is they who can set standards and determine relationships with the rest of society. The young Marxists, even though they are the genuine scholars, are deprived of authority, despite the fact that they live in a Marxist-proletarian state. It seems that a prerevolutionary situation exists, the non-Marxists governing and willy-nilly suppressing Marxism so that a revolution in scholarship, corresponding to the October Revolution in politics, is necessary.

Pokrovskii's picture, no matter how ingeniously contrived, must be rejected as a misrepresentation of the facts. Although his picture in some respects describes the situation as it existed even as late as 1924, it is a grossly misleading account of the situation in 1929. Pokrovskii passed over the fact that Marxist historians could enlist the support of the state and command the lion's share of resources. He did not trouble to remind his listeners and readers that destruction of a non-Marxist or semi-Marxist institute was at issue, as well as the creation of a Marxist Institute. The non-Marxists were barred not only from the classroom but from the means of carrying out their investigations and presenting their findings. They were being silenced by administrative means.

Pokrovskii's mode of argument, his choice of pedagogic tasks rather than the requirements of investigation as the frame of reference, has some important implications. Basic facts of age and chronology control the situation. The non-Marxists—by definition nonscholars, for the revolutionary triumph of Marxism in the October Revolution rendered their methods and assumptions obsolete—hold authority simply because they are senior. Young scholars, who because they are Marxists are alone capable of genuine scholarship, are fated by virtue of their youth to be in subordinate positions. Such arrangements are inevitable unless the state overthrows them. Pokrovskii does not describe this disposition of ideological forces as a "law of building socialism," but his account by implication describes what he considers to be a lawful or natural outcome of the October Revolution. He would expect to find similar arrangements after future socialist revolutions. If taken as a basic pattern or model, Pokrovskii's account, despite its crudity with respect to the facts of the moment, is noteworthy. It provides a base for comparing the cultural histories of societies which claim to be governed by proletarian states that officially sponsor Marxism as a method of scholarship. Pokrovskii's account than can be construed as a development of Marx's theory of ideology: it is an enlargement though not necessarily a refinement of that theory.

Pokrovskii's model of the evolution of ideas helps provide a context for some of the enduring features of Soviet historiography. It affirms, as does its rival, the traditional liberal model, the inevitability of conflict of ideas. It departs from the rival theory in postulating that truth emerges as a result of the triumph of a particular set of ideas and evaluations. It is the victory of Marxism-Leninism that assures attainment of truth, or at least of the closest approximation of reality. Establishing truth, then, requires annihilation of conflict among ideas. Pokrovskii's model is not without merit when compared with the liberal model. By repudiating the assumption that truth inevitably results from the continued conflict of ideas refined in the light of gradually accumulated experience, Soviet historians discard unneeded baggage. Without it, they are less likely to lose sight of the capacity of our species to forget its experience as well as to learn from it. Pokrovskii's use of the Leninist figure of a conductor's baton calls attention to still another aspect of reality glossed over by the liberal model. It denies the contention that there can be free and equal competition in a marketplace of ideas. An establishment inevitably exists, as does a corresponding orthodoxy. Pokrovskii implies that there is inevitably a dominant set of values; the governing part of society employs its power to assure that education in the leading institutions proceeds in conformity with them. Pokrovskii's model not only derides liberalism; it seeks to point up its limitations.

The closing of RANION's Institute of History was a major event, and Pokrovskii's part in it was crucial. Had he decided earlier, the institute would have been liquidated earlier. We cannot, of course, know what might have happened had he opposed its liquidation, but enunciation of possibilities helps show the range and limits of his authority. First, the demise of traditional non-Marxist institutions did not inevitably lead to the death of semi-Marxist institutions such as RANION. After all, they did educate many Marxist scholars, which in itself was a strong argument available to their supporters. Although it is difficult to imagine RANION's not being impaired by 1931, when Stalin intervened directly in scholarly matters, the fierce disputes among Marxists might not have occurred or, at least, probably would not have taken the same form, had RANION's Institute of History not been liquidated. Unfortunately, there are not enough facts available to allow even a preliminary judgment as to whether Pokrovskii's decision to close the institute was one of the matters that mobilized his opponents against him.

Second, had Pokrovskii prevented the liquidation of RANION, this would not have spared him posthumous denigration. He had always been an antagonist of non-Marxist scholarship, even when he had been among its patrons. His decision removed all ambiguity from the relationship: he was an enemy. Justifying his decision, he helped develop a rhetoric of abuse that would be turned against him. Nevertheless, had he decided in favor of RANION, his denigration might have taken a different form. His opponents might not have so relished the campaign and promoted it with so much zest.

A further thought about the demise of RANION's Institute of History—Pokrovskii's decision was not simply an inevitable response to circumstances not of his own making. It was a species of ingratiating behavior: it seems that Pokrovskii sought to appease those who held power over him for the purpose of retaining his own power and protecting his good name. If we can take his earlier observations about the uses of non-Marxist scholarship as a statement of a requirement for the development of proletarian scholarship—a proletarian interpretation of history was to be forged in opposition to and not in the absence of bourgeois interpretations—then we can say that he acted in a fashion inimical to the development of proletarian scholarship in his own understanding of the concept. We cannot escape the conclusion that he behaved irresponsibly.

Rout of the Non-Marxists

Pokrovskii's new theory of cultural revolution was a sign of the times. Even as he stated his thoughts, the venerable Academy of Sciences, initiated by Peter the Great, came under the powerful sway of Soviet authority. The autonomy of the Academy of Sciences had begun to erode almost at the outset of the Soviet regime. The authorities took an important step in June 1927, when they drafted a new charter that impaired the right of the academy to elect its own members. Once vacancies were published, scholarly institutions of all the Republics as well as public associations and individual scholars could nominate candidates for membership. The statute also greatly enlarged the number of departments, with the result that in 1929 there were forty-two vacancies. The communists nominated nine members, including Bukharin, Pokrovskii, Riazanov, Lukin, Friche, and Deborin, a former Menshevik who was now head of the KA's Institute of Philosophy. In open discussions all these candidates won approval, but in the closed elections three of them—Deborin, Friche, and Lukin—were rejected, while all the non-Marxist candidates, including Petrushevskii, were approved.[12] Pokrovskii, shortly after the election, became head of the academy's Archeographic Commission.

Pravda interpreted the elections as "*a political demonstration* against the working class," and initiated a campaign against the old Academicians. The campaign can be followed on the pages of *Pravda* of late January and early February. Letters appeared from almost all party-led scholarly institutions; even the nonparty workers of the Red Triangle Factory protested—all to the effect that "the Academy should cease being a state within a state." Finally on February 8, the presidium of the academy announced that new elections would be held in the near future. It had capitulated.[13] The uneven struggle was resumed in the summer. *Pravda* reported that sixty-one research workers had been removed in the course of a purge not quite half completed. In September the OGPU announced it had uncovered a monarchist plot by former Tsarist officers in Leningrad (20 Sept. 1929). In November the press accused some of the Academicians of concealing documents of historical significance and of not cooperating with the government purgers. At an open meeting a few days later speakers denounced the accused as Black Hundreds. S.F. Ol'denburg then lost his post as permanent secretary of the academy and S.F. Platonov surrendered his position as head of the academy's library.[14]

Sotsialisticheskii vestnik, the well-informed émigré Menshevik journal, reported that on October 1, 1929, the Council of People's Commissars issued a decree, never to appear in the press, closing all non-Marxist historical societies and institutes (1929, 23:15). Some of the non-Marxists, such as B.D. Grekov, N.Ia. Marr, S.B. Veselovskii, and S.V.

Iushkov,[15] completed their apparent conversions and succeeded in insinuating themselves into the rival camp. Other unsheltered scholars were engulfed in successive waves of arrests, some of them becoming victims in the show trials of the era. Tarle fell victim in the Industrial-Party Trial in November and December 1930. Testimony was given implicating him in an alleged counterrevolutionary plot. A number of secret parties, the Soviet authorities would have one believe, designated Tarle as minister of foreign relations in a future bourgeois government. He was exiled to Central Asia.[16] Assuming momentarily the validity of the charges, it is still puzzling that Tarle was condemned not for his own acts, but because others had intentions that involved him. D.B. Riazanov, head of the Marx-Engels Institute, had just enjoyed a nationwide celebration of his sixtieth birthday (*Na boevom*, 1930) and then fell in connection with the Menshevik trial of March 1931. He, like a number of others, found employment in Leningrad under the patronage of S.M. Kirov (Nicolaevskii, 1965:44).

Numerous historians were arrested in the Academic Case, sometimes called the Platonov Case, which has been described by the émigré scholar V.V. Tchernavin (1935:359–68). A series of arrests spanned a two-year period from the purge of the Academy of Sciences in the fall of 1929 until 1931. Charges of a monarchist plot were issued, yet no confessions were published nor were sentences announced—and no trial was ever held. Some of the victims were shot; the majority were sent to camps. The most fortunate merely endured exile in remote provinces. In the 1930s many of the historians were restored to society and resumed their professional activities.

In 1930, Platonov and his assistant S.V. Rozhdestvenskii were arrested (Shteppa, 1963:49). The eminent Ukrainian historian M.S. Hrushevskii was exiled the same year. He died in Kislovodsk in November 1934. Numerous students of his were also brought to trial. G. Vasenko and the Byzantinists V.N. Beneshevich and M.A. Shangin suffered arrest. In August it was the turn of Moscow historians. The émigré historian Constantine Shteppa estimates that in 1931 more than 120 historians were arrested, including N.P. Likhachev, V.I. Picheta, and S.K. Bogoiavlenskii (Shteppa, 1963:49).

It should be noted that some Soviet historians have denied these claims or at least considered them exaggerated. According to M.E. Naidenov only three historians were arrested—Bakhrushin, Platonov, and Tarle. Not their beliefs but their behavior was at issue, and since their acts were not illegal, they were released in short order. Platonov died not in exile but at home. While many non-Marxists lost their jobs, most found new ones at the State Institute of Material Culture (GAIMK) or in schools.[17]

Pokrovskii and the SMH dispensed yeoman service for the party in the course of this purge. In articles and public discussions, the Marxists unmasked the scholarly ineptitude and political chicanery of their opponents.[18] These works will forever hold a place in the history of human unreason as monuments to the abuse of learning. In the opening discussion of the SMH, S.A. Piontkovskii quoted the minutes of a meeting of the Archeographic Commission in 1918. At that meeting, a letter from the recently deceased head of the Commission, Sheremetiev, to Platonov was entered into the minutes. Sheremetiev had written, "God grant that the armistice be replaced by a proper peace." Piontkovskii interpreted this as follows: "He is evaluating negatively the foreign policy conducted by Soviet Russia and the dictatorship of the proletariat in 1918" (*IM*, 1930, 28–29:159). Platonov also entered another remark of Sheremetiev into the minutes: "I die with a profound faith in Russia—she will be reborn." According to Piontkovskii, this "clearly means" he considered Russia in a state of ruin. "In these words there is a definite political program." For the commission to read these words was "a political demonstration, a hostile evaluation of the dictatorship of the proletariat, a hostile evaluation of our internal and external policy" (*IM*, 1930, 28–29:159). Piontkovskii's tendentious interpretations are the vilest sort of gossip-mongering. That the passages of Sheremetiev quoted here were so innocuous suggests perhaps the disposition of the non-Marxists to adjust to any authority. The only possible redeeming feature of such discussions is the possibility that some of the accusers spoke with tongue in cheek in order to reveal the total absurdity of the allegations.

The only work of any scholarly merit was Pokrovskii's contribution to the campaign, an article entitled "The Rise of the Muscovite State and Great-Russian Nationality" (1930c). It represents his last sortie against the national school. Though one-sided and ill-tempered, it is a somewhat technical criticism of the use of sources on the rise of Muscovy by the non-Marxists as far back as Kavelin and Soloviev. This article and *Russian History from Earliest Times* are two works that represent an able, though one-sided, criticism of the national school that reigned before and after the Pokrovskii interlude.

There are of course numerous other incidents in this campaign, but to cite them would serve only for a study of social psychology or to trace the development of the rhetoric that would predominate in the Great Purge Trials. No pattern of ideas emerges from these events; it was wholly a pogrom and cannot be considered even class warfare. An all-powerful state intimidated and even imprisoned a few defenseless individuals in the name of science. Certainly these events mark a low point of Soviet historiography, a step down the ladder to Stalin's *Short Course* on party history.

Expansion of the Communist Academy

As the Academy of Sciences temporarily writhed in pain, the Communist Academy reached its pinnacle. Pokrovskii's scholarly apparatus was no longer merely "a library, plus a journal, plus a general meeting," but the coordinating center of an elaborate network of institutes and societies. Clearly a new era had dawned since the gloomy Conference of Marxist-Leninist Research Institutions had met early in 1928. By 1930, the academy registered a membership of 100; it employed 800 research workers and had enrolled 700 graduate students. Its structure incorporated not only the institutes of RANION, but the Institute of Red Professors as well. The number of people associated with the academy was 1500 all told, if one counted those who merely listened to reports.[19] It published its own books as well as ten or so journals. One heard no more complaints, for the time being, about material facilities. In the summer the Central Committee designated the Communist Academy the national center for scientific planning. The presidium of the KA was assigned a month to work out a system of planning that would coordinate the efforts of scientists with the needs of the People's Commissariats; it was given two weeks to draw up the material requirements for implementing the plan ("O meropriatiakh," 1929) a prodigious assignment that reflected the spirit of the first five-year plan.

The leaders of the KA found their tasks so varied that they set up a number of administrative organs to coordinate the work of specialists. For example, by 1930 they created an Information Department to supply the press with news. A Department of Mass Work arranged for the academy staff to participate in lectures and social campaigns (anniversary celebrations, etc.; *VKA,* 1930, 42:149). In time the academy published its own newspaper, *Teoreticheskii front* (*The Theoretical Front*) and a bulletin for internal communications.

The Comacademy's new Institute of History opened in the fall with a staff of forty and an enrollment of thirty-six graduate students.[20] It was governed by a collegium headed by Pokrovskii and including Vanag, Volgin, Gorin, Lukin, S.M. Monosov, Udal'tsov, Fridliand, Piontkovskii and M.A. Savel'ev.[21] Unlike in the old institute, the conventional classification of ancient, medieval, and modern history was eliminated. The institute was organized, like the Society of Marxist Historians, according to problems—methodology, the history of imperialism, industrial capitalism, sociology, the proletariat of the USSR, the East. The SMH and not the institute, in most matters, was still the foremost organization on the historical front.

The Institute of History was only one of the rewards the Marxists reaped from the new policy; for Pokrovskii it was just one of the prizes that enhanced his authority. Specialized historical commissions, almost vertical trusts, for archival work, research, and the publication of professional and popular works, were created or enlarged at this time. Within the Communist Academy a special section coordinated all the work on war, armed uprising, and the Civil War (*BKA,* 1929, 33:274). A commission headed by Pokrovskii, organized under the Central Executive Committee of the USSR, undertook to publish diplomatic documents of the era of imperialism.[22] The Society of Marxist Historians itself created a commission for the study of the Russian proletariat (*Plan,* 1928:79). Pokrovskii exercised general supervision, while the day-to-day leadership was in the hands of A.M. Pankratova, who had established herself at the First Conference of Marxist Historians as the chief authority in this field. These commissions, plus a few others, would attain full bloom in the late 1930s, some as scholarly institutions, others as propaganda enterprises.

Armed with so many auxiliaries, the Society of Marxist Historians grew more formidable than ever. Admittedly some of its claims were specious. While it did manage to found chapters in 22 cities, the total membership outside the capital was 120.[23] Moreover, the membership was so embroiled in current campaigns and organizational matters that production fell off. In the year ending October 29, 1929, only 28 of 64 projected reports were delivered, a mere 43.7 percent of quota.[24] The society nevertheless became increasingly fit for its militant tasks. A branch was finally established in Leningrad, and the local Institute of Marxism was converted into the Leningrad Department of the Communist Academy (LOKA). The most important innovation was the creation of a section on the History of the Party, Leninism, and the Comintern (referred to here as the Party Section). Published sources admit nothing distinctive about this section, aside from the special timeliness of its subject matter, but a work that utilizes archival materials reveals its special character (Nosov & Zakharikov, 1962:62–64). In addition to research and publication, it was authorized to supervise education and to train activists to lecture on party history, Leninism, and related topics. Moreover, it participated in the work of the SMH in leading the struggle against "revisionism, pseudo-Marxism, and bourgeois doctrine." It presumably assured that work in all fields was consonant with findings and dictates in party history. In addition, it was to supervise party history in other institutions, even those specialized in this field. It was urged to mobilize forces for the realization of the plan of the Lenin Institute, which now included Istpart (*PR,* 1930, 4:199). The Party Section spearheaded the drive to unify the Marxist camp. Yet there was an anomaly in the makeup of the section from the outset: Emelian Iaroslavskii, who was to become the chief opponent of Pokrovskii, was a member of the section's governing bureau (Nosov & Zakharikov, 1962:63).

Divergent Hypotheses

As the events unfolded and just after, some of the participants sought to justify the demise of non-Marxist historiography, and their explanations affected ongoing events and then became working assumptions of Soviet historians. According to Ts. Fridliand, the immediate cause of the demise was an offensive by the non-Marxist historians against Soviet power. The offensive was a response not only to the success of Marxist historiography but to the victories nationwide of socialist construction—the triumph of the party over the kulaks, nepmen, bourgeois and petty-bourgeois intellectuals. Fridliand's hypothesis is somewhat more complex than the bare suggestion that the bourgeoisie had gone on the offensive. The indecisive Marxist response exacerbated the crisis. The activity of "pseudo-Marxists" would not have been dangerous had "communist-historians presented a united, well-knit front." Far from closing ranks, some of the Marxists resisted the decision to unmask Petrushevskii and Tarle. Some expressed opposition by remaining silent, and others openly attacked "extreme struggle" on the historical front. They accepted the slogan *laissez-faire, laisser passer* and felt that "the free play of forces would be the best exit from the present situation." One communist, Fridliand alleged, had declared "that the task of Marxism by no means consists of suppressing other points of view. 'Live and let live' " (1928b:69).

Pankratova, who participated in the events reviewed here and had ample time to reflect on their meaning, produced still another explanation. She viewed the destruction of non-Marxist historiography as a consequence of the party leadership's effort to clear its own house of contraband theories. The "history and perspective of the proletarian revolution" became crucial matters "only when the party was involved in the struggle against Trotskyism." It fell to historians to undertake, "under the supervision of the party, a rebuff of the opportunistic revision of the Leninist teaching concerning the possibility of building socialism in our country" (1934:69). This presumed affinity between Trotsky and the non-Marxists explains why, in Pankratova's opinion, historians had to go beyond "unmasking the Trotskyite schema." It was necessary at the very same time to demonstrate the ideological-political identity of this schema with bourgeois and petty-bourgeois conceptions of the October Revolution. That is why, struggling against Trotskyism, the Bolshevik historians conducted a struggle with the historical schemata of the bourgeois restorationists and the petty-bourgeois liquidators. In other words, non-Marxist historiography proved to be an obstacle both to the long-range aspiration of socialist construction and to the immediate exigencies of state building. The "rebuff" the non-Marxists had to endure was a by-product of intraparty conflict. Merely going about their business, the non-Marxists impinged on party prerogatives.

Among the questions raised by these events, the following stand out. Were many non-Marxist historians being drawn to the banner of Marxism? Are there indications that those who were not were using their pedagogic authority to instill a worldview in their students? Were Marxist historians satisfied by their own efforts at historical construction? Is it possible to determine whether students and professors were becoming less or more ideology minded? In general, were the party's cultural policies succeeding, and was the expectation that noncommunists could be employed in the building of communism being borne out by experience? Finally, were the forebodings expressed about non-Marxist historiography genuine or contrived?

The question of whether there was a resurgence of non-Marxist historiography could be the object of a separate investigation, but the materials at hand for this study indicate a negative answer. The allegation should not, however, be viewed entirely as a contrivance. In the conflict between Marxist and non-Marxist historians, factors combined in a peculiar fashion. The growing strength of the Marxist historians manifested itself in their increasing numbers, enlarged resources, and effective organization. The growing strength of the non-Marxists expressed itself in the fact that their influence persisted despite meager resources and the absence of autonomous organization. Few non-Marxists embraced the official creed. Although no evidence of an offensive exists, the attitudes and methods of the non-Marxists had not evolved in the direction foretold by the Marxist theory of cultural revolution. This itself created anxiety in the Marxist camp.

The expanding organizational power of the Marxist historians may well have engendered favorable sentiments about the old way of looking at things. The post-Civil War generation of scholars, no matter how pleased they might have been with Soviet power, could not exactly duplicate the sense of commitment of the generation that had made the Revolution. The student youth may have been skeptical of a Marxist commitment like Pokrovskii's. It is generally agreed that the non-Marxist historians were the best trained and most accomplished among the teachers at the Institute of History. Did the students view them sympathetically as underdogs? It would seem that the dynamics of generational conflict in at least some of its aspects were working against the Marxists.

Under other circumstances, the persistence of non-Marxist historiography would not have resulted in its demise. The outcome of the conflict between Marxist and non-Marxist historians apparently was determined by its context—the struggle for power within the party. Suppression of the opposition required not only the "discrediting" of their views, but the elaboration and inculcation by the victorious faction of a comprehensive yet highly specific view of the past. The new interpretation included both the specifics of party hagiography and a comprehensive revaluation of Russian history that would sanction the doctrine of "Socialism in One Country." In a broader sense, the new interpretation had to legitimate political authority by reaffirming the scientific character of Marxism; it had to prove that the outcome of the Revolution and the subsequent evolution of Soviet society was in accord with Lenin's prerevolutionary prognosis. The circumstances of party life gave rise to the new system of ideas, but developing and enforcing it required the suppression of all opposition, not just party opposition. In the course of this process, historical writing became wholly, or almost wholly, subordinated to the party.

8   The Gap between Theory and Practice

The events of Pokrovskii's life and the fate of his ideas not only show the impact of the first five-year plan and ensuing socialist construction on Soviet historiography; they exemplify the dominant trends in Russian intellectual life. In some respects, this book tends to confirm a hypothesis already formulated about Soviet intellectual history. According to Robert Daniels (1956), the history of ideas in the Soviet Union up to about 1953 encompasses three distinct periods. Ideological competition endured throughout most of the 1920s; in 1929 pluralism was forsaken in the face of an effort to proclaim a single orthodoxy in each intellectual discipline. Taken together the new orthodoxies constituted an "extreme Marxism." The "intellectual content of the orthodoxies varied: in some fields 'vulgar Marxism' prevailed; in others, Marxism with voluntarist overtones which had roots in Lenin's pre-revolutionary thought" was the rule (1956:101).

Along with "extreme Marxism, *partiinost* . . . and service to the party were imposed on intellectual activity as the supreme criterion of value and truth." For example, Pokrovskii "set up a virtual dictatorship in history, terminating the fairly broad tolerance which had been accorded the activities of non-party historians during the NEP" (1956:100, 106).

In the third period, after 1932, "in each field a breakdown of practical work threatened as a result of the imposition of extreme Marxism." As a result, "the extreme Marxism of the First Five Year Plan period was successively repudiated in various fields, while the people who had espoused and imposed these views in the name of the party were denounced as anti-Marxist wreckers and in many cases liquidated." Extreme Marxism was "replaced by a surprisingly obvious and thorough traditionalism," which continued to carry the name of Marxism. "In this fashion, the machinery and justification of control built up during the process of imposing extreme Marxism were retained, but turned around to operate in the opposite direction" (1956:102). While Daniels' three-period division is generally acceptable, it has some limitations. The liquidation of RANION, the communization of the Academy of Sciences, and the accompanying expansion of the Communist Academy were major events of the second period. Pluralism was set aside as a governing principle and replaced by a striving for monolithic unity. "Service to the party" was becoming the "supreme criterion of value and truth." It is not, however, altogether suitable to speak of a dictatorship of Pokrovskii. The increasing activity and authority of the KA, which can be understood as a striving for domination, went hand in hand with increasingly successful defiance of its authority. There was opposition to Pokrovskii even in the SMH itself. More important, despite the great publicity attending Pokrovskii's name and writings, his historical synthesis was being increasingly and ever more systematically criticized. Pokrovskii himself had repudiated economic materialism, but he had succeeded in replacing it only with exhortations about the need for a more flexible understanding of the historical process. Pokrovskii's 1927 reinterpretation of the Russian Revolution—his formulation of what is referred to as the theory of growing over—made the concept of merchant capital problematical. He would soon, moreover, begin to yield ground on the question of Russian imperialism. It would indeed be difficult to summarize Pokrovskii's system as it stood in 1929 and 1930, and the variety of controversies among Marxist historians makes it impossible to state what constituted "extreme Marxism" in the field of historiography.

A Rival Coalition

The enhancement of authority brought on by the rise of Stalin created a base for numerous Stalins writ small. But even as circumstances conspired to increase Pokrovskii's stature and popularize his historical views, they set obstacles in his path. Some historians wished merely to be left alone; others sought the mantle of leadership for themselves. How they responded to his growing influence can be described best in terms of Europe's balance-of-power system. The simplification of the historical sector into a Marxist camp enhanced Pokrovskii's authority. The possibility of his achieving hegemony brought about an opposing coalition within the Marxist camp.

In 1928 Istpart merged with the Lenin Institute,[1] creating a large center for the study of party history. In 1930 the Lenin Institute established its own facilities for training specialists, an IKP of its own. It could scarcely conceal its disdain for the tutelage of the Party Section of the Society of Marxist Historians.[2] Riazanov's Marx-Engels Institute also failed to express gratitude for projects conceived in the Communist Academy. And the members of the Society of Former Political Prisoners and Penal Exiles who published *Katorga i ssylka* were impervious to calls for unity. Yet it would be an error, in my view, to exaggerate the organizational dimension of the conflict. Although there was a tendency for specialists in party history to line up against Pokrovskii, the battle lines cut across institutions. Opponents turned up in Pokrovskii's own bailiwick, and he received occasional support from *Proletarskaia revoliutsiia*, the main journal on party history.

Pokrovskii most likely had misgivings about the election of Iaroslavskii to the Communist Academy late in 1928. An event of singular importance occurred in 1929 when L.M. Kaganovich, the patron of Iaroslavskii, took over as chief of the Academy's Institute of Soviet Construction, the body concerned with legal scholarship.[3] This betokened an active concern on the part of Kaganovich with questions of theory and matters of personnel on the theoretical front. The former head of Kaganovich's institute, E.B. Pashukanis, was to rise to the presidium of the Communist Academy, where he was to be a persistent obstacle to Pokrovskii. Then hostile criticism of Pokrovskii began to reach the public. In May S.M. Dubrovskii gave a report on "Asiatic, Feudal, and Peasant Modes of Production." After a special meeting was held to evaluate this report, Dubrovskii published a book critical of Pokrovskii's concept of merchant capitalism (1929). Dubrovskii, one of the first graduates of Pokrovskii's IKP seminar, was a specialist on agrarian history, whose emphasis was on the Stolypin era. In 1929 he was elected to membership in the Communist Academy, and he became deputy chairman of its newly formed International Agrarian Institute. His book sustained the debate on historical materialism initiated by the discussion of Petrushevskii.

I.A. Teodorovich, an old Bolshevik who had served as one of the first People's Commissars and who was now chief editor of *Katorga i ssylka*, was Dubrovskii's superior at the International Agrarian Institute. That summer, he published an article to commemorate the jubilee of *Narodnaia volia*, which gave rise to the noisiest struggle on the historical front (1929). The legacy of Russian populism was among the most difficult problems for Marxist historians until Stalin finally ended the discussion in 1935.[4] We have seen that it was the subject of Pokrovskii's most controversial book, *History of the Revolutionary Movement*. Controversy arose also in 1928 in connection with the celebration of Chernyshevskii's jubilee. Pokrovskii had been criticized on that occasion by Y.M. Steklov, a former independent Social Democrat who had played an important role in the Petrograd Soviet in 1917. Steklov was a master of the sources, but he exaggerated the similarities between populism and Bolshevism. Pokrovskii was compelled to modify his own stand slightly, admitting some affinities with Marxism on Chernyshevskii's part, and he abandoned his attempt to stigmatize Chernyshevskii as a proto-Menshevik. Pokrovskii gave ground grudgingly, fearing lest the supraclass theory of the state, which he felt permeated populism, become respectable among Marxists.[5] Teodorovich's article, which reopened the conflict, led to a wholesale assault on Pokrovskii's views. Another sign of the emerging conflict was the appearance of some volumes of an authoritative party history, edited by Iaroslavskii. This anthology was the chief manifestation of "Iaroslavskii and his school."[6] Its authors included two of Pokrovskii's prize students, A.L. Sidorov and I.I. Mints.

Pokrovskii responded by taking the offensive. In November he wrote to the party unit of the Institute of Red Professors' historical section. The only correct line was

> to cleanse Marxist historical literature of all vestiges of bourgeois ideology of which there are still very many, and to carry on a merciless struggle with bourgeois ideology when it has the effrontery to manifest itself openly, as has happened with particular frequency in the last few years. Opposition to carrying out of this line, I have noted up to now only on the part of Trotsky and partly by the followers of N.I. Bukharin.[7]

An event whose origins lay outside the historical front redounded to Pokrovskii's advantage by heating up the atmosphere and driving his campaign forward. On December 20 Stalin addressed a Conference of Marxist Agronomists. Just after the capitulation of the Right Bolsheviks, in the very speech in which he called for the elimination of the kulaks as a class, Stalin commanded scholars and scientists to close the gap between theory and practice—the coming watchword in the intellectual life. In effect, he called for the ferreting out of unorthodox ideas:

> But while we have reason to be proud of the practical successes achieved in socialist construction, the same cannot be said with regard to our theoretical work in the sphere of economics in general, and of agriculture in particular. Moreover it must be admitted that theoretical thought is not keeping pace with our practical successes, that there is a certain gap between our practical successes and the development of the theoretical thought. Yet our theoretical work must not only keep pace with practical work but must keep ahead of it and equip our practical workers for their fight for the victory of socialism.

Except for the gap between theory and practice how can we explain the fact that

> in our social and political life various bourgeois and petty-bourgeois theories on problems of our economy are still current? How can we explain the fact that these theories are not yet meeting the proper rebuff? . . . Is it so difficult to understand that unless a merciless fight against bourgeois theories is carried on on the basis of Marxist-Leninist theory, it will be impossible to achieve complete victory over class enemies? (Stalin, 1953:389, 390)

Some months later Pokrovskii observed that the conference at which Stalin spoke "had opened our eyes to many sides of our work which we simply had not noticed" (*VKA*, 1930, 39:15). On December 30, possibly having heard reports of the speech, he wrote to Gorin from Berlin, where he was being treated for a bladder disorder: " 'The signs multiply,' as Lenin once wrote, that a great attack is impending on the right flank" (Gorin, 1933:102). Then on January 8 he predicted the "evaporation from the Bolshevik kettle of the final remains of the democratic elements that joined [the party] . . . in 1905 . . . and during the Civil War. They will disappear only with disappearance of their class base—the wealthy peasants" (Gorin, 1933:104). Before Stalin's speech there were disagreements; after it, deviations. As phrased in an SMH resolution, "The line between ideology and politics is wiped away" (*IM*, 1930, 15:165).

The Narodnaia Volia Dispute

The controversy between Pokrovskii and Teodorovich arose during the fiftieth anniversary celebration of the founding of *Narodnaia volia*—the most famous of all revolutionary terrorist groups. The Communist Academy had appointed a committee headed by Iaroslavskii and including Pokrovskii, Gorin, Riazanov, and Krupskaia, Lenin's widow, to arrange a jubilee program scheduled to last from late 1929 until March 1, 1931, the anniversary of Alexander II's assassination. The polemic was ended officially by a resolution of the Culture-Propaganda Department (APPO) of the Central Committee, published in *Pravda* on April 9, 1930. It reverberated, nevertheless, until June and echoed even into 1931. Pokrovskii, already infirm, did not participate directly, though at stake was his authority. Instead he exhorted his followers into action; Gorin bore the brunt of the struggle.

The chief editor of *Katorga i ssylka*, I.A. Teodorovich, had himself been a member of *Narodnaia volia* and then later a prominent Bolshevik. He had been commissar for food in the first Soviet government, then commissar of agriculture for the RFSFR and head of the Peasant International before he became chairman of the International Agrarian Institute. His demotion to the Agrarian Institute in the spring of 1928 was probably the result of "rightist" policies on his part, particularly his opposition to the extraordinary measures being used to obtain grain from the peasants. Perhaps Teodorovich's most dramatic moment as a historical actor had been at the Stockholm Congress in 1906, when, on behalf of Lenin, he replied to Plekhanov's famous warning that counterrevolution would ensue from Lenin's land policy.[8] Teodorovich possessed a judicious mind and showed mastery of the subject; he was an able polemicist.

Teodorovich attempted to identify the ideas shared by *Narodnaia volia* and Bolshevism.[9] Everyone agreed that continuities between the two were discernible, but Teodorovich asserted that *Narodnaia volia* anticipated the following typically Bolshevik ideas: having taken power, the party should (1) destroy the old state apparatus, (2) create a new form of state, on the order of soviets, (3) use the new state to cultivate the socialist elements of the economy, (4) take into account that the nurturing of the new economy "presupposed the existence, more or less extensive, of a so-called 'transition period' " (1930:77–78). Such a brief summary of Teodorovich's ideas seems to authenticate the charge of his opponents that he modernized the history of Populism and, in doing so, idealized small-scale production; hence he was guilty of a right-wing deviation.

To offset this notion it is necessary to show how Teodorovich qualified his thesis. For instance, he wrote that "as a result of its long political experience *Narodnaia volia* sensed (*nashchupyvala*) in some instances more, in others less clearly" the four ideas presented above. Proletarian hegemony was another example: *Narodnaia volia* did not formulate this notion, "but in *rambling, rudimentary form,* they understood the need and the inevitability of the hegemony" (1930:78, 86). Thus Bolshevism and *Narodnaia volia* shared ideas in a special way; the latter sensed and groped for concepts that could be formulated only in a subsequent stage. Teodorovich did not attribute these ideas to the entire *Narodnaia volia* but to its extreme left wing in its final phase of development.

Although Teodorovich stressed the similarities between Bolshevism and *Narodnaia volia,* he never lost sight of the differences. He considered *Narodnaia volia* an instance of allegedly utopian socialism that existed in Europe before the rise of Marxism; as such, its members were guilty of numerous errors owing to their gross misunderstanding of capitalism. Teodorovich noted that had *Narodnaia volia* triumphed over tsarism, the result would not have been socialism but the American pattern of capitalist development, that is, a republic based on widespread distribution of private property. This brings us to Teodorovich's major point: despite the fact that *objective circumstances* would not have permitted the triumph of socialism, the members of *Narodnaia volia subjectively were socialists* (1930:49). Thus Teodorovich challenged Pokrovskii's view that the members of *Narodnaia volia* were tied by their world view to the bourgeois order.

The kulaks would have found scant comfort in Teodorovich's ideas; it is difficult to perceive any sense in which they supported Bukharin's program or to see in them an attack on Stalin's abandonment of the NEP. Yet the inflamed imaginations of the time were capable of conjuring up Teodorovich's past history to accuse him of being a Rightist—the most timely means of misrepresenting and discrediting his ideas. The political content of his essay, however, applied only to the politics of historical scholarship.

Stalin's speech to the Marxist-Agronomists assured a lively reception for Teodorovich's essay. The initial round was fought out in the newspapers. Then the editors of *Izvestiia* (9 Jan. 1930) decided that the debate should go on, but in scholarly journals rather than in the daily press. Discussions were held under the auspices of the Society of Marxist Historians on January 16 and 25 and February 4, 1930.[10] Not surprisingly, Teodorovich failed to convince the followers of Pokrovskii in the course of these discussions, but he upheld his views and continued to make them known. In February he found a broader forum at a Conference on the Teaching of Party History, the Comintern, and Leninism organized by the Party Section of the SMH, but including representatives of other institutions.[11] A resolution was adopted censuring Teodorovich. Angry and disgruntled he fought on, extending his criticism to Pokrovskii's basic assumptions about Russian history and calling attention to the tactics of his opponents. Finally he was censured by resolution of the Central Committee.[12] He then assembled and published his various statements—his final public act in the dispute. In an appended note he suggested, not wholly unjustifiably, that he had been the victor. Teodorovich continued to edit *Katorga i ssylka* until its demise in 1935.

Pokrovskii was displeased and apprehensive. Not Gorin alone, but Teodorovich, through his somewhat unwilling ally Iaroslavskii, who was one of its editors, had access to the pages of *Bol'shevik*. Writing to Gorin from Berlin, just after Teodorovich's work had been criticized in *Pravda,* he noted that V.F. Malakhovskii, an SMH specialist on the revolutionary movement, "had taken fright and decided to make peace" with Teodorovich. He indicated also that Riazanov, the influential head of the Marx-Engels Institute, was sympathetic to the opposition. Assuring Gorin that he himself would join the issue when he returned home after recuperating from his impending operation, he stipulated that his efforts would be confined to his writing table; ill health prevented public debate. He went so far as to raise the question whether there should be a formal change in the leadership of the Society of Marxist Historians (Gorin, 1933:101). Pokrovskii sent a note to the Secretariat of the Central Committee, in which he stated: "Com. Teodorovich, it seems to me, repeats the things I heard from the SR's in 1905, that the members of *Narodnaia volia* were above all socialists, and we should honor them as our predecessors in this respect, etc." (Sokolov, 1970:196).

In February Iaroslavskii sent a letter to the leadership of the SMH. He noted that he, Bubnov, and Popov[13] did not wholly agree with Teodorovich, but they felt that he had at least posed the problem of *Narodnaia volia* in a new way. The SMH should not label him a revisionist, especially "while being silent . . . about the errors of other comrades," whose writings contained "no fewer" errors (Teodorovich, 1930:249). In the same letter, or a separate one to Pokrovskii, he urged Pokrovskii "not to mutilate an old Bolshevik," Teodorovich (Sokolov, 1962:75). Pokrovskii's reply has been preserved in Central Party Archives:

> Dear Comrade Emelian—
> No one is mutilating Comrade Teodorovich. He is being "criticized" (*prorabatyvaiut*) as I was "criticized" in *Bol'shevik* in 1924, as I have been "criticized" since then in the Institute of Red Professors (the last time three days ago in the first-year seminar), as I was criticized in the Society of Marxist Historians (the dispute about Chernyshevskii) and most recently in connection with Dubrovskii's book. They did not pass a resolution about me because the majority upheld as correct my point of view. It is also true that, as concerns my errors, insofar as they were proved, I submitted willingly, never depicting myself as an infallible Pope. . . .
> If you consider the judgment about Teodorovich—[that he] is theoretically close to Populist authors—incorrect (in the draft resolution accepted only "as a basis," there is no direct reference to a *rightist deviation*) you can bring the question before the C.C. But should I take it upon myself "to suppress self-criticism" by my personal authority then I assure you, dear Comrade Emelian, nothing will come of it, except my loss of this authority.[14]

At his writing desk Pokrovskii could maintain civility, but he grew increasingly irate as the controversy dragged on. Finally in March he addressed a plenum of the Society of Marxist Historians. He urged the verification of personnel "to guarantee genuine Marxist-Leninist" pedigree. "Comrades, I think that it has long been time to approach this purge (*chistka*). . . . Those comrades who turned out to be close neighbors of our opponents need not feel insulted" (1930b:16). Not all our opponents, Pokrovskii continued, hold views unequivocally Populist, there are many intermediate points. But

> Don't stand beside [the enemy], don't confuse the public, because if you stand there one has the impression that you are his friend or ally! Stand aside; or, better, come over to us, because we will also strike neutrals. There cannot be neutrality in these sphere [just] as there cannot be neutrality in class struggle. And if you don't come over to our side nothing can be done if you receive a lump. (1930b:13–14)

At the Teaching Conference that censured him in its resolutions, Teodorovich opened an attack on Pokrovskii. Not only should one not idealize Populist groups, "one should not idealize bad (*durnyi*) textbooks on the history of the revolutionary movement. [One should] in good conscience discern who is responsible for idealization."[15] He went on to cite long passages that affirm the communist character of writings of the 1860s. Then he cited another work that stressed their bourgeois character. Who was the idealizer?

> Comrades, I have no basis to rely on the disinterest of the Presidium [of the Conference]. But you, having heard these citations . . . will say, "of course the idealizer is the first author; the modernizer is the first author and the second author is completely justified in criticizing the first." Permit me to take off the masks and say—the first author is M.N. Pokrovskii, I am the second.

He called attention then to the fact that he, not Pokrovskii, faced censure. His words, he noted, must be particularly unpleasant for Gorin, I.L. Tatarov, and Fridliand: "One is struck in the face by the fact that you are not governed by the search for truth but by some sort of group interests." When the conference chairman, Savel'ev, indicated that Teodorovich had used up his allotted time, according to the stenographic report, "loud voices from all over the hall: 'let him continue.' " He concluded by urging everyone to read his article, otherwise not to believe a word they might hear about it.

The Teodorovich affair persisted throughout the Teaching Conference, with Iaroslavskii morally supporting the protagonist. Iaroslavskii was an elder of the Society of Former Political Prisoners and Penal Exiles; moreover he was a close friend of Teodorovich—they had worked together in the underground and had shared imprisonment.[16] Friendship must have been an important factor bringing Iaroslavskii into the dispute, for, though Teodorovich's cause may have been popular with rank and file historians, it did not represent a timely way of closing the gap between theory and practice. Iaroslavskii dissociated himself from Teodorovich's interpretation of *Narodnaia volia* while he stressed the need to study the question anew. He rejected the prevailing interpretation, thereby giving comfort to those who had disagreed with Pokrovskii. "It even happens that the Menshevik interpretation, the Menshevik criticism of Populism is substituted for Bolshevik criticism. It even descends, moreover, to a liberal understanding and interpretation of Populism" (*Voprosy,* 1930:16). Later on the pages of *Bol'shevik,* the party's theoretical journal, Iaroslavskii adversely criticized the evolving norms of the historical profession.

> The discussion showed how *dangerous* the situation is for Bolshevik research into the facts of our past when one or another group of comrades declares revisionist anything that does not fit its scheme. Among other things, one of the conclusions of this dis-

cussion, with which, it seems, all comrades agree, is the necessity in our historical journals to guarantee more balanced illumination of numerous controversial problems in the history of our party, the history of the class struggle, and the history of the revolutionary movement. We hope that in *Proletarskaia revoliutsiia* and in *Istorik-marksist* there will be possible more enlivening and more objective discussion of a number of unclear and controversial problems in the history of our party and in the history of the revolutionary movement, without attaching to each other unsuitable labels. (Iaroslavskii, 1930:122)

Such observations implicitly censured the leaders of the historical profession but, again, not in the spirit of Stalin's speech at the Agrarian Conference. Evidently Iaroslavskii went even further in private, urging that those who have their own point of view about the theory of merchant capitalism should not be accused of revisionism (*Voprosy,* 1930:196).

At the Teaching Conference, the absent Pokrovskii did not lack defenders. In one discussion Pankratova denounced "imperialist" tendencies in the speeches of Adoratskii, Popov, and Kin, party historians close to Iaroslavskii.[17] The chairman, Savel'ev, broke in immediately to call her out of order. Gorin made the main defense, a heavy-handed, tedious statement with ill-concealed threats. Surely it aroused sympathy for Teodorovich and discomforted Pokrovskii when he heard about it. "We would not have the right to call ourselves the Society of Marxist Historians," began Gorin, had we not unmasked Teodorovich's "falsification of Bolshevism." Despite trivial flaws that Pokrovskii himself has corrected, Gorin continued, his schema is the "Marxist-Leninist explanation of the historical process":

> It is not, therefore, accidental that we have frequently observed harsh attacks on the schema of Com. Pokrovskii on the part of L. Trotsky, and A. Slepkov, and others. The controversy often begins, as it were "over minor points" . . . that is why Com. Iaroslavskii is wrong to regard our polemics so lightly. (*Voprosy,* 1930:183, 184–85)

We will continue to criticize "all who seek, under the badge of Marxism, to introduce a world view alien to us." Then Gorin went on to cite shortcomings in Iaroslavskii's own writings, which showed an inflated estimation of his own authority.

In due course, Teodorovich rejected entirely Pokrovskii's depiction of the background of the Revolution. At the same time, his remarks became increasingly personal. There is a serious danger "of strangling self-criticism on the historical front." He objected to distortion of his views by Tatarov, Fridliand, and Gorin. His own condemnation he attributed to cliquishness (*gruppovshchina*): had he, he felt, "invited Gorin to a cup of tea," he could have had his name stricken from the resolution. "That fierce hydrophobia with which some of my opponents pounce on me is explained, of course, by the fact that I 'finally' decided to call the attention of Party society to the need of exposing these com[munist] mandarins of historical scholarship." Pokrovskii's "henchmen" had created "a conspiracy of silence" around him making criticism impossible. The purpose of the resolution censuring him was "to butt a person who would not doff his cap to the 'Apis of God,' because he saw that 'Apis' as a most ordinary bull" (1930:247, 246, 240, 244–45).

Tatarov drafted the Central Committee resolution that brought the dispute to a climax.[18] It sought to balance the continuities and discontinuities between Bolshevism and *Narodnaia volia*. While the resolution mentioned Teodorovich by name, it also took note of a tendency to sustain the Menshevik analysis. The dispute can be considered at best a Pyrrhic victory for Pokrovskii.

Opposition in the Communist Academy

Just after the *Narodnaia volia* dispute ended new opponents of Pokrovskii came into the open from an unexpected quarter—the Communist Academy itself and its presidium. At the June plenum in 1930, Pokrovskii met a barrage of criticism. It is unlikely that he expected such a hostile response to his opening speech. A.I. Angarov, a member of Kaganovich's Institute of Soviet Construction, complained that Pokrovskii's report had neglected the achievements of his institute.[19] The contrived character of the response from the floor became evident when E.B. Pashukanis, who was both a member of the Institute of Soviet Construction and a member of the Communist Academy leadership, and also a leading member of the Marxist intelligentsia, followed Angarov with a general assault on Pokrovskii, implying that Pokrovskii's infirmity disqualified him from leadership. He went on to charge that the presidium failed to assert leadership in pressing ideological discussions and expressed the hope that "with the infusion of new members into the Comacademy the matter will change" (34–36). He sounded a note that would be heard with increasing frequency in the next few years: "In each institute there should be inculcated the kind of discipline [exercized] in any major enterprise; a division of labor should be introduced; norms of production; there should be control." We have not achieved this. "And if at sometime, and I think the time will come, a work brigade arrives to inspect us, then . . . it will not pat us on the head" (36).

Other leaders such as A.I. Bubnov, E. Varga, a Hungarian émigré and head of the newly formed Institute of World Economy, and K.V. Ostrovitianov, head of the Economics Institute, followed Pashukanis' lead (44–48, 67–70). They were joined by A. Martynov, a former Menshevik, who spoke on behalf of the Comintern (60–64). A note of generational conflict was injected by M. Bronskii, who complained that while the leadership was overloaded with work, it was reluctant to assign important tasks to young people (53).

Fridliand argued in Pokrovskii's defense that the tendency even in party circles to derogate the Communist Academy in comparison with the Academy of Sciences isolated the leadership and weakened the organization (64–65). Others, including Pokrovskii's old colleague L. Kritsman and a former Bogdanovite, P. Kerzhentsev, defended Pokrovskii (42, 70–73, and passim) but in an unexpected manner. Staying on the defensive, in a posture of self-criticism, they sought to soften the criticism and deflect it from the leadership. They refrained from attacking their opponents and demanding self-criticism from them.

Pokrovskii stood his ground; in the new bureau of the presidium he could maintain a majority with votes from Miliutin and Kerzhentsev, over Pashukanis and Ostrovitianov, who could probably get support in the presidium from Bubnov, Varga, and Riazanov. Pokrovskii apparently counted on support from the remaining membership—Deborin, Gaister, Kritsman, Krizhizhanovskii, Lukin, Ronin, Savel'ev, Stetskii, and Schmidt. The plenum admitted thirty-seven full members and twenty-four corresponding members into the academy. These included some of Pokrovskii's supporters, but some of his opponents gained access as well (88).

Though meeting the challenge, Pokrovskii clearly had an uncertain future and cause for alarm. After the plenum, he was overtaken by illness. In October he underwent his fourth operation and also experienced difficulty with his eyes. He complained to Gorin that another working year was disrupted, and that once again he would be confined to literary work.[20] Public encounters were beyond his strength.

Cultural Revolution and the Concept of Truth

The dispute about *Narodnaia volia* yielded a by-product for historians—the notion of *partiinost'* (party-mindedness). The resolutions of the Teaching Conference contain the following passage:

> Leninist history of the Party is alien to bourgeois "objectivity" torn from contemporary concerns. Bringing to bear in research the point of view of the strictest *partiinost'*, which singularly assures the authentic scientific character of research, the history of the party facilitates the militant tasks of extermination of capi-

talism, the building of socialism in our country and the struggle
for international revolution. (*Voprosy,* 1930:313)

This concept of Lenin's, which may have roots in Marxism itself, was
first applied to Soviet scholarship in the philosophical discussions in
which Iaroslavskii actively participated.[21] The passage quoted here may
be the first time it was used formally by historians.

With the introduction of this term into current discourse, Pokrovskii
had to refine his own understanding of the connection between politics
and scholarship. Earlier he had used the figure of ideology as a curved
mirror, suggesting that any ideology distorts reality.[22] Even when he
renounced this image, and granted Marxism a special status, he did not
state any principle by which one could distinguish Marxism from other
ideologies. His notion that historical scholarship can and should help
fulfill other aspirations than merely our desire to comprehend the past—
what we might call usufructory scholarship—is not exclusively Marxist.
And within the Marxist school differences arise as to what needs are
legitimate and what means are sanctioned. Pokrovskii had clearly stated
the forms of service that are excluded. He enunciated a norm that has
been upheld as a principle, even if violated in practice, at least with
respect to party history—one must not falsify facts. As Pokrovskii said
to an assembled body of archivists:

> I should say, as a communist and as an historian, that we should
> disassociate ourselves from any such principle. We have no right
> to put into the hands of peasants and workers falsified docu-
> ments, not containing things actually written. Our first duty to the
> proletariat and the peasantry is to be truthful. *If we find it unsuit-
> able* to print one or another document, for one or another reason,
> *then we do not have to print it* at all.[23]

The clauses emphasized here might be taken as a slip of the tongue—an
unconscious expression of a basic assumption. Historical truth is subordinate to a presumed greater truth about human destiny and human
values.

Pokrovskii derived still another norm from this underlying assumption: the historian's choice of subject should properly serve the needs of
a class and its party. Pokrovskii deemed it natural for Marxist historians
to treat contemporary themes, and he felt that all worthwhile historical
writing must have a polemical dimension. Nevertheless, he was misunderstood on this point in his own lifetime and after.[24] He did not consider modern history the only legitimate domain for Marxists.

In 1930, after Stalin's speech to Marxist agronomists, Pokrovskii became more specific about the relationship between theory and practice,
scholarship and politics. To close the gap between theory and practice

one should first choose practical, timely themes: "We stand in Western Europe, undoubtedly, before an immense revolutionary wave, and it would be in the highest degree strange and for us shameful, if in this immense uprising, we historians, *i.e.* representatives of the most political and most revolutionary science, did not participate" (1930b:8–9). For both Western and Russian workers, Pokrovskii continued, a mass of reports, lectures, journals, and books should be prepared. The demand can be met only by abandoning handicraft methods of historical production in favor of collective works. The other method for closing the gap between theory and practice is relentless struggle against contraband theories. We must manifest "historical sensitivity and a political scent" so that "from a book, from a printed line or from a report, from a word on a tribune, we can immediately discern [whether] he is one of ours or not one of ours, a friend or an enemy" (1930b:10). Pokrovskii's feelings found reflection in an SMH resolution: "People who only yesterday we considered merely our ideological opponents, turn out to be active participants in anti-Soviet organizations. Drawing a line between 'disagreement with Marxism' and direct wrecking becomes less and less possible."[25] Pokrovskii's feelings are clear enough, but one may doubt whether the words quoted reflect his thoughts. It is unlikely that he believed literally that wrecking and disagreement were almost indistinguishable.[26]

Despite his stress on militant scholarship, Pokrovskii shied away from the term *partiinost'*. Was he a victim of habit? Was it recollection of the curved mirror kept in the "unventilated corners of his mind"? For whatever reason, he would not sanction polemics as a higher form of objectivity. Militance did not assure truth; assertions made in the service even of the highest cause were subject to the same laws of probability as all other assertions.

As in the case of the *Narodnaia volia* dispute, Pokrovskii's encounter with Pashukanis compelled him to elaborate further his understanding of the relationship between politics and scholarship.[27] In his opening speech at the June plenum of the Communist Academy he addressed himself to the problem offhandedly in a discussion of planning. He expressed bewilderment as to how the presidium could develop plans for all the institutes. "How can I supervise research work in the area of higher nerve activity? What would be the result?" he asked. "I can be an object of this work but a subject I cannot be" (28). He proposed decentralization of the supervision of research by grouping related disciplines, each group having its own bureau. Political supervision should derive from the academy's higher organs (28).

Pokrovskii, in his concluding remarks, modified and sharpened his formulations. "Dear Comrades, I understand science not in bourgeois fashion," as you do:

> One cannot imagine political leadership of Marxist-Leninist insti-
> tutions without methodological leadership . . . we will carry on
> methodological leadership, and in this will consist the specific
> politics of our Communist Academy. (80)

He attributed to Varga and Ostrovitianov the opinion that the presidium
should hold three or four sessions on every controversy and promptly
resolve the matter. That would be an "aristocratic approach," he
argued. Public debate has a distinctive value. The *Narodnaia volia* dispute, for example, "taking place in a broad arena of scholarly society,
drew in not only our scholars but wider circles of all comrades who
wished to express themselves." Once a resolution is adopted "the Presidium should have its word, should affirm whether this resolution affirms Marxism-Leninism or not. This is a methodological problem, and it
is the concern of the Presidium." The presidium's task is to assure that
"no document that might be subject to legitimate reproach" should ever
appear under the imprint of the academy (80). The same principle holds
for long-term planning: "What we shall study, and why we develop
along this line and not another. This is methodological leadership and at
the same time political [leadership]. To separate methodology from politics is impossible" (80).

To defend himself against charges of negligence, Pokrovskii turned his
attention to the problem of scientific planning of scholarship. He sought
to devise procedures that would enable section heads in the institutes
and the presidium itself to intervene in disputes among specialists on the
staff. That is, those in line positions could decide which hypothesis best
accorded with the interests of the proletariat and its advanced representatives. Leaders such as Pokrovskii would be responsible for resolving
questions of fact as well as matters of value. This was but a step away
from Stalin's personal intervention in scientific issues. Ironically, this
process created precedent and machinery for Pokrovskii's own posthumous fall and denigration.

Pokrovskii's proposals should also be thought of as an explication of
the emerging concept of *partiinost'*. They raised thorny philosophical
problems in the effort to define truth by distinguishing implicitly between ideological and empirical truth. He asserted the existence of a
meaning of truth about nature gained somehow other than by means of
investigation. The authoritarian premises that denied autonomy of conscience to investigators and sought means of supplanting appeal to nature as the arbiter of truth were not new in human history. As proposals
for the advancement of science, however, they were innovations.

9   A Besieged Fortress

> Back in 1926 when I spoke in the Communist Academy about the
> remarks of the opposition, I said that [their position] was theoreti-
> cally incorrect, since it contradicted the resolutions of the Party
> Congress. Then my words provoked laughter. . . . Now one can,
> in scientific discussions, refer to Comrade Stalin and to the reso-
> lutions of our Congresses and the C.C.[1]

Writing history of timely, practical subjects grew in vogue in 1930, and
the "unmasking of contraband theories" ranged wider than ever. Contemporary political themes crowded out all others, even economic
studies. Party history and works on the Comintern and the Civil War as
well as detailed histories of revolutionary activities of workers in plants
and factories held a central place. Overcoming the lag between theory
and practice was Pokrovskii's final task. His opponents, in a struggle of
unprecedented intensity, sought to discredit his ideas and to supplant his
leadership of the historical front with their own. Pokrovskii, for his part,
sought to annihilate their influence. The outcome was a stalemate and
cessation of orderly work—compelling the political authorities to resolve
the issue of leadership directly.

Rules and Issues of Conflict

Stalin's speech to the Conference of Marxist Agronomists late in 1929
had given rise to controversies in all areas of scholarship, not only
history. Polemics raged in law, economics, literary criticism, psychology, orientology, and, especially important, philosophy. In 1929 Deborin, head of a school of philosophers known as the dialecticians, triumphed over his rivals, the mechanists. Then in October 1930, at a
conference in the Communist Academy, Deborin suffered a setback; he
was finally overthrown in January 1931 by a Central Committee resolution in favor of a new group of young philosophers.[2] Predictably, Pokrovskii had given guarded support to Deborin, while Iaroslavskii and
Pashukanis had supported those who sought to replace him.[3] Deborin's
fall must have caused acute anxiety among Pokrovskii's associates and
have prompted some historians to go over to Iaroslavskii's camp.

Pokrovskii would have us think that at heart his opponents sided with the non-Marxist historians and represented a rightist deviation. They challenged his authority in order to discredit the campaign against the non-Marxists (Pokrovskii, 1931c:3). He may have been correct in attributing this motive to Slepkov and other editors of *Bol'shevik* in 1928, but he offered no evidence that this motivated the group of historians that clustered around Iaroslavskii. It is more likely that Pokrovskii's own vacillation and his long friendship with Bukharin weakened his authority and opened the door to his opponents. The balance-of-power analogy between the historical front and the European state system is helpful up to a point. Though the coalition against Pokrovskii was in some measure a spontaneous reaction reflecting the feelings and interests of historians, it ought also to be thought of as a contrivance and a result of policy. It became increasingly an instrument of intraparty conflict. Each side sought to convince officials that it was best suited to fulfill the party will. This aspect tapers off into party history itself—Stalin's standing (he still needed historians), his relations with his lieutenants, and their relationships with each other.

Before 1930, opposition to Pokrovskii consisted mainly of disagreement with and criticism of ideas associated with his name. In 1930, Teodorovich sharply attacked specific writings of Pokrovskii, and Pashukanis led an almost undisguised attack against his leadership. The quick transition seems to have surprised even Pokrovskii. Hindsight reveals that political change had enabled this to happen. Party history and the history of scholarship were becoming ever more interlocked. After the discrediting of the leaders of the Right Opposition in 1929, lesser known men moved into top positions in the party. One, L.M. Kaganovich, had long been associated with Stalin. He was a Politburo and Orgburo member and a secretary of the Central Committee. As an organizer of the special political departments used to implement policy in the countryside, he came to be associated with the most uncompromising tendencies of the collectivization drive. In April 1930 he was made secretary of the Moscow Committee. Some of the new leadership, such as P.P. Postyshev, became national figures only during collectivization and the struggle against the Right. There are some hints that Postyshev was discovered in the Ukraine by G.K. Ordzhonikidze, chairman of the Central Control Commission, and that he represented something of a moderating tendency during collectivization (Mariagin, 1965:209, 215–17, 221). At any rate, Postyshev's rise was meteoric. Brought to Moscow in 1930, he became a member of the Orgburo of the Central Committee and supervisor of the party's agitation and propaganda work. He also headed the extremely important Orgotdel, the Central Committee's department in charge of party assignments. He was a party secretary and then became a candidate member of the Politburo.

The years from 1929 to 1932 are among the most obscure periods of party history. Stalin had triumphed over the Left and Right Oppositions to emerge as the party's head. He held even more power than Lenin had possessed after the Treaty of Brest-Litovsk, but he still ruled as head of a faction and was far removed from the preeminence he would attain by 1938. Control over academic disciplines, including the writing of history, was one of the informal powers he used to attain that preeminence.

Historical writing, like other instruments of mass and elite communication, was important to Stalin and almost as important to his lieutenants. Though the other Politburo members and secretaries depended on Stalin for their status, their control over such instruments affected their value to him and their standing with each other. It would be misleading to suggest that the historians who sought to diminish Pokrovskii's authority represented a particular party faction. It will, however, become clear to the reader that Iaroslavskii willy-nilly became a rival leader on the historical front who sought to displace Pokrovskii and his close associates. Behind Iaroslavskii stood Kaganovich. Perhaps Kaganovich sought the overturn on the historical front for his own purposes; perhaps he acted at the behest of Stalin. At any rate we shall see that at a crucial moment, P.P. Postyshev spoke up to frustrate Kaganovich's initiative.

Rivalry among historians was at no point a struggle of disembodied principles. As ever the historical front was an arena of personal likes and dislikes, political and professional ambitions and anxieties. Yet the story is not one of passions and material calculation only. The struggle always retained an intellectual dimension, and should properly be considered a struggle for Marxism, or at least for a particular version of Marxism.

The Soviet historians who argue that the young historians had a better mastery of Lenin's writings than did Pokrovskii are probably correct. Lenin's works were becoming increasingly available. The young historians assimilated from them a sense of voluntarism, a spirit that was becoming increasingly timely and stood at odds with the mood of Pokrovskii's original synthesis. They were genuinely troubled, also, by some of the untidy details of Pokrovskii's system, his understanding of Russian imperialism, for example. His notion that Russia was the object rather than the subject of modern forms of imperialism stressed the underdeveloped character of the Empire and was unwelcome on several grounds. Finally, an increasing number grew skeptical about the entire construct of merchant capital, as it became ever clearer that this notion was out of keeping with the theory of growing over. The discussions of this theory turned out to be more than an explication of Lenin's interpretation of revolution. It was a set of definitions, assumptions, and generalizations about Russia's transition from feudalism to capitalism to socialism. That is, it treated the same subject matter as that addressed by the concept of merchant capital. They were rival concepts.

Every step taken by Pokrovskii in the fall of 1930 was impeded by his opponents, who must have been a sizable minority among the Marxist historians by winter 1931. Yet the conflict was less evident publicly than it had been when Teodorovich first brought it into the open, or than it would be in the final stages. In a letter to the Central Committee, Gorin described the rules of the game:

> Slander, double-dealing, irresponsible public defamation of one's opponents, etc. are means; unfortunately, they have been conventional means of struggle. I think it is unnecessary to prove that it is very difficult to work under such circumstances. They vote for our resolutions but in practice sabotage them; they declare their full political confidence in Comrade Pokrovskii . . . and simultaneously disseminate underground "cribs" (*shpargalki*) which discredit Pokrovskii politically; they talk about the correctness of the political line of the leadership of the Society and await the fall of that line, etc. . . . . These means of struggle are practiced before the eyes of about three-hundred graduate students, future historians, whom we should educate as steadfast, principled fighters on our theoretical front.[4]

Similar complaints against Gorin and Pokrovskii very likely found their way to the Central Committee. In the *Narodnaia volia* discussion, it had been Pokrovskii who set the ground rules. And as early as March 1930 he had urged a purge of historians, to assure the predominance of Marxism-Leninism, as being overdue. He stooped to the level of courting support with a hint that such a purge would open up teaching positions for young historians (Pokrovskii, 1930b:16).

Iaroslavskii had numerous means available for his campaign. His long-term association with Stalin is well known; Kaganovich's concern with the personnel of the theoretical front has been brought out by Soviet historians,[5] and the link between Iaroslavskii and Kaganovich is an inescapable inference. As already noted, Iaroslavskii held important positions in Pokrovskii's own apparatus, as a member of the Communist Academy (since 1928) and its Institute of History. He held a leading position in the Society of Marxist Historians and in the bureau of its section on party history. He was an editor of *Istorik-marksist*. In addition, he was a leading member of the Lenin Institute and as such gave an account of its activities to the Sixteenth Party Congress in 1930. He was a member of the editorial boards of *Pravda*, *Izvestiia*, and *Bol'shevik*. Since 1923 he had been a secretary of the Central Control Commission (the presidium of which Pokrovskii had become a member of in 1930) and, like Pokrovskii, a member of the Central Executive Committee of the USSR. Whereas Pokrovskii was a consultative delegate to the Sixteenth Congress, Iaroslavskii was a voting delegate.[6]

Pokrovskii's advanced age and ill health may have been assets for him. To be sure, his infirmities slowed his activity, and by early in the autumn of 1931 the scene of his writing and disputation was his deathbed in the Kremlin hospital. These indications that he would soon leave the historical front argued against removing him by decree. On the other hand, if Pokrovskii had not been ill, his anxiety might have been less acute. He wrote to Gorin:

> We search out heresy everywhere and will soon find ourselves in the situation of the Deborinites. They, of course, also sought out heresy everywhere and thought that they didn't have to do any work. And then the screws were put to them (*ikh prizhali*). And they will put the screws to us if we do not come to our senses in time and understand that serving the masses in our area is the most important thing. I very much hope that [our] comrades grasp this. (Gorin, 1933:107)

Yet not long before he had expressed dissatisfaction with the popularization effected by the society. Referring, most likely, to a collection of readings which bore the imprint of the SMH and contained a selection by the non-Marxist A.E. Presniakov, he wrote to Gorin, "You can easily guess what Dubrovskii will do with us when this book appears. His book is exemplary Marxism in comparison" (Gorin, 1933:105). He complained about Fridliand's inactivity, and of Vanag's failure to keep up their correspondence. He praised Pankratova for her extensive activity but pointed out that she failed to write every ten days, as she had promised. He grew increasingly suspicious when the publishers were slow with a brochure of his about the Revolution of 1905; he sensed a plot. He urged Gorin to speak to Stetskii, head of Kultprop of the Central Committee, and affirmed his intention to write to Molotov. Later he suspected deliberate sabotage when he received his copy of *Bol'shevik* from the editorial office of *Istorik-marksist*, with Gorin's article excised (Gorin, 1933:107–8, 111). It would be incautious to assume that his suspicion was groundless.

Under Attack

Kaganovich, in his capacity as party secretary, early in January 1931, requested Pokrovskii to report to him on the state of the historical front. On January 15, before he had completed the report, Pokrovskii attended a meeting of the KA presidium, where unexpectedly he found a note from three members calling for a thorough investigation of the historical sector.

The three alleged the existence and concealment of theoretical errors and further charged the absence of criticism and self-criticism.[7] How Pokrovskii responded at the meeting is unknown, but the proclamation, combined with the resolution that condemned Deborin just ten days later, made him decide to assume the offensive. Resolving to bring the dispute to the attention of the highest authorities, he wrote two letters to the Central Committee, the first in January, the second on February 5. Evidently the first letter concerned pedagogical matters; the second was an eighteen-page complaint that he wrote and rewrote before sending it to Kaganovich with his report. He sent copies to all the other secretaries of the Central Committee and to the chairman of the Council of People's Commissars, Molotov. The letter, on the one hand, is a reasoned defense by Pokrovskii of his understanding of Russian history, an attempt to demonstrate the consistency of his theory of merchant capitalism with the assumptions of Marxism-Leninism.[8] On the other hand, the letter is a defense of his own leadership and criticism of his opponents.

Pokrovskii began by explaining why his report to Kaganovich had been late:

> It was unavoidable, for in that time three members of the Com-academy Presidium came out against me. (I have heard through the grapevine that others are beginning to join them.) One must, therefore, cast out all academism and speak directly and candidly [and] thus speak more concisely, and forcefully. I am sending all copies to you. If you find it worthwhile to distribute [them], please do so. (Sokolov, 1962:78)

Pokrovskii complained about a dangerous tendency of "working over" (*prorabatyvat'*) one's colleagues, "hurrying to earn a reputation for irreproachable Leninist fidelity." He wrote that "recognition of my individual errors" by no means vindicated his opponents: "They should have to prove that a '*pokrovshchina*' in history is the same as a '*rubinshchina*' in economics, or a '*deborinshchina*' in philosophy. That it is a straightforward distortion of the Leninist understanding of the historical process in general and of Russian history in particular."[9] He continued, "For a number of years, I have been accustomed to exercising self-correction and I am profoundly grateful to all who assist me in this" (Sokolov, 1962:75). He went on to cite the documents in which, beginning in 1925, he had criticized his own errors. Some errors persisted, he admitted, but none that could invalidate the Leninist character of his work (Nosov & Zakharikov, 1962:87–88). He declared an intention to further rework his views. "However," as Sokolov summarizes his words, "the slanderous campaign of a small group within the Institute of Red Professors, and the Society of Marxist Historians . . . extremely encumbers normal constructive work" (Sokolov, 1962:78). Pokrovskii called for the censure of Iaroslavskii, accusing him of confusing questions of principle by sheltering friends with the authority of his name (Nosov & Zakharikov, 1962:88), an allusion to the Teodorovich affair.

It seems that Pokrovskii urged that his opponents be compelled to undergo the ordeal of public self-criticism, and some of them were consequently rebuked. Just as in 1930 Pokrovskii had urged self-criticism— "not in an administrative office" but before society (*IM*, 1930, 15:16)— now in 1931, undoubtedly alluding to actual events, he spoke of improper self-criticism by his opponents. Their remarks, he complained, remained unknown to the public, and they had used the occasion to attack him (1931c:4–5). Not until the end of the year, when Stalin personally intervened, did Pokrovskii's critics endure public self-criticism, and then it was in another connection.

Ambiguity marked the outcome of Pokrovskii's initiative. The secretariat did not see fit to publish his letter; public airing of his complaint did not occur;[10] the baiting of Pokrovskii continued. However, just a month later, the Central Committee reaffirmed his leadership.

The Central Committee Resolution of March 15, 1931, which affirmed Pokrovskii's leadership, represents a landmark in the history of the KA and its historical sector ("Postanovlenie," 1931). It stimulated further dispute while it stabilized a stalemate at the top, showing the marks of an unsuccessful compromise. At the same time that Pokrovskii retained the leadership, the academy was urged anew to close the gap between theory and practice. The academy was commended for "pursuing a correct political line" but reproached for lassitude "in the reconstruction of its work in connection with this correct line." This might be considered Pokrovskii's second chance. Once again the party provided the KA with sufficient material resources, but it did not give Pokrovskii a free hand. His opponents, far from being silenced, retained important positions. One would still predict in retrospect an overturn on the historical front. Most likely, Pokrovskii's opposition grew in the aftermath of the resolution.

Either a conspiratorial view of history or faith in the conscious design of historical actors might lead one to construe the situation in 1931 not as an unworkable compromise but as a trap set for Pokrovskii. The tasks at hand were more urgent than ever, while the means for their realization were clearly insufficient. Sometime in the spring, Pokrovskii sent still another letter to the Central Committee; this one to Wilhelm Knorin, a Central Committee member who was at the time head of the Culture-Propaganda Committee of the Moscow Branch of the Communist Party. He complained that the condition of his eyes was such that he could work only three or four hours a day, and only during daylight:

It goes without saying that under such circumstances I do not refuse to edit the brochure of Mints and works of the Institute of Red Professors. In addition to the brochures, which I've already scanned and will make the basic revisions in the next few days (before I'm sent to the South, then to spend a week in the Kremlin hospital) the galley proofs should reach me at the end of July or the beginning of August, when, with luck, my eyes will be better. This is the way I hope to scramble out of the present situation.

The situation concerning the social-studies textbook for secondary schools is considerably worse. Very thorough editing in my study is necessary for this, in order to scrutinize each line . . . keeping in mind the extraordinary theoretical illiteracy of social-studies teachers (this fact in its full grandeur became evident to me only recently when I read a few of their works), the consequences of which could turn out to be very surprising: in the field of history, the one responsible is I. It is necessary, therefore, that those who are in positions of supervision are people I can rely upon.[11]

Pokrovskii's proposal to Knorin, that he be permitted to edit the works in question by having them read to him aloud, was not approved.[12]

Pokrovskii's letter to Knorin grew out of the circumstance that his lieutenants were proving vulnerable to criticism. The colleagues he relied on most—Fridliand and Gorin—lost their authority in the spring. Fridliand was demoted in 1931. Gorin had come under criticism even earlier, and his rivals pressed for his removal from Moscow. He blundered in 1930 by republishing his book on the Soviets in 1905 without even consulting Pokrovskii. The archives evidently reveal Pokrovskii's disappointment that Gorin did not remove errors and formulations that had gone out of fashion since 1927.[13] Gorin, the son-in-law of the chairman of the Belorussian Soviet, was designated to become president of that republic's newly formed Academy of Sciences. Ostensibly a promotion, this was in fact a demotion, as is evident from a letter of Pokrovskii published posthumously by Gorin. Pokrovskii assured Gorin that he had protested to Molotov as forcefully as possible, suggesting to him that the removal would be a "catastrophe for the Society, and risks its disintegration" (Gorin, 1933:109–10). By May, Gorin resigned from his positions as secretary of the SMH and secretary of the Institute of History.[14] It is not clear when he took up his duties as president of the Belorussian Academy of Sciences. If he did so immediately, then he spent much time commuting back to the capital. His voice would be heard until 1936.

Accompanying the eclipse of Pokrovskii's lieutenants was the rise of his opponents, notably Pashukanis and Ostrovitianov. Not only were they reaffirmed in the KA presidium, but they were more active than ever and tended to overshadow two other presidium members who were more favorably disposed to Pokrovskii, V.P. Miliutin and M.A. Savel'ev. Ostrovitianov became chief editor of the *Vestnik* of the KA. Pashukanis was the most active of all members of the presidium. At the same time Pokrovskii's associate N.M. Lukin acquired increasing prominence. He was not only a member of the Academy of Sciences, but he became chief spokesman about work on the western sector of the historical front (European history). He was deputy director of the KA's Institute of History, in charge of its research activities, and he became increasingly important in the Society of Marxist Historians. He was fated to replace Pokrovskii as leader of the historical front and to govern until 1938, when the purges reached their climax. It will be recalled that he, like Pokrovskii, had graduated from the historico-philological faculty of Moscow University and had worked in the revolutionary underground. Thus he had professional stature of his own and credentials as an old Bolshevik. He was not a creature of Pokrovskii. Yet like Pokrovskii he had been a Left Communist in 1918, and he championed Pokrovskii's legacy until 1936. Though he should not be thought of as a member of the opposition to Pokrovskii, it is likely that the opposition considered the removal of Fridliand a victory and found Lukin less objectionable.

A growing dispersion of forces within Pokrovskii's own camp became noticeable. Owing to Pokrovskii's illness and protracted absences from the capital, the Institute of History and the Society of Marxist Historians became increasingly distinguishable and remote from each other. The institute became the intellectual center. Its major activities conformed to the general pattern of all sectors for the intellectual front. Just after the Central Committee Resolution of March 15, a meeting was held to revise all research plans. The new plan placed greater emphasis on contemporary themes—the history of the Comintern, the postwar history of German Social Democracy ("social fascism"), the Spanish Revolution, and colonial policy (*BKA*, 1931, 20:14). Specialists in all fields were instructed to concentrate on Lenin's teachings and their bearing on their particular subject matter (*BK*, 1931, 6–7:159).

Another innovation for the Institute of History was its establishment of permanent ties with specialized party and state organs. Among other institutions, the institute sought to cooperate with the Culture-Propaganda Department of the Central Committee. It edited, in collaboration with the Commissariat of Foreign Affairs, various documents of tsarist diplomacy. It sought to coordinate its research with the needs of the Great Soviet Encyclopedia. After the removal of Tomskii from the Politburo and from his leadership of the trade unions, the institute collaborated with the All-Union Central Council of Trade Unions in rewriting the history of trade unions. With the overthrow of the rightist leadership, it had been "discovered" that the trade unions' own historians had depicted the history of the movement from a Menshevik standpoint. The task of the institute was to demonstrate that the "party had stood at the cradle of the trade union movement" (*BK,* 1931, 6–7:159).

The Society of Marxist Historians grew spectacularly and for the first time met with success in the provinces. We can doubt the claim that it attained a membership of 800, including 300 non-Muscovites.[15] If, as claimed, chapters existed in twenty-four localities, it is probable that many were largely paper organizations. Prodded by Pokrovskii, the SMH constantly sought new means to fulfill the party aspirations. In 1931, it began to publish *Bor'ba klassov* (*Class Struggle*), a popular historical journal, which contained, in addition to conventional articles, writings and transcribed remarks by workers about revolutionary experiences in the factories in which they were employed. Similarly the Commission on Plants and Factories began to publish its own journal. The SMH, in becoming a specialized vehicle for popularization, ceased to be a "voluntary tribune" of historical discussion.

We observe then, with reference to the balance-of-power analogy, that after 1928 the Marxists, by silencing the non-Marxists, created a homogeneous front. The Marxist camp, which had been but one of two poles, became the single center of the historical front. Simultaneously, polarization within the Marxist camp took place. As the process approached its climax, dispersion took place at each of these poles.

Revolution of 1905 Reconsidered

Gorin, it will be recalled, spoke unfavorably of Iaroslavskii's writings at the Teaching Conference in February 1930, the conference that had condemned Teodorovich.[16] In context, Gorin's word had seemed a threat. A new dispute arose behind the scenes late in 1930. In connection with the celebration of the twenty-fifth anniversary of the Revolution of 1905, Iaroslavskii and his associates prepared a set of theses outlining what the Marxist understanding of the event should be. Pokrovskii rejected the draft and succeeded in amending it before its publication in *Pravda* on December 10.[17] The final text appears to be a compromise containing formulations that foreshadowed arguments by both sides. That Pokrovskii succeeded in asserting his authority could be taken as a victory. But the fact that Iaroslavskii, still the challenger, managed to uphold some of his interpretations is a more definite victory. He created a stalemate.

Gorin shifted the dispute to the public arena, where it rankled for about eight months. An essay review of a multivolume history of the party

written by Iaroslavskii's followers and published under his name[18] began
Gorin's attack (1930). He charged that Iaroslavskii's interpretation of the
Revolution of 1905 represented a ''Populist misunderstanding of the peasant movement.'' He attributed to Iaroslavskii the view that the vestiges of
serfdom were the ''basic cause'' of the peasant movement and that the
development of capitalism was an ''indirect precondition.'' If it was the
development of capitalism that moved the peasants to action in 1905,
according to Gorin, then the peasants were fighting to preserve the commune and small-scale production. Such an interpretation shares Populist
assumptions; it depicts the peasant movement as reactionary (Gorin:
1930:165). What Gorin apparently suggested was that the peasants had
already become enmeshed in capitalist relations by 1905. They were striving to remove remnants of feudalism—the commune and small-scale production. Their revolutionary strivings were progressive.

Iaroslavskii replied effectively to this point. He demonstrated that
Gorin had distorted his meaning. With an abundance of citations, he
demonstrated that his view was that the peasants were fighting a progressive battle for a particular form of capitalism. Repaying his antagonist in kind, he asserted that it was Gorin who slighted the peasants and
thus approached the Menshevik view (1930:151–52). Iaroslavskii's article is more scholarly than Gorin's; one senses that the imputation of
Menshevism was tongue-in-cheek, a means of underlining the absurdity
of Gorin's charge of a Populist deviation. As the dispute grew hotter,
Iaroslavskii managed to discredit Gorin. He demonstrated that Gorin in
a book of his own had incorporated without acknowledgment long extracts from Trotsky's works for the sake of bolstering his narrative.

The dispute raised basic questions about the Revolution of 1905 and
about the revolutionary process in Russia in general. Gorin, in his quib-
bling fashion, noted that his opponent affirmed the establishment of the
American pattern of capitalism[19] as the immediate goal of the Bolsheviks
in the Revolution. To let this stand alone, not to affirm that the final goal
was socialism, is a falsification, Gorin argued. It ''creates the danger of
depicting the Bolsheviks only as the most thoroughgoing petty-bourgeois
revolutionaries.'' Here a serious question is at issue: Gorin affirmed the
possibility of a socialist revolution in Russia in 1905, even without a
revolution in the West: ''So far as we know Lenin . . . never denied that
the proletariat, in the event of a successful bourgeois-democratic revolution, should fight for a socialist revolution.'' Gorin went even further: to
deny the possibility of the revolution ''to grow over'' into socialism is a
Trotskyite position, for it affirms the need for a European revolution as
a precondition for a socialist revolution in Russia (1930:167, 169–70). In
other words, not to affirm the possibility for the Bolsheviks to have
come to power in 1905 is to be a Trotskyite.

Gorin's thesis had various and even contradictory political ramifications. On the one hand, it represented a refinement of the interpretation of the Revolution outlined by Pokrovskii in 1927. The international revolution was banished once and for all as a precondition to a socialist revolution in Russia. On the other hand, the assertion that the Revolution could have grown over into a socialist one implied that Russia even in 1905 was in a considerably advanced state of capitalism. This contradicted Pokrovskii's theory of imperialism, which stressed the underdevelopment of Russia.

Gorin was not Iaroslavskii's equal as a polemicist, but he had found a chink in the latter's armor, and he probed it relentlessly. Nor was Iaroslavskii unaware of the political ramifications of Gorin's thesis. In 1931 any assertion of Russian backwardness "provided grist for the Trotskyite mill" by implying that it was impossible to build socialism in Russia. But until autumn 1931, it was not evident just how many theories could be interpreted to imply Russian backwardness. Iaroslavskii agreed as to the widespread development of Russian capitalism, but he denied that it was sufficiently extensive to permit "growing over":

> Objective and subjective conditions made "impossible a *rapid* full liberation of the working class," a rapid transition to the socialist revolution. . . . In 1905, the proletariat of Russia needed the help of the Western-European proletariat for completing the socialist revolution.[20]

Only during World War I did Lenin suggest the possibility of socialism in one country. Iaroslavskii supported this argument with extensive quotations from Lenin's and Stalin's writings. At issue, then, were rival interpretations of Leninism. Only Stalin could decide which of them best supported the theory of socialism in one country.

Pokrovskii urged Gorin on. From afar, he offered tactical advice, suggesting which arguments he should pursue and warning against certain stylistic devices that left openings for Iaroslavskii. He even commented on Gorin's diction.[21] But Pokrovskii's authority did not prevail. An editorial note in *Bol'shevik* answered both Gorin and Iaroslavskii. It affirmed that on balance Iaroslavskii's book correctly interpreted the Revolution of 1905. But, it went on, even though it is true that Lenin did not "pose the question of the victory of a socialist revolution in Russia alone, it is wholly untrue that in Russia in 1905 the material preconditions for socialist revolution did not exist." Gorin, for his part, was rebuked for misrepresenting Iaroslavskii's views and especially for his unacknowledged quotations from Trotsky (*Bol'shevik*, 1931, 9:78, 82). Thus, we see, at the end of the debate the stalemate persisted.

Leninism and European History

A simultaneous discussion about European history raised parallel issues. In the academic year 1930–31 probably half a dozen formal discussions were held among specialists, with reports delivered by Karl Radek, R.G. Manuilskii, the Comintern leader, and W. Knorin. These discussions constituted still another arena in the leadership struggle and provided the immediate occasion for Stalin's intervention. They were significant also for wiping the slate clean of views considered egregious by 1931.

This time the Marxists set about unmasking each other. It appears that a free-for-all took place, more noteworthy from the psychological than from the ideological standpoint. One encounters the accusation that such old-guard Marxists as Zaidel and Fridliand had written works containing deviations, as well as remarks "openly hostile to Marxism" ("Rezoliutsiia Prezidiuma," 1931). Similar unlikely accusations abounded in the discussion. A historian named Arkman was alleged to have denied that imperialism represented a distinctive and final stage of capitalism. Volgin was accused of isolating the development of socialist thought from class conflict (*BK*, 1931, 6–7:154–55). More than a dozen historians are denounced in similar terms. Stetskii, head of Kultprop, noted that the criticism ranged too broadly, as though the *"general line* of the work of the Society of Marxist Historians is incorrect" (*VKA*, 1931, 2–3:16). Yet the disputes were not wholly personal, and matters of principle underlay the denunciations.

The main subject was German history—the evolution of social democracy into social fascism on the one hand and into communism on the other. So various were the political implications of this history that it was more difficult to establish basic premises than had been the case with regard to Russian history. Answers were sought that would lead the German workers to the Comintern, while at the same time affirming the correctness of the break with social democracy undertaken by Stalin in 1928 and opposed by Trotsky. An interpretation that might meet one set of criteria need not satisfy the other. The ambiguity did provide scope for those who opposed Stalin's rise to power. Even the terminology posed difficulties for historians. In discussing the "centrism" of German social democracy one had to be mindful of Rakovskii's use of the concept in the theory of revolutionary degeneration he was seeking to formulate in Trotsky's *Bulletin of the Opposition*.[22]

The proper understanding of the legacy of Rosa Luxemburg was another problem. Was she close to or remote from Lenin? By upholding her authority one might build a bridge to Leninism for the German workers. But one also might court the danger of setting up a rival leader and a rival theory and thereby sanction deviations within the Comintern.

Inevitably, one had to study Lenin's understanding of the evolution of German social democracy, and this brought up the problem of socialism in one country. When did Lenin understand that the European revolution did *not* constitute a prerequisite for the growing over of the Russian Revolution into socialism?

Historians tread warily. The study of German Social Democracy became more institutionalized and received more public attention in the late 1920s. In 1928 the Lenin Institute organized a group of historians, led by Bela Kun, former head of the short-lived Hungarian Communist Government, to study the history of the Comintern, including the international role of Bolshevism during the world war. When the Institute of History was shifted from RANION to the Communist Academy in 1929, a *sector* on the history of imperialism, which contained a *group* on German Social Democracy, was created. The academic secretary of the group was A.G. Slutskii, a former Menshevik who had become a candidate member of the Communist Party. In addition, Lukin conducted a seminar on German Social Democracy in the Institute of Red Professors. Work proceeded in accordance with a comprehensive plan that provided for study in German Archives by number of Soviet scholars (Dunaevskii, 1966:494–96).

By 1930, after a significant number of works had been published, sharp differences of opinion emerged, the thorniest problem being Lenin's attitude toward German Social Democracy in the prewar period. The question was broached in formal discussions at the Institute of History in the first half of 1930. At about the same time, volumes 2 and 3 of *Istoriia VKP(b)*, edited by Iaroslavskii, appeared. They had been the occasion for the polemic between Iaroslavskii and Gorin, and they also fueled the dispute among Soviet westernists. It should be remembered that this was the period of all-out collectivization; the turmoil in the countryside was accompanied by the rout of the Right Opposition and by signs of conflict even among party members who favored collectivization.

In the course of discussion, three responses—they cannot be considered clear-cut interpretations—emerged. We can call the first response either rightist or realist. E. Tsobel pointed out that in Lenin's works there are numerous remarks censuring opportunism and reformism in the German party. The fact that he did not consider the party as a whole revisionist after 1907 does not mean that German social democracy preceding World War I "was a genuinely revolutionary party and that *qualitative* change took place only after the beginning of the War."

> In my opinion, it is necessary to recognize that although Lenin even before the War carried on energetic, merciless struggle against reformist, petty-bourgeois, trade unionist tendencies

within German social democracy, the full scope, the full depth, the full practical *predominance* of opportunism before the War was not evident to him. Were there errors on Lenin's part, that he did not even before the War call for a split within the Second International and within German social democracy? That is a question which for the present we will have to leave open. ("Diskussiia," 1930a:137)

A variant of this response was the suggestion that Lenin, though aware of the predominance of centrism, remained silent for tactical reasons. This provoked the other extreme response, voiced emotionally by Ludovik Magyar, an immigrant historian from the short-lived Hungarian Soviet Republic.

This is slander of Lenin, because if Lenin were able to remain silent on a basic problem of the workers' movement, on the problem of opportunism, due to tactical considerations, if he identified himself or did not identify himself with the official direction owing to tactical considerations then this is opportunism and Lenin was not an opportunist. ("Diskussiia," 1930a:103)

Kathe Pol', a party historian who had only recently graduated from Bubnov's course in the IKP, supported the first response, but late in the conference she took the floor again and sought to document Magyar's position. She adduced a variety of statements that show clearly that Lenin was aware of the existence of centrism and that he opposed it. None of them, however, bore out the conclusion that she urged upon her listeners—that Lenin thought the party as a whole was opportunistic and that he unequivocally supported only the revolutionary currents ("Diskussiia," 1930a:108, 138–40).

Fridliand, who should have provided the definitive answer, tended to skirt the issue in his remarks. In passing, however, he did stake out a middle ground: Lenin was sensitive to the various currents in the German party. It is true he supported the Center as he opposed the revisionists. He could do so because the Center was not at the time revisionist ("Diskussiia," 1930a:134). The general tendency of Fridliand's remarks was to transform the matter from a factual problem into a methodological one, implying that the entire matter required further study. He suggested, thereby, that a conclusion could not be stated for the moment. Clearly the middle ground involved fence-sitting.

It was in connection with these discussions that Fridliand was replaced by Lukin as principal spokesman on the western sector of the historical front. It fell to Lukin to uphold the leadership and to prove the constructive character of the discussions. He did so in the spirit of self-criticism, citing repeated shortcomings in the work of "westernists." He went so far as to repudiate some of his own work. He conceded the backwardness of the sector—insufficient militance and too low a tempo of production. At the same time, he went out of his way to praise Pokrovskii. The drift of his criticism was that the leadership was sound with respect to methodology and the political line; this had enabled the leaders to overcome the backwardness, to unmask a host of ideological deviations (Lukin, 1931).

All the commentaries within the Communist Academy stressed these points and rejected any suggestion that the current line was incorrect.[23] It was upheld in *Proletarskaia revoliutsiia* ("Za povorot," 1931) and in *Bol'shevik* ("Zadachi," 1931) by Wilhelm Knorin. The contrary standpoint, which affirmed the backwardness as a consequence of the existing leadership's policies, found expression in a short-lived journal of the Institute of Red Professors ("Zapadno," 1931). The author of the article, I. Fileev, was a party secretary in the IKP. That his views could find expression in print probably resulted from the influence of Mints, head of the party unit in the institute, and from Pashukanis, chief editor of the journal.

That the initiative for the discussions lay with Pokrovskii's opponents is attested to by his attempt to tone down and reduce the scope of criticism. It was probably illness that prevented his participation in the KA presidium's deliberations on the work of the westernists. But archives preserve a letter he sent on July 16 that succeeded in having a draft resolution revised:

> Having familiarized myself with the draft of the Presidium resolution with respect to the discussion on the Western-history front, I associate myself wholeheartedly with the positive side of that draft: the assignments to historians of the West are posed entirely correctly, and they certainly could not be more timely. But I must protest most unqualifiedly against the critical portion of the draft, in which monstrous accusations in the realm of theory are directed at old comrades known to all and holding leading positions in the field, without the slightest attempts to validate these accusations. Thus, comrades Rotshtein and Volgin are proclaimed non-Marxists (this is not said directly, but this is precisely their meaning). Really, is the Communist Academy (after all, this is a draft of a resolution of its Presidium) going to seek the removal of Volgin from his post as Permanent Secretary of the Academy of Sciences and of Rotshtein from the editorial board of the *Bol'-shaia Sovetskaia Entsiklopediia?* And if practical measures of this order are not envisaged, then what is the point of casting such severe accusations, without, I repeat, documenting them in any manner whatsoever? Or, with respect to Comrade N.M. Lukin, it is said that his understanding of imperialism is not Lenin's but

Hilferding's. It is, of course, very pleasant to learn that my notion of years ago that there is a fundamental divergence between Hilferding's Menshevik formulation and Lenin's Bolshevik definition of imperialism has gained general acceptance. But in this connection doesn't the question of when Comrade Lukin made this mistake become of tremendous importance? For the fact is that seven or eight years ago, the overwhelming majority of comrades held that view—and if necessary I will undertake to offer quotations from the most prestigious publications. But if N.M. [Lukin] thinks that way now—that's bad. Once we name specific persons as committing errors, we are required to provide completely specific and concrete characterizations of the mistakes they have made. This would, of course, make the resolution more cumbersome—but that consequence could and should have been foreseen at the outset. . . . [24]

The campaign on the Western sector left the entire historical front in a state of disarray. Disagreement was so widespread that important work ceased. No further issue of *Istorik-marksist* for 1931 appeared after August, a sign of deadlock. The inability of the editorial board to evaluate Lenin's response to the crisis in German social democracy held up the publication of the leading historical journal. Slutskii's article on the subject, published in 1930,[25] was a lengthy, overly subtle analysis that staked out the middle ground Fridliand coveted in the ensuing discussions. Pol', who changed her position in the course of the discussions, published a rejoinder in *Proletarskaia revoliutsiia* (1931). She saw Slutskii's work as a species of Trotskyism.

Slutskii sought to publish his reply in *Istorik-marksist*. He was supported by Iaroslavskii[26] but opposed by other members of the editorial board. Perhaps the board split down the middle. Iaroslavskii impeded publication. His strategy seems to have been to bring the conflict to a climax and thereby provoke intervention from above. He very likely expected the outcome to duplicate the overturn on the philosophical front. For Pokrovskii, the failure of *Istorik-marksist* to appear was itself a mark against his leadership. He deemed the matter serious enough to write to the Central Committee on September 28, 1931:

A scholarly Marxist historical journal is now exceptionally important in international relations. Bourgeois historical scholarship is now thoroughly disorganized. There is widespread interest in us. Articles about us, translations of our brochures appear almost every day, and we have a marvellous opportunity for propagandizing Marxism-Leninism in history. But in order to have influence among European and American historians, it is necessary to have available a press organ in which would be located genuine research works. (Sokolov, 1969a:47)

The journal did not go to press: a perfect stalemate. The same state prevailed in the Marx-Engels-Lenin Institute. Even though the editors of the institute's journal, *Proletarskaia revoliutsiia,* had dissociated themselves from Slutskii's interpretations, they affirmed the need for further study of Lenin's evaluation of German Social Democracy. A discussion was schuled in the institute sometime in autumn. Slutskii and his opponent, S.S. Bankte, prepared abstracts of their reports, which were duplicated and then circulated. According to V.A. Dunaevskii (1966:505), a Soviet historian who has had access to some of the unpublished materials related to this matter, "One may suppose that the abstracts . . . fell into the hands of I.V. Stalin." At any rate, as late as October 20, 1931, and even though the June issue of *Proletarskaia revoliutsiia* had not yet appeared, its editors reiterated the need for discussion. A week later they reversed their position completely (*PR,* 1931, 6:13, 199). In the interim (October 20–27), Stalin had spoken, causing "blows of steel" to fall upon historians.

10   Renewal of Mandate

Stalin's Intervention

In October 1931 Stalin wrote a letter to the editors of *Proletarskaia revoliutsiia* "Concerning Certain Problems in the History of Bolshevism,"[1] protesting the publication of an article by A. Slutskii, "The Bolsheviks on German Social Democracy in the Period of the Pre-War Crisis" (1930). Stalin called the article "anti-party and semi-Trotskyite" for suggesting that Lenin had underestimated the extent and danger of centrism in prewar German Social Democracy. Such an imputation implies that Lenin "underestimated the danger of camouflaged opportunism, the danger of conciliation with opportunism." Slutskii had implied, according to Stalin, that "in the period before the war Lenin was not yet a real Bolshevik; that it was only in the period of the imperialist war or even at the close of the war, that Lenin became a real Bolshevik." Stalin went on to protest *Proletarskaia revoliutsiia*'s providing a forum for such views, "for the question of Lenin's *Bolshevism*, . . . the question as to whether Lenin *was* or *was not* a real Bolshevik, cannot be made a subject of discussion" (1953:483).

Expounding his own interpretation of the international significance of Bolshevism in the prewar period, he concluded,

> even some of our historians—I mean historians without quotation marks, *Bolshevik* historians of our party—are not free from mistakes which bring grist to the mill of the Slutskiis and Voloseviches. In this respect even comrade Iaroslavskii is not, unfortunately, an exception: his books on the history of the C.P.S.U.(b), despite their merits, contain a number of errors in matters of principle and history. (1953:497)

In these remarks, Stalin quite clearly vindicated Gorin. But because the remarks were susceptible to further interpretations they required still further clarification. And soon they gave rise to new disputes which called for further authoritative announcements.

Stalin's letter also contained precepts for the writing of history. After asking why the editors of *Proletarskaia revoliutsiia* provided the likes of Slutskii with a forum, he answered: "Perhaps for the sake of a rotten liberalism, so that the Slutskiis and other disciples of Trotskii may not be able to say that they were being gagged? A rather strange sort of liberalism, this, exercised at the expense of the vital interests of Bolshevism" (1953:484). Stalin commented on Slutskii's assertion that more documents were required in order to define Lenin's position:

> He employs this bureaucratic thesis as an irrefutable argument in favor of the postulate that Lenin (the Bolsheviks) underestimated the danger of centrism in the Second International. . . . Is it not perfectly clear that by his talk about the inadequacy of documents Slutskii is trying to cover up the utter inadequacy and falsity of his so-called conception?
>
> Let us assume that, in addition to the documents already known, a mass of the documents were found containing, say, more resolutions of the Bolsheviks urging the necessity of wiping out centrism. Who save hopeless bureaucrats can rely on written documents alone? Who, besides archive rats, does not understand that a party and its leaders must be tested primarily by their deeds, and not only by their declarations? (1953:492)

Immediate Aftermath

Stalin's letter was a "militant political weapon" of immense international importance in the struggle against bourgeois reaction and its Trotskyite vanguard. The letter played

> *an exceptional role in mobilizing the historical front around the struggle for the general party line,* against deviations and distortions of the history of Bolshevism and its role *in the international revolutionary movement,* and also in inducing historical scholarship to confront tasks of party and socialist construction. ("Rezoliutsiia," 1931)

L. Flidner, a Leningrad historian, proclaimed that all values are transvalued (*pereotsenivaiutsia*) (Mekhlis, 1932:12), as if throwing up his hands to suggest the absence of basis for any beliefs. After the letter's publication, "extermination of cadres of historians began. Many historians were slandered, then repressed. Many were compelled to admit 'errors.' "[2]

A host of meetings were convoked immediately; in due time Stalin's letter was discussed in every institute of the Communist Academy (*VKA*, 1933, 6:101) and in every party unit throughout the country.[3] On November 2 a preliminary meeting of the Society of Marxist Historians demanded a review of all existing historical literature. Then a cycle of reports on the political significance of the letter was organized with more than 130 people being dispatched throughout Moscow to deliver reports; even more were sent, subsequently, to outlying republics. A decision to convoke still another meeting—one that was to last for three days—of the party faction of the Society of Marxist Historians was the final act of the preliminary meeting (*VKA*, 1931, 1–2:42).

When the party faction met, Iaroslavskii and his associates seized the initiative, even though they had been mentioned disapprovingly by Stalin. They had, it seems, considerable support and pressed for resolution upholding their position.[4] Finally, a resolution was adopted censuring the authors of Iaroslavskii's four volumes for *gruppovshchina* (*VKA*, 1932, 1–2:42). Within a short time, Iaroslavskii recanted in letters to the editors of *Pravda* (10 Dec. 1931) and *Bol'shevik* (1931, 21:84–86). He was restored to the good graces of the party when the presidium of the Central Control Commission resolved that his declaration was satisfactory.[5]

Although Iaroslavskii's faction was checked and rebuked, this did not signify an unequivocal victory for Pokrovskii's faction. Both within the meetings and in subsequent statements from above, the leadership of the SMH was censured. Attacks on the dominant faction provoked Gorin to state that he did not "share the views of comrades who consider everything in the historical sector absolutely bad, that the situation is completely hopeless, that the historical realm is found in the hands of Trotskyites and all sorts of opportunists" (*VKA*, 1932, 1–2:56). An editorial in *Bor'ba klassov* took note of an attempt to smuggle in Trotskyite contraband by means of attributing "rotten liberalism" to the existing leadership ("Za boevuiu," 1932). The leadership, however, judged itself not guilty of any major dereliction of duties. An authoritative statement in the *Vestnik* of the Communist Academy affirmed that while the SMH leadership "unconditionally pursued a correct political line . . . , Bolshevik convictions had not been manifested to a sufficient degree" (*VKA*, 1932, 1–2:43). The editorial in *Bor'ba klassov* criticized the failure to maintain a satisfactory emphasis on "*practical* work," adding that the leadership failed to compel a "Bolshevik tempo of literary production and reports" ("Za boevuiu," 1932:13). An editorial in *Istorik-marksist* noted the inability of the leadership to bring self-criticism to bear within the SMH. The "basic leadership" of Pokrovskii was sound, it continued, but Gorin and Fridliand failed to reveal the crudest mistakes in the ranks ("Za reshitel'nuiu," 1932:8–9).

Personal recriminations, even within factions, was an especially unpleasant aspect of the discussions. Iaroslavskii turned on Mints and blamed him for the errors in the now infamous *Istoriia VKP(b)*, alleging that he had not had time to read carefully the work that appeared under his name. Gorin, in turn, denounced his comrade Vanag in an attempt to dissociate himself from the latter's interpretation of imperialism (*VKA*, 1932, 1–2:57). Public confessions of error abounded throughout the winter in the press, the historical journals, and in

Bol'shevik. The incomplete notes of one of the meetings in the Communist Academy reveal a glimpse of the process. One of Vanag's books came under attack by Ostrovitianov. At the outset Vanag defended his work by admitting the presence of Trotskyite errors while denying that the work as a whole was Trotskyite. He categorically rejected the suggestion that his work was Trotskyite until it could be proved to him. Then Savel'ev joined the criticism. After a resolution was adopted, Vanag took the floor to recognize his mistakes. The entire book was at fault, he conceded, and badly conceived (*VKA*, 1932, 1–2:63–67). Vanag's failure to call the book Trotskyite may be considered the only bright spot in this performance.

Previously it had been Iaroslavskii and his school then Pokrovskii and his school that were subjected to criticisms (Sidorov, 1964:136). Pokrovskii himself escaped open censure, but a participant reported decades later that materials harmful to Pokrovskii had been circulated among historians, which would be expanded upon later in the two volumes devoted to his denigration.[6]

Issues

Anarchy is one's first impression as the discussions moved toward a war of each against all. In fact all authority among historians did collapse in the wake of Stalin's letter. But a higher authority asserted itself, as the Central Committee intervened directly: teams of IKP students, experienced party workers, were mobilized immediately and undertook to review all major historical works. The reviews identified contraband Trotskyites and decided which historical interpretations were true and which false.[7]

What was at issue in the discussions? What was their outcome? There are three major problems. The discussions were, first of all, a conflict of ideas—"a battle for Marxism,"[8] or, more accurately, a battle for a particular interpretation of Leninism and a condemnation of other possible interpretations. It represented an effort to work out an understanding of the Russian Revolution that presumed that Lenin had expected the confinement of a socialist revolution to an underdeveloped country. These views were summed up in the theory of growing over. The theory was an assignment to historians to show that the building of socialism in one country was a program that had taken shape even before the Revolution.

The discussions that followed Stalin's letter were, secondly, a statement of professional norms, almost a constitutional convention. The premises of historians and politicians about the relationship between scholarship and politics became universalized in the doctrine of partiinost'. The rewards and the full range of sanctions that would be administered to back up the doctrine were made evident to all. The final problem of concern here is the organization of historical scholarship and the problem of leadership. The discussions expressed a conflict between individuals and groups, and a bitter and in some respects infantile personal rivalry between Pokrovskii and Iaroslavskii. Their respective schools contended for advantage as well.

The meaning of partiinost' was elucidated more fully in the behavior at meetings than in any of the stated definitions. Mints received the greatest amount of abuse and criticism, compelling, we have seen, even his patron Iaroslavskii to abandon him temporarily. He was condemned for his false opinions, for *gruppovshchina*, but most persistently for his theory about objectivity and expediency. At issue was party hagiography and the creation of the cult of personality. Mints was taken to task for not affirming in Iaroslavskii's volumes an identity of views between Lenin and Stalin in March and April 1917. Refusing to recant, he created a sensation in a closed meeting by saying that Stalin's position did differ from Lenin's but that it would be inexpedient to say so at present.[9] Not a word of this found its way into print. The sources reveal only the charge that Mints had distorted the concept of partiinost' by contrasting expedience and objectivity.[10] Shortly thereafter, Iaroslavskii was personally instructed by Kaganovich and by Stalin as to just how he should revise his *Istoriia VKP(b)* and how he should present Stalin's role in that history.[11]

As concerns doctrine, the crystallization of the theory of growing over and the unequivocal commitment of Soviet historiography to the doctrine of socialism in one country is the most enduring consequence. Almost all public confessions and almost all reviews written by IKP teams reiterated this point as the "root question of Bolshevism." Kaganovich's formulation is typical. He condemned Iaroslavskii for treating

> falsely the question of the Revolution of 1905 and likewise falsely presenting the role of Lenin and his estimate of the character of the Russian Revolution; the presentation of our Bolshevist treatment of the question of the hegemony of the proletariat and especially of the growth of the bourgeois-democratic revolution into the socialist revolution is also false.[12]

The necessary corollaries of the doctrine were sanctioned as well. Vanag's (and Pokrovskii's) thesis that Russia was the object rather than the subject of modern imperialism, it was found, provided grist for the Trotskyite mill. In a letter to the editor of *Istorik-marksist*, Vanag stated that he considered it "necessary by decisive means to censure the standpoint which portrays tsarist Russia as a colony of Western European imperialist countries. This theory would serve as a basis for the Trotskyite thesis on the impossibility of constructing socialism in our country."[13]

The theory of growing over persisted in this form from 1931–32 until 1936, when Stalin changed his mind about Russian imperialism. Just as Vanag was purged, his original interpretation found official sanction. In accord with the new national motif, the Russian Revolution was accorded the significance of having delivered the Soviet peoples from the threat of foreign domination ("Zamechaniia po," 1936). The theory underwent further modification in the discussions of Peoples' Democracies after World War II, and is an issue in the controversies between Moscow and the resurgent West European Communist parties.

Stalin's letter marked a turning point in the evolution of Soviet historical ideas. Completing the evolution of a particular understanding of the Rusian Revolution and of Bolshevism, it provided historians with a set of assumptions that would affect findings on all questions of modern history. Because it brought attention to the concept of feudalism, it affected findings on even remote topics. Going back as it did to the national origins of the Revolution, it proved to be a seedbed for the revived national school, and it marked a turning point for the norms of historical investigation. A short-lived consequence was the reorganization of scholarship to assure the primacy of timely, practical research. This can best be seen through a brief description of the work of the Institute of History in 1932.[14]

During the early months of 1932, the Institute of History was reorganized; the sections were replaced by teams. For a given historical problem a production plan was adopted and a team formed. The institute employed 100 scholars who worked on the following problems: the fifteenth anniversary of the October Revolution, Lenin's legacy with emphasis on the methodology of history, the history of plants and factories, the trade unions, and the Civil War. The express purpose of these teams was to overcome the lag between theory and practice. The team dealing with the problem of "The History of the Proletariat in the Epoch of Its Dictatorship" had eight members plus a captain. Its first assignment was the completion by October 15 of a collection of articles entitled *The Proletariat in the October Revolution*. Six members were to contribute articles, while presumably the others did bibliographical work and editing. The team's second assignment was the preparation by January 1 of a collection of documents on the proletariat in the first period of its dictatorship. After a vacation, the members who assembled the collection were to edit the documents for publication. By October 15, 1933, the same team was to supervise the preparation of a collection of autobiographies of workers who had participated in the Revolution.

The Institute of History administered the teams through a number of controls. It negotiated an agreement with each team captain determining the composition of the team and the duration of its work and then worked out agreements with each of the members in order to affirm the obligation of each to the team and to arrange for other work that he or she might do for the institute. The purpose of these individual contracts was to avoid the debilitation of individual responsibility and initiative: to assure, on the one hand, that the historian did not "hide behind the backs of the team," and to encourage him, on the other hand, not to confine his research to the team assignment. Because of the institute's need for teachers and the historians' needs for additional income, the institute also permitted the historians to teach. Some of them undertook the teaching of six or seven seminars, which had a deleterious effect on their research. Consequently, the institute ruled that no one could lead more than three seminars without special permission. "Control by the ruble" supplemented "control by contract." When a researcher failed to meet his obligations, the institute withheld part of his wages—fifty rubles the first time, twenty-five the second time; a third failure resulted in dismissal. Bonuses rewarded overfulfillment. The party discreetly abandoned this mode of organization in 1934, when history faculties in the major universities were restored.

Another organizational trend, more significant as a sign of the times than for its practical consequences, deserves mention—the demise of the Society of Marxist Historians. As the society specialized increasingly on popularization of scholarship, the most able historians associated themselves with the Institute of History. Presumably, they retained their membership in the society but simply devoted less time to its activities. After the publication of Stalin's letter, many found the meetings of the society unpleasant and stopped attending.[15] The death knell sounded just after Pokrovskii's own death when the Culture-Propaganda Department failed to hear the society's report, signifying that its plan was not ratified. The presidium of the Communist Academy then created a team to reorganize the society, which in effect made it an adjunct of the Institute of History (Doroshenko, 1966:21). It ceased to be a voluntary organization. The society's activities then become difficult to follow. It sponsored a Soviet delegation to the plenum of the International Historical Committee in the Hague (*IM*, 1932, 28:148). Still in 1932, we find mention of activities by the Leningrad and Georgian chapters,[16] and the Black-Soil District chapter even held a conference that same year (*Pervaia*, 1934). The following year the society's members encountered the following judgment about voluntary societies in general: "Absence of leadership, drift, leads to parallelism, to the absence of a clear plan, to the preservation of old classification and units in societies" (Novinskii, 1933:28). Beginning in 1933, the journal *Bor'ba klassov* ceased bearing the society's imprint; presumably it was taken over by the Institute of History. Early in the year the society did participate in a commemoration of the fiftieth anniversary of Marx's death, held at Moscow University.[17] The Leningrad chapter lasted until 1934.[18]

A "free" Marxist tribune implied the existence of other centers; a special organ to work out the Marxist view of history implied competition of ideas and ideological rivalry. The Society of Marxist Historians had lost its reason to be.

Leadership

The offspring perished with the parent. After Stalin's letter Pokrovskii's own standing was ambiguous and his legacy indeterminate. We have seen that he alone among the leading Marxist historians escaped public censure. We can only guess that the word of mouth criticism included the themes of his denigration as well as the themes of his more recent rehabilitation. More than likely his ideas were condemned while his militance and practical leadership earned praise. We can judge the standing of Pokrovskii's historical works from reviews by the IKP brigades. This can be perceived most clearly in an essay on a book by Pokrovskii's associate S.A. Piontkovskii.[19]

Piontkovskii's work, the critics charged, contained Menshevik-Trotskyite and right-opportunist distortions. The author ignored dialectics and "counterpoised history to practice, history to politics." "He formally and mechanistically approached the study of events and the facts of class conflict, and therefore the entire schema of the history of the peoples of the USSR is conceived by him in a vulgar-mechanistic spirit [that] has nothing in common with the Leninist understanding of the historical process of the USSR." He shares the "Bogdanov-Rozhkov treatment of the problems of socio-historical formations (the depiction of merchant capital as an independent sociohistorical formation in general and in particular in Russia autocracy as the dictatorship of merchant capital)." "Merchant capital in Russia in the epoch of feudalism, as everywhere else, played the role of middleman in exchange. It played a significant role in both the economic and political history of Russia; nevertheless, her ruling class remained the class of serf-owning landlords." This error led to the author's depicting of the Pugachev Rebellion as a movement against merchant capital, and his failure to comprehend the 1861 reform as a consequence of the peasants' struggles. Just what sort of formation merchant capital is "is known to him alone."

The author treats Russia as a semicolony. He depicts the Revolution as a spontaneous process, which minimizes the role of the proletariat and exaggerates the role of the bourgeoisie, while it neglects the role of the party. He distorts the teaching of the growing over of the bourgeois-democratic revolution into a socialist revolution. In suggesting that

Lenin only after returning to Russia posed the problem of a socialist revolution, he sanctioned Trotsky's notion of the rearmament of Bolshevism in 1917, when Lenin allegedly adopted Trotsky's theory of permanent revolution.

We see then that Stalin's letter wiped the slate clean of old interpretations just as it implanted the doctrine of growing over. But there is still some ambiguity as to the standing of Pokrovskii's ideas: if historians were warned away from them, they were still the system best known to the public. They found expression in almost all published works, and Pokrovskii's *Brief History* was widely accessible to all. The theory of growing over was still merely a set of assumptions, a general perspective, the embryo of a new course of Russian history. Pokrovskii's *Brief History* would be republished as late as 1936 in the Ukraine[20]—even after Pokrovskii had been publicly repudiated. For some still unclear reason the Marxist historians had difficulty in constructing a new course and writing new textbooks. The situation was remedied only after the rehabilitation of the former non-Marxists.

There is a definite sense in which Stalin's letter represented a victory for Pokrovskii: it signaled the defeat of Iaroslavskii. Since Pokrovskii's school won the battle for leadership, it seems likely that in the closed discussions Pokrovskii's leadership was praised. Iaroslavskii, after his brief discomfort, remained historian in good standing and continued to publish articles in the leading journals, mostly publicist works about past defeats of opposition groups within the party and new trends in their makeup. He continued to hold a seat on the editorial board of *Istorik-marksist* even after its shakeup late in 1932. He did, however, give up his position on the board of *Bor'ba klassov*. Most of his time was devoted to the Commission on the History of the Civil War. Though still a leader who could demand deference, he did not concern himself with the day-to-day supervision of the historical sector. In 1933 he became a member of the Central Purging Commission (Iaroslavskii, 1933:54), whose membership included Kirov, whose assassination led to the purges, N.I. Ezhov, who conducted the purges, Kaganovich, and Knorin.

Iaroslavskii's followers fared less well. Some of their names are not to be encountered any further, but his chief lieutenants suffered only temporary eclipse. Mints, after losing his position as party secretary in the Institute of Red Professors, for "softness," went to work for Iaroslavskii in the Commission on the History of the Civil War, and later attained eminence as a member of the Academy of Sciences. A.L. Sidorov and N.L. Rubinshtein "went off to do practical work" (Sidorov, 1964:136) for a few years.[21] Dubrovskii most likely endured the same fate; he was not to be heard from for a few years until he emerged as a practicing historian and dean in Leningrad.[22] El'vov was reassigned to

Kazan and later liquidated.[23] K.A. Popov and Piontkovskii, it seems, were lost in the purges.

It was Lukin who replaced Pokrovskii as the leader of the historical front. He emerged as head of the Institute of History and chief editor of *Istorik-marksist*. He retained this position even after 1936 when the institute was placed within the Academy of Sciences and amalgamated with its various historical departments. Gorin and Fridliand remained in the background, where they had fallen in 1931. Gorin continued to make general pronouncements, but they carried less weight when echoed from Minsk. In 1934 Fridliand regained authority as one of the senior members of the newly formed History Faculty of Moscow State University. Lukin relied mainly on Vanag and Pankratova to enunciate the current tasks in Russian history.

Soon after the dust settled in 1932, the perennial complaints about lack of coordination between the Institute of History and the Marx-Engels-Lenin Institute resumed.[24] The latter institute was reorganized as a department of the Central Committee in 1932, and much of Riazanov's work was undone. General supervision of the field of party history was entrusted to Wilhelm Knorin. He seems to have collaborated harmoniously with both Lukin and Kaganovich.

In sum, after Stalin's letter the party refashioned historical scholarship so that old forms of leadership were no longer necessary or even possible. Pokrovskii's prescriptions now became descriptive: research was centralized and bureaucratized with publication, selection of topics, and disposition of personnel controlled by historians in a hierarchical framework that reflected political priorities. A distinctive interpretation of Marxism-Leninism that constituted a set of axioms was formalized or at least made explicit and universally recognized. All historians now had a single starting point, which narrowed the range of tolerated opinion; they were relieved of all anxiety as to the character of sanctions that might be employed against them.

Scholarship and Politics

We have reviewed some of the effects of Stalin's letter—its impact on ideas, the structure of the historical profession, and the standing of individual historians. We ought finally to consider why it led to these consequences. This can best be approached by asking how it was possible for Pokrovskii to forestall the overturn on the historical front that seemed to be impending in 1931. Though the final answer lies in the recesses of party history and in closed archives, it is possible to make some suggestions from the sense of direction one gains from materials at hand. Pokrovskii was a better manager and a cleverer strategist than

Iaroslavskii; His incessant and aggressive activity, even while ill, his extensive knowledge of history and of the historical profession, his purposefulness and refined sense of timing were unmatched assets. He had more to offer the party leadership than did his rivals.

Pokrovskii conducted a nearly flawless campaign; Iaroslavskii joined battle on the wrong issues and in support of the wrong people. He quite clearly allowed personal sympathies to influence his judgment and therein showed want of tact with regard to the feelings and interests of those above him. To champion Teodorovich, who, it will be recalled, had been dismissed from the Commissariat of Agriculture of the RFSFR in 1928, during the enactment of extraordinary measures for grain collection, was to invite the accusation of rightist deviation. To force a showdown over the right of the ex-Menshevik Slutskii to reply to critics may suggest integrity; it was, nevertheless, a blunder. These indiscretions proved a windfall for Pokrovskii—they greatly weakened Iaroslavskii's credentials as a claimant to leadership of the historical front.

Pokrovskii's leadership had been effective. He and his supporters could point to a variety of successes of the Institute of Red Professors, the Communist Academy, and the Society of Marxist Historians; he could, moreover, claim credit for the scholars produced in RANION. He could also deflect charges that RANION had been a seedbed of deviationism by showing his initiative in disbanding it at the proper moment. In keeping with the spirit of the first five-year-plan, Pokrovskii had helped launch major projects on the history of the Civil War and the history of plants and factories. He encouraged regular publication of popular historical works, including the reminiscences of workers themselves. It should be recalled that Pokrovskii's name had international renown; nevertheless, he had demonstrated the flexibility of his own historical ideas.

What did Iaroslavskii have to commend himself, except past favors? He had been a faithful agent of Stalin in party work since the early 1920s, and he had done presumably commendable, if not notoriously successful work as head of the anti-religious campaign. In addition, he headed a small circle of young historians who were unburdened by any such albatross as the concept of merchant capital; they had demonstrated ample talent in their research and disputation on Russian imperialism and had helped refine the theory of growing over. But they could not write party history correctly. Mints' factually accurate portrayal of Stalin in 1917 proved a disservice to Iaroslavskii's cause. Iaroslavskii had thus done little to prove his ability to manage the complex of individuals and institutions that made up the historical front.

Pokrovskii, in addition to taking credit for successful policies, could extol the theory of cultural revolution he had elaborated in connection with the liquidation of RANION's Institute of History. It could be considered the Marxist-Leninist justification of policies being carried out in a variety of fields. As chairman of the Communist Academy he devised procedures for the planning and control of science that embodied the principle of partiinost'. Clearly Pokrovskii had comprehended the spirit of the times better than his rival had. Stalin's call to close the gap between theory and practice contained no mysteries for him and provided no obstacles. In the developing conflict, Pokrovskii represented militance and partisanship; his sense of the moment made him strive not to be outflanked on the left. The fact that Iaroslavskii advocated open discussion made his the voice of toleration. It may have won support and congratulations for him among some historians, but it was a cause of his defeat in the Central Committee.

Pokrovskii labored, nevertheless, under a number of disadvantages in his rivalry with Iaroslavskii. First, his vacillation in the first half of 1928 had suggested a lingering sympathy for Bukharin. Second, the theory of merchant capital—no matter how he twisted and turned, he was hard pressed to show its continued usefulness. Finally, Pokrovskii's remoteness from Stalin coupled with the anomalous disgruntlement that seemed to be his mood the final year could not escape attention. These not entirely unimportant matters were evidently outweighed in Stalin's mind by Pokrovskii's superior credentials.

It should be noted, however, that the discussions that ensued after the publication of Stalin's letter were shaped significantly by the party secretaries Kaganovich and Postyshev. In a widely publicized speech in December 1931, Kaganovich sought to heat up the atmosphere. He rebuked and then forgave Iaroslavskii. He also observed:

> It is now difficult for one to come forward openly under the flag of Trotskyism. One must now come forward under other flags, slogans, theses, formulations. One must now cast doubt on the consistency of the Leninist Bolshevist theory in order to besmirch the actual realization of the general line of the Party. Opportunism attempts at present to creep into our ranks under various guises; it attempts to fawn and ingratiate itself, to grovel, to slip through the wicket gate of the history of our Party.[25]

In January Postyshev echoed the call for a cleansing of theory, but he did so in such fashion as to suggest opposition to the most strident forms of the ongoing cultural revolution and opposition to Kaganovich. Though armed with quotations from Stalin, he suggested that too many party cells were dealing with the matter by administrative means. Too often people are being expelled from the party, he said, without examination. Too often when a comrade errs, instead of being given comradely aid in correcting the error, he is just excluded from the order. Those acting in this fashion have misunderstood the meaning of Stalin's letter: "One must be able to distinguish separate errors of a person from the system of views. It is one thing to uncover concealed Trotskyites and another to criticize a comrade. This must be done in comradely fashion in order to help them correct themselves."[26]

Do these political speeches help us understand the outcome for historians? Kaganovich, in urging militance, was supporting Iaroslavskii by calling for an overthrow of Pokrovskii's leadership. Postyshev, in counseling moderation, was in effect upholding the status quo. There is an apparent paradox in this alignment of forces, for Pokrovskii, in seeking renewal of his mandate from the Stalinist Central Committee, preempted the role of militant. Iaroslavskii seemed the moderate. On the face of it, Pokrovskii had comprehended the spirit of the times better than had his rival. Stalin's charge to close the gap between theory and practice contained no mysteries for him and provided fewer obstacles than opportunities. Pokrovskii stood for partisanship. His sense of the moment made him strive not to be outflanked on the left. Iaroslavskii's defense of the rights of Teodorovich and Slutskii made his the voice of toleration. As commendable as this was, and though it probably won him support from some of the practicing historians, it was very likely an important cause of his defeat in the Central Committee.

Was the Pokrovskii-Iaroslavskii rivalry but one arena of an extensive conflict among Stalin's lieutenants? Were his subordinates eager to prove that their subordinates in turn could do the job he wished? Affirmative answers provide the most plausible explanation and require the least speculation. It may be that Pokrovskii's militance enabled Postyshev to make a more persuasive case to Stalin than Kaganovich. Perhaps Postyshev and others persuaded Stalin that it would be pointless and wasteful to duplicate the overturn among philosophers that had subordinated the discipline directly to Stalin. Deborin, after all, was an ex-Menshevik. Postyshev could argue that historical scholarship was in the hands of a tested and true Bolshevik. We should not ignore the possibility, however, that Pokrovskii was upheld not because of Stalin's decision or inclination, but despite it. Pokrovskii's academic credentials and his success as a leader of the front may not have endeared him to Stalin at all. Iaroslavskii, in contrast, was almost entirely Stalin's creature. The bare facts are, after all, that Stalin's rise, 1927–38, coincided with the weakening of Pokrovskii's authority and then his posthumous fall and denigration. Pokrovskii's victory in 1931 was exceptional and temporarily reversed a clear trend.

Stalin's known opponents had been removed from positions of authority by 1931, but he had not yet become all-powerful. Though the limits of his authority are not clear, it is evident that he chafed and had them removed by 1938. Stalin did not have a free hand in disposing of opponents. Some Politburo members, even though they had supported Stalin against the Left and Right Oppositions, did not wish to enhance his power further. It is sufficiently clear at least that at a later date they sought to stay his hand. Even a Soviet textbook puts Postyshev in the foreground of Stalin's opponents during the purges (*Kratkaia*, 1964:271). There are hints that he emerged as a moderating influence during the period of collectivization.[27] There is even the suggestion by Boris Nicolaevsky (1954) of a Kirov-Postyshev axis that sought to block Stalin's attempts to use terror within the party. Can we hypothesize a projection of this situation—Iaroslavskii-Kaganovich-Stalin against Pokrovskii-Postyshev—onto the historical controversies?

Stalin's later wholesale incursion into the writing of history, the publication of the *Short Course* in 1938, supports the view that previously he had possessed only limited control. Was Kaganovich, sponsoring Iaroslavskii's attempt to effect an overturn on the historical front, acting on his own initiative? Or is there any point in assuming that Kaganovich acted at Stalin's behest and that Iaroslavskii's failure represented a defeat for Stalin as well? The term *defeat* is probably too strong. The assertiveness of Postyshev may simply have persuaded Stalin to let matters stand as they were, not to force the issue. This line of reasoning, suggesting that in 1931 Stalin merely postponed setting up the arrangements he deemed most desirable, is highly speculative. It receives a measure of confirmation not so much from Postyshev's fall, which could have had many causes, but from the subsequent rise of Iaroslavskii, particularly when he replaced Lukin as leader of the historical front during the purges. This fact at least accords the argument the status of a hypothesis.

11 Pokrovskii's System in Ruins

Discussion of Socioeconomic Formations

Public events in the historical profession—the discussions affecting historians most directly, the matters they were talking about—have been the object of our attention. Another series of events that received little publicity and whose impact was not felt immediately took place at the same time. This undercurrent, the debate about socioeconomic formations, in due time led to a reformulation of the tenets of historical materialism. Pokrovskii's interpretation of Marxism was replaced by a new one. These discussions as well as the events treated in the previous chapters compelled Pokrovskii to reconsider his synthesis of Russian history and led finally to its disintegration. Before considering Pokrovskii's final system of ideas, it is necessary, therefore, to examine the debate about socioeconomic formations as a context of Pokrovskii's intellectual evolution.

A variety of circumstances produced the discussion. First, the agony of the Chinese Communist Party brought attention to a particular formation—the Asiatic mode of production. Second, the theory of growing over, which was an analysis of one particular mode of transition from feudalism to socialism, needed as an underpinning a general doctrine about the transformation of one system into another. Third, the mere presence during the five-year plan of numerous disputes that could not be settled by appeal to the facts impelled a reconsideration of methodology and fundamental principles. Furthermore, the study of Lenin's writings and the familiarization of historians with the voluntaristic elements in them exacerbated the long-standing discontent with economic determinism. Pokrovskii himself exemplified this discontent. Closely related to this was Stalin's need for a doctrine that countenanced a greater role in history for the state and the exceptional individual. The encounter of Soviet Marxist historians with Western social theory in the Petrushevskii affair, which forced a reconsideration of economic materialism, was the first event in the discussion of socioeconomic formations.

The second event in the debate was the appearance of S.M. Dubrovskii's *On the Question of the Existence of an "Asiatic" Mode of Produc-*

tion, Feudalism, Serfdom and Merchant Capital (1929). Dubrovskii's duties at the International Agrarian Institute put him in close touch with foreign communists, mainly Asians. He conceived of his book as a refutation of their theories.[1] The stir that resulted from its publication surprised him and caused him to remark, "When I wrote my book, I did not intend to discover any sort of America" ("Diskussiia," 1930b:156). In the course of the debate, his opponents labeled him a right deviationist, making the charge not only in historical journals but on the pages of *Izvestiia* (24 Feb. 1930).[2]

Dubrovskii's theses were that Asiatic society, the "so-called Asiatic mode of production," was not a genuine socioeconomic formation but rather a species of feudalism and that serfdom was a socioeconomic formation, one that normally appeared between the feudal and capitalist formations. This second thesis called for reevaluation of the notion of merchant capital and led to a clash with Pokrovskii. When Dubrovskii first tested his theses at a meeting of the IKP, Pokrovskii challenged him. Dubrovskii replied, "I'll write the entire book, and you will see that I am right."[3] When his book did appear, his colleagues discussed it at two open meetings of the sociology section of the SMH on May 17 and 24, 1929 ("Diskussiia," 1930b).

In late 1929 or early 1930, Dubrovskii's thesis that serfdom constitutes a socioeconomic formation was rejected in a discussion following a report by Mints at the IKP.[4] But discussions held in Leningrad and Kharkov in 1930 and 1931 supported Dubrovskii's thesis about Asiatic society.[5] Even Grekov's special report in 1932 that posited the feudal essence of Kievan society can be considered an event in the dispute.[6] A.G. Prigozhin, in an authoritative report to GAIMK, reviewed the debate and codified the doctrine.[7]

This debate about Dubrovskii's book was urgent and candid. The thesis that serfdom was a genuine formation—Dubrovskii's most original idea—was dispatched without prolonged debate; its rival conception—merchant capital—demanded more attention. But the problem of the Asiatic mode of production overshadowed all else. Within this first stage of the discussion, the emphasis shifted from particular formations to the very notion of socioeconomic formations as such. Dubrovskii defended his idea of serfdom by attacking the theory of merchant capital. There had been in Russian history clashes between industrial and merchant capital, but in light of the recently formulated interpretation of the Revolution, Dubrovskii argued, these must be considered intraclass maneuvers. They were not instances of genuine class struggle, because the industrial bourgeoisie had never been a "basic moving force" of the Revolution. Even in the democratic stage of the Revolution, the basic force was peasants under the leadership of the proletariat.[8] In other words, the clash between industrial and merchant capital was insignificant: it could not play an important role in the transformation from one social order to another.

Merchant capital, "which soared in the clouds," did not create its own mode of production, according to Dubrovskii; rather it "penetrated the pores of existing societies" (126). Dubrovskii considered it a phenomenon that could exist within various formations; it was not a formation itself. Even Pokrovskii's defenders agreed with this evaluation of merchant capital. In effect, they argued that Dubrovskii took over Pokrovskii's evaluation as his own, while imputing to Pokrovskii ideas foreign to him. Pokrovskii, they contended, had never considered merchant capital a formation in its own right ("Diskussiia," 1930b:111–13, 126). Strictly speaking this was not true. Although Pokrovskii had not called merchant capital a formation—the term was not current when he created his system—he had treated it as one. The ways of merchant capital, not those of feudalism, determined the nature of autocracy in Pokrovskii's system. Thus in defending Pokrovskii's conception, his supporters diluted it.

Dubrovskii also contended that Marx had never considered Asiatic society a "special formation, but only a coincidence of productive means that predominated in both Asia and Russia during the epoch of feudalism" (123). Asiatic society, according to Dubrovskii, was an instance of a dictatorship of the landlords, with state-owned land representing one particular form of predominance by landlords. Taken as a whole, it was a species of feudalism: "Of course, the forms of feudalism varied in Asia, Western Europe and Russia, but class relationships were the same" (124, 126).

The source of confusion concerning Asiatic society, Dubrovskii argued, lay in his critics' failure to distinguish between actual societies and the abstract notion of an Asiatic mode of production. Actual societies contained elements of various social formations. Any capitalist society contained vestiges of feudalism and rudiments of socialism. An abstract formation, however, existed nowhere, but if it were a genuine one, its characteristics could be seen in various societies. For example, slavery, potentially a formation in its own right, existed both during the Middle Ages in Europe and in the southern United States under capitalism. No one, challenged Dubrovskii, could cite an instance where the Asiatic mode of production existed in a society as a subordinate element. Hence it was not a genuine formation (124).

A.D. Udal'tsov endorsed the conclusion that Asiatic society was not a special formation, but he formulated the argument differently. He interpreted Marx's writings on the subject as follows: Asiatic society was a species of the communal structure that preceded slave-owning society. It was a variant of the German *mark* and the Slavic *mir*. Consequently, the feudal system that evolved from this commune was a variant form of feudalism, one characterized by strong collectivism (117–18). A. Efimov upheld the conclusion that Asiatic society was not a distinctive mode of production. Like Dubrovskii, he considered it a form of feudalism. Unlike Dubrovskii, he emphasized the distinctive characteristics of this species. At a certain stage, he argued, collective labor and land ownership triumphed over the formation of private property. This resulted in the emergence of a powerful state that succeeded in preserving the primitive commune. The need for centralized irrigation and the widespread influence of merchant capital were the main reasons for this pattern of evolution (135–36). Efimov occupied a middle ground in the debate. He denied the existence of an Asiatic formation; by stressing the distinctive features of Asiatic feudalism, however, he countenanced the view that the future evolution of Asiatic society would also be distinctive.

Ludovik Magyar, armed with quotations from volume 1 of *Capital*, argued that there was an Asiatic mode of production and that it took the place of feudalism in China. The prevalence of irrigation, he contended, gave rise to a social system in which private property in land was absent (107–8). Thus the differences between Efimov and Magyar were minor; their respective descriptions of Asiatic society were similar, as were the implications of these descriptions with regard to subsequent evolution. What differed were their systems of classification.

A.V. Shmonin defended the Asiatic theory in its most radical form: "Any formation so stable that it lacks the possibility of evolving into capitalism is called the Asiatic mode of production." Such stability, in his view, characterized China, India, and Russia. Russian merchant capitalism attained such extensive development that it "impeded the transition to industrial capitalism." Shmonin did not consider the existence of the Asiatic mode of production an exceptional state of affairs. "Where the disintegration of the old mode of production and the transition to industrial capitalism is possible—there the Asiatic mode of production is absent." The chief problem, in his view, was to discern where the Asiatic system did *not* exist and account for this departure from the predominant pattern. By raising the question, "How does Marx explain the transition from feudalism to industrial capitalism precisely in the west?" (153–55), Shmonin came very close to suggesting that the evolution of European society was a unique phenomenon.

Political overtones to the discussion of the Asiatic theory, even in the SMH meetings in May 1929, were evident to the participants. A. Mukhardzhi, an Indian communist who addressed the assembly in English, stated that to agree that Eastern nations have

> a special mode of production is to agree with the chauvinistic elements of India and other countries, who insist that Eastern nations are distinguished by some specifically Asiatic organization of production, and that, in consequence of this [there is] a special form of evolution for India, completely different from capitalist Europe. (110)

The theory would comfort Gandhi, whose own program stressed the distinctiveness of India, and his Indian followers who insisted on the cooperation of classes and the creation of a national party.

I. Reisner, a specialist on Indian history and British colonial policy, interpreted the political implications differently: Dubrovskii's thesis "denying the distinctiveness of eastern development . . . leads us not forward but backward." Marxist theory permits one

> to uncover the basic elements of class contradictions, and having torn from stagnant Asian history her sacred halo, placed there by bourgeois scholarship, reveal economic laws, which, it is true, [operate] in slightly different fashion. But they are revealed in their immutable efficacy. (115)

In the first round of discussions, neither interpretation of Asian society and neither set of political interpretations received official sanction.

Prigozhin's report, delivered in Leningrad in March 1933, represented the final stage of this discussion of socioeconomic formations during Stalin's lifetime. He "sought to clarify the essence of the synthesis of Roman and Germanic elements in the process of the establishment of feudalism in various parts of Europe" (*OI*, 4:613). In doing so he formulated a number of propositions about historical evolution which can be taken as a summary and a codification of the principles of historical materialism. At the time "many [historians] considered it necessary to express their agreement with the basic propositions of his report." The report itself was summarized in a passage that echoed Marx's *Critique of Political Economy* and at the same time went beyond it:

> Socio-economic formations constitute a definite socio-economic system, at the base of which lies the predominance of the mode of production. This mode of production, as the totality of production, forms the economic structure of society, the real base upon which rises the entire superstructure. But this definition of socio-economic formations expresses only the general regularity (*zakonomernost'*) of all formations and is, thus, only a theoretical abstraction. Marxism-Leninism . . . demands the unveiling of the regularity of each formation as a specific regularity,

which reflects the specific form of movement for each stage of society.[9]

Prigozhin's point of departure was the assumption of universal regularity (or law-governed patterns); he asserted that the "objective world is eternally moving and developing matter." From this, one could affirm the regularity, not only of nature, but of thought and society. The distinctive feature of the regularity of social life was that it was carried out by people. Only a consideration of both the general pattern of history and specific forms of its regularity would reveal the mode of human participation in society. The basic regularity of social evolution was "the regularity of the development of material production." The regularity of the development of material production stood behind the rise, development, and disappearance of all particular formations. Material production developed as the contradiction between the productive forces and relations of production. The forces or instruments of production constituted the content of the economy. The relations of production, the division of labor, constituted its form. Taken together they represent a dialectical unity. Material production developed through the conflict between form and content of the economy (4–6).

This development was regular and uninterrupted, but because it was dialectical it imitated the figure of a spiral rather than a straight line. This conception of universal history as conforming to a spiraling pattern led to a consideration of social evolution as a series of definite progressive degrees or stages. The interdependence of the various stages, the fact that each stage inhered in the previous one and foreshadowed the subsequent one, constituted the determinism of history (6–8). Thus the development of material production constituted a regularity for all history—preclass societies, antagonistic class societies, and classless societies. At the same time, there was a distinctive, specific regularity for each formation which occupied a central place in the doctrine of socioeconomic formations. This aspect of the doctrine, which examined "*society at a definite stage of development and is concerned with the specific forms of movement inherent in each stage of society,*" was emphasized by Lenin, according to Prigozhin. Lenin did not merely reiterate the theory of Marx and Engels but was responsible for "the further development of the doctrine of formations" (14).[10]

Repeatedly citing Lenin, Prigozhin defined a formation as the "totality" (*sovokupnost'*) of relations at a given stage of development, not only the relation of people to material objects, tools, and the products of labor, but their relations to each other, "the relations of people in the socially organized process of production." Each formation was a live, constantly developing, concrete social organism; each had its own laws of development determining its disintegration and transformation into a higher form. To discern the laws of a given formation—to comprehend a specific regularity—required concrete investigation. It was an inductive process, calling for a description of material production at a given stage of development (14–15).

Prigozhin suggested a number of means of differentiating among various formations. First, the division of labor evolved in connection with material production, and each division of labor expressed itself in a specific form of property (11). Second, at each stage of material production there was a specific means of combining labor force with the instruments of production. Both these formulations share the notion that there were distinctive modes of production; each represented material production at a given stage of development. Each mode of production was a distinctive combination of the forces of production and the relations of production. Each mode of production was distinctive but not unique; each shared characteristics with the others. The broadest categories were antagonistic and nonantagonistic modes of production. Prigozhin's chief interest was the antagonistic modes, whose common characteristics were "monopolistic possession of tools and instruments of production by one part of society." The possessors drew the actual producers into one or another form of dependence. Thus each mode of production has its corresponding "forms of exploitation" (18).

There were three antagonistic modes of production and, consequently, three such social formations—slaveowning society, feudalism, and capitalism (15).[11] Thus the distinguishing characteristics that Prigozhin emphasized and with which the working historian presumably should concern himself were not the instruments of production—the level of technology—but the forms of exploitation. Slavery was the simplest form of expropriation: the labor force itself was an instrument of production (20). A more complex and higher form was feudalism: the actual producer had his own instruments of production, but a nonproductive class monopolized the land, the real basis of wealth. Extra-economic compulsion was necessary to expropriate the producers. Capitalists required only economic compulsion, the wage system, to expropriate the producers (28, 81).

This doctrine was a more comprehensive and subtle depiction of the historical process than the one that governed the creation of Pokrovskii's synthesis. It armed Soviet historians with a fresh perspective for examining current problems. The most notable of these, once the national school was reestablished, was the problem of Russian feudalism. All societies at a certain stage of development bear characteristics of this formation. Each society manifested these traits in its own way. Thus each feudal society is in some respects distinctive, but no feudal society is wholly unique. The distinctive features derived from both the traditions of a given society and the conscious action of individuals. Hence this doctrine restored the nation, the state, and the exceptional individual as effective historical agents. They determined the specific form of the socioeconomic formation in each society. The doctrine then was deterministic, but neither mechanistic nor fatalistic.

The doctrine had both strengths and weaknesses when applied to world history or to Russian history. Its chief strength was its breadth, its ability to perceive any specific problem in the light of a vision of the past and future, almost under the aspect of eternity. One of its principal weaknesses was its rigid delimitation of phases of development and the application of this pattern to all societies. It may be that Marx himself considered the pattern of European evolution unique rather than universal (Lichtheim, 1961:154). Another weakness was the well-known difficulty in demonstrating that material production developed as an independent variable.

As regards Russia, the doctrine was at once liberating and stultifying. It was liberating in that it resulted in a refinement of the problems of feudalism that had troubled the minds of numerous Russian historians in the twentieth century, including Pavlov-Silvanskii, Iushkov, Grekov, and Pokrovskii. By calling attention to uniformities on a European scale, the doctrine presented Russian history within a framework broader than national history. It employed the terms nation and class in such fashion as to show the limits of both concepts. The presence of Russian feudalism could be affirmed without stretching the facts of Russian history to fit the Procrustean bed of French feudalism. It sufficed for historians to discover traces of the essential characteristics of the feudal model; they need not deny the distinctive features of the Russian past—the simultaneous existence of centralized monarchy and serfdom, and even perhaps the exceptional power of the state at certain stages of its development; nor need they identify Western absolutism and Russian autocracy, to argue as Pokrovskii had that the Russian state was normal in that it was the instrument of social classes.

The new doctrine was stultifying in that it led to the conclusion that feudalism existed in Russia from the ninth to the twentieth century. It thus rendered inexplicable the immense changes in Russian culture in those centuries and the variegated pattern of twentieth-century Russian culture. Such a conclusion implied that diverse personalities like St. Sergius, Peter the Great, and Alexander Herzen derived from the same mode of production. Even allowing for subhypotheses concerning stages within a formation, or rudiments and vestiges of other formations, such a conclusion implicitly denied the economy the role in social change that it probably deserves.

Last Writings

Pokrovskii wrote more than a dozen articles in 1931. Although some were ceremonial addresses and prefaces, others were serious works, the outcome of study and reflection, that, taken together, constitute a reconsideration of his entire historical synthesis. It was a year of intense intellectual activity. Pokrovskii continued to meet his seminar at the Institute of Red Professors, even though his health drastically reduced his activity in the Communist Academy and its branches.

We have seen Pokrovskii as a combatant in the controversy regarding the Revolution of 1905, aiding and comforting Gorin and directly supporting him in his writings. It should be noted, however, that Gorin's ideas, even though designed to uphold Pokrovskii's authority, contradicted some of Pokrovskii's own interpretations. Pokrovskii, for example, had never previously held that Lenin had envisioned a transition to a socialist revolution in 1905,[12] but late in the day he equivocated. It seems that Pokrovskii was not fully at home with the new ideas. In a speech delivered on December 11, 1930, in the early stages of the Gorin-Iaroslavskii dispute, he stated: "It is absurd to imagine that Lenin intended to obtain a bourgeois republic and then to lie down and rest. Lenin said quite explicitly that on the day after the victory of the democratic revolution, we would immediately pass on to the socialist revolution."[13] At the same time he affirmed Iaroslavskii's contention:

> Socialism was advanced by us as our slogan in 1905. We never wrote a single proclamation, a single leaflet where we did not speak of socialism. To imagine that we called the working class to carry out a revolution in favor of the bourgeoisie is a piece of nonsense, invented by Trotsky. . . . *But we honestly stated that at that given stage of the revolution the bourgeoisie could not be overthrown. We did not propose to introduce socialism at once.* (*BH*, 2:305–6; emphasis added)

Pokrovskii thus answered yes and no to the question whether the Revolution of 1905 could have grown over into socialism.

A passage about the revolution in 1917 contains an even more curious lapse:

> The workers together with the peasants, and together with the soldiers, with the army, overthrew tsarism and would have overthrown the squires if the SR's and the Mensheviks had not come to the rescue and supporting them on both sides begged those gentlemen: please, don't go, be so kind. The squires took compassion on the SR's and the Mensheviks, agreed to stay and stayed another eight months, when they were at last kicked out for good, all of them together. (*BH*, 2:329)

This is nothing else than lapse into his 1923 interpretation of the Revolution, according to which it had in no sense ever been a bourgeois revolution. It was socialist *de facto* in March, *de jure* in November.

In the final stage of his career, Pokrovskii was again out of step, further than ever before. His position was equivocal, suggesting that he recoiled from the full development of the program for closing the gap between theory and practice. In May 1931, at a meeting convoked to implement the March 15 resolution of the Central Committee concerning the KA, Pokrovskii addressed the Society of Marxist Historians for the last time. He commended the society for its part in curbing and uprooting non-Marxist scholarship. "Here the society . . . acted completely in the spirit of the directive on the linking of theory and practice." His only regret was that the society had not played a larger role in these events and in the fall of the "dyed-in-the-wool reactionary historians." They "were taken care of by the appropriate institutions, and the frank confessions they have made relieved us of any obligation whatsoever to unmask them."[14]

Concerning the selection of research topics, he objected to specialists in European history

> sitting amidst the debris of the French Revolution or of the history of German Social-Democracy in the old days, or in other remote places, which both by their remoteness, and by the manner in which they are being investigated, represent a break between theory and practice. Here chronology is not the question at issue. (1931c:7)

He went on to enumerate what he considered to be the urgent questions. They included "feudalism, the natural economy, and even the question of tribal customs as it relates to the study of the peoples of the USSR. . . . The question is not one of chronology, but of approach. . . ."

> Unless we can solve these many concrete questions . . . our historical work can easily degenerate into polemics that are quite superficial, requiring no historical knowledge. If such degeneration be allowed, one fine day we may hear this question: why do we have historians here at all—the all-party press handles this kind of thing magnificently. (1931c:7)

Again, the rhetoric was radical, but the program was conservative. If only contemporary themes are treated, "historical works can easily degenerate into polemics." It is not evident from this speech in itself that Pokrovskii felt reservations about the dominant trend—exclusive study of recent political problems—but taken in connection with other statements, it is the most plausible conclusion.

In a popular article written for the first issue of the journal *Bor'ba klassov,* Pokrovskii wrote:

> Why is it necessary to study history? Many consider that it is by no means necessary—that it is necessary only to study the contemporary scene; or that history serves only as entertainment, or, at best, as a "precept." If one says that without some historical education . . . one cannot be a Marxist, some people just stare. Recently there was a dispute about whether history should be taught in schools, even though Lenin insistently and absolutely demanded this. (1931a:1)

In his reconsideration of merchant capital, Pokrovskii expressed dismay at "the fact that in our universities, Communist universities, and even in the Institute of Red Professors, very little attention is paid to the middle ages (the Marxist cannot afford to ignore even them!)" (*BH,* 1:289). In his preface to the tenth edition of the *Brief History of Russia,* written on July 15, 1931, Pokrovskii commented on the state of Russian historiography. Noting the abundance of fresh documents, he commented that they were "still *raw* material, and it looks as if it will have to wait some time before our young historians, who are much more keen on enquiries of a very different kind, have digested it with the aid of Marxist-Leninist methods" (*BH,* 1:11).

These passages are not, of course, outspoken denunciations of the course of events on the historical front, but considering the immediate circumstances under which Pokrovskii wrote them, they can be said to constitute an equivocation regarding the wholesale subordination of research to current needs of state and party organs.

Pokrovskii's review in *Bol'shevik* (1930a) of Trotsky's autobiography, *My Life,* represents another curious lapse on his part. It is a bristling, sardonic essay, in its meanness closer to a Stalinist diatribe than anything Pokrovskii had ever written. Yet only one very naive or one schooled in aesopian communication could have included the following passages:

> Our party is proletarian—at its head cannot stand a philistinish individualist, in as much as his philistinish individualism did not burn itself out fully in the fire of proletarian revolution. . . . Can a person enjoy the confidence of the *party* who does not deserve any *personal* confidence? A person not a single word of whose can be relied upon?
>
> Trotsky did not and could not lose power from such a single cause [untimely illness], for he did not and could not possess such power over the Bolsheviks. For our party is not a feudal fief and did not delegate power *over itself* to any single person. (1930a: 144–45)

Despite occasional references to Stalin, there is evident an indisposition on Pokrovskii's part to laud the party's leader. His rectitude in its context is a failure to live up to his responsibilities as leader of the historical front. It involves only a small measure of speculation on our part to see in his remarks about Trotsky the employment of a rhetoric that could only have been distasteful to Stalin.

It should now be clear that Pokrovskii's views were always in a state of flux. He had adopted Vanag's theory of imperialism as a means of buttressing his interpretation of autocracy (merchant capitalism), but this theory had been a steppingstone to a new understanding of the Revolution. By affirming it normal and predictable for the Revolution to have been confined to Russia, Pokrovskii then had to review his understanding of agrarian history. He had been troubled by this problem for some time, and in his final articles on the Revolution of 1905, he came very close to rejecting explicitly his original analysis of peasant behavior in 1905. In a popular speech included as an appendix to his *Brief History*, he noted that shortly after the Revolution of 1905, the Free Economic Society published two volumes of letters from rural correspondents, which described peasant uprisings. The letters, he maintained, had "been arranged" to indicate that the kulaks had led the movement. Only after the Revolution, when he studied the problem anew, did he understand that "the movement was directed against the kulaks": "It was only against the squires that the peasants formed a united front; as soon as the latter were ousted, if only for a moment, the class struggle blazed up in the villages with extraordinary rapidity" (*BH*, 2:313).

In these remarks Pokrovskii endorsed the view that the peasants were enmeshed in capitalist, not feudal, relations. He implicitly apologized for ever having held the view that the kulaks led the struggle in the villages. He alluded to the sources as if to say that he had held incorrect views in the years when he depended on bourgeois sources—the letters of the Free Economic Society.

Pokrovskii's modification of his interpretation of the Revolution of 1905 bore implications for other components of his synthesis, most notably for his interpretation of imperialism. If the composition and struggle of the peasantry were those typical of capitalism, how could one uphold an interpretation of imperialism that stressed the dependent, underdeveloped character of Russia and assumed or implied the predominance of precapitalist relationships in the countryside? But it was not Pokrovskii's susceptibility to logic alone that caused him to rethink the matter. The political command expressed explicitly in the 1928 Comintern program and implicitly in the rapid-tempo industrialization embracing the entire population and summed up in the criticisms of his own writings also invited a response. Pokrovskii no doubt wished to be done with any assertion implying that Russia was underdeveloped, too backward to build socialism unaided.

Pokrovskii's last writing, an article written in November 1931 and published the following spring in the very issue of *Istorik-marksist* (1932) that commemorated his death, took up the matter. It was a review of an unsigned chapter in the second edition of volume 3 of *Istoria VKP*(b) edited by Iaroslavskii. Pokrovskii made much of the anonymity of the chapter, though he knew, in fact, that it was written by his former student A.L. Sidorov. It is a vigorous polemic, in which Pokrovskii sought to dissociate himself from Vanag's theory of imperialism, while turning the charge of Trotskyism back onto Sidorov. It is at the same time a complicated set of clever and subtle arguments that not only modified but amplified and refined Pokrovskii's meaning and marked a progressive stage in the discussion of imperialism. He introduced a number of new distinctions and new metaphors to describe the situation.

Pokrovskii began by reversing himself as to how one should study Russian imperialism. Whereas in 1929 he had recommended study of the role of the Russian Empire in world diplomacy, he now suggested that the central question was to decide whether modern forms of capitalism or only the more primitive forms had existed in Russia. "The essence of the matter is the question, did we have only comprodore capitalism [a primitive form derivative from foreign imperialism] . . . or did we have present, in more or less developed form, all the forms of European capitalism, including industrial and financial capitalism" (1932:19). The answer to this question would solve the problem of whether Russian imperialism was the kind that Lenin equated with the highest level of capitalism or with the military-feudal imperialism characteristic of merchant capitalism.

Pokrovskii's answer is complicated and a bit hazy. For reasons stated above, he could not affirm the predominance of primitive forms of capitalism, nor did he wish to capitulate to his detractors.

> Leninism affirms that in Russia (up to 1917) large capital "predominated" but was entangled with all sorts of pre-capitalist survivals. And, it should be added, the most modern forms of capitalism were enmeshed with very primitive forms. (1932:20)

Pokrovskii stipulated, quoting Lenin, that capitalist imperialism of the newest type predominated in Russia's relations with Persia and Mongolia. Generally, however, military-feudal imperialism predominated in Russia (1932:20). Did he then simply reaffirm his old thesis about the role of merchant capital? No. He further stipulated that Russia was backward only with respect to the most advanced capitalist countries. "Thus Russia was not only a capitalist country, but a country of monopoly capital, an *impe-*

rialist country. But among the imperialist countries it occupied a special place" (1932:19). In other words, "not being a 'hireling,' Russia was also not a fully equal, independent member of the anti-German imperialist coalition" (1932:16). Russia was "an 'unequal partner,' a 'junior' member. The policy of the 'firm' was set not by it [Russian imperialism], but it was obliged to subordinate itself to this policy. Russia, in comparison with England, France, Germany, the United States, and Japan, was a backward imperialist country" (1932:18–19).

In Pokrovskii's final version, then, Russia's backwardness was not an absolute condition. He situated Russia near or above the middle of a continuum between backward and advanced countries. Though subordinate in her policies, she fitted into the category of advanced societies.

On reflecting on the significance of his own work on imperialism, Pokrovskii sought to deny that he had provided grist for those who affirmed Russia's backwardness. He partly misrepresented his own legacy in so doing. "I, of course, never denied this [the existence of bank capital in Russia]—on the contrary, I persistently stressed the role of bank capital in Russia between the first revolution and the war" (1932:21). If this can be understood as a claim that his theory of imperialism had brought to the fore the importance of modern capitalism, it is untrue. Although there are isolated passages that suggest this, the burden of his effort was to prove the contrary—the feebleness of modern forms of capitalism. He had argued, especially since his encounter with Slepkov's theory of the "social regeneration of autocracy," the predominance of merchant capital. In the end he came close to asserting an absurdity—urging that the significance of his theory of *merchant capital* was the stress that it placed on *finance capital*.

These two modifications of Pokrovskii's synthesis required further revisions. Just as important, the discussion of socioeconomic formations impelled a reformulation of the conception of merchant capitalism and even his theory of the state. Late in the hour and on the basis of an intensive study of Lenin's writings, Pokrovskii undertook to salvage what he could of his system in order to avoid the erosion of his reputation and to further renew his mandates as leader of the historical front.

As with Pokrovskii's final statement on imperialism, he grudgingly and halfheartedly revised his ideas, claiming that he was reaffirming his own views while merely removing rhetorical exaggerations. He insisted that in its essentials his system had "never departed from Lenin's" (*BH*, 1:13, 284). He upheld the validity of the essentials of his synthesis in his plea to the Central Committee on February 5, 1931:

> The "schema" of Pokrovskii mainly concerns the history of Russia up to the Revolution . . . *the development of capitalism.* It

seeks to demonstrate that capitalism is not a phenomenon brought
to us [from without], which arose either owing to the influence of
the West, or owing to autocracy, "which implanted" here industry and commerce, but [that it] had deep national roots. Merchant
capital began to take shape here even in the second half of the
sixteenth century; the rudiments of industrial capitalism, *i.e.* capitalist production stem from the beginnings of the nineteenth century. By 1905 Russia was already a country "of relatively highly
developed capitalism" (Lenin). (Lutskii, 1965:364)

Pokrovskii affirmed that his synthesis was "fully Marxist and Leninist,"
but he conceded that

to arrive at such a formulation as that autocracy was "merchant
capital in Monomakh's cap" means to obscure completely the
feudal base *of production,* and in this is the entire essence. Autocracy in the eighteenth century undoubtedly relied on merchant
capital and in part met its requirements in foreign policy. But in
itself autocracy was the dictatorship of feudal land-owning and
not merchant capital. (Lutskii, 1965:364)

In seeking to draw out the national roots of the Russian Revolution,
Pokrovskii tampered with the fundamentals of his system. Up to this
point, however, we can still discern his underlying theme—the state as a
creature of social forces.

More, indeed, was at issue than rhetorical exaggerations. Pokrovskii
seemed to acknowledge as much when he said to his students: "Is this
final conception of mine free from error? I cannot guarantee that. It is
free from those errors I have had time to notice and to correct, but there
may be others that I have not yet noticed" (*BH,* 1:282). In a number of
writings and addresses, some of them published posthumously,[15] Pokrovskii elaborated his reinterpretation of autocracy. While in the process
of liquidating his old synthesis, Pokrovskii embraced certain ideas that
suggested the outline of a new synthesis. What is remarkable is that the
new synthesis foreshadowed the one that was to emerge with the revival
of the national school of Russian historiography.

What was this final conception? First of all, Pokrovskii disavowed the
very term *merchant capitalism,* designating it an "illiterate expression."
One can only speak about "merchant capital"; "capitalism is a system
of *production,* and merchant capital produces nothing" *(BH,* 1:289).
That is to say, merchant capital should not be thought of as a socioeconomic formation. The purpose of this redefinition was to underline the
significance of feudalism in Russia. He described the underlying reality
of modern Russian history as the transformation and disintegration of
feudal society and the gradual emergence of capitalist relations within it.

Pokrovskii suggested a reconsideration of the chief events of Russian history in the light of this new perspective. For example, he rejected his older view that the Pugachev Rebellion had been a "bourgeois revolution of the epoch of merchant capital." "In reality the *Pugachevshchina* was a typical rebellion of the feudal peasants, one of the last uprisings of this type in European history." Only in the slightest degree was it a result of the development of capitalism. "One must emphasize that there was an intensification of *feudal* exploitation, intensification of *barshchina* and other feudal obligations" (*BK,* 1932, 4:36–37).

It was too late in life, there simply was not enough time, for Pokrovskii to reconsider his treatment of Russian intellectual history. Yet from the following statement it is evident that he considered a revision in order:

> As concerns ideology, the bourgeoisie existed . . . as a scarcely discernible rudiment (Novikov, Radischev): not only was our literature up to the second half of the nineteenth century basically landlord (Pushkin, Turgenev, L. Tolstoi), but so also were our publicists (Kavelin, Chicherin and the Slavophiles); the epoch corresponding to the French "age of encyclopedists" took place in the 1860s.[16]

Thus in the treatment of particular historical events, such as the Pugachev Rebellion, and in the delineation of trends in intellectual history, Pokrovskii recast his interpretations to a considerable degree.

Another element in Pokrovskii's final outline should be considered here—the social evolution of autocracy. Here we find Pokrovskii employing the perspective of feudalism to provide grounds for his assertion that in 1905 the mass of peasants turned against the kulaks as well as against the landlords. In this connection, one can observe the connection between this new perspective of feudalism and Pokrovskii's final interpretation of the 1905 Revolution and imperialism, both of these being crucial components of the theory of growing over. The most important social process, viewed from the standpoint of disintegrating feudalism, was the immersion of the peasants in capitalist relations:

> In 1917 there still remained a considerable amount of feudalism. Nevertheless, to describe the Russian economy at the latter date or indeed at any time after 1861 as "natural" economy would mean utterly to ignore the facts of history and the teachings of Lenin.[17]

The Reform of 1861 was not simply "an episode in the substitution of the bourgeois mode of production for the serf (or feudal) method of production." Its significance was its impact on the lower classes: the peasants were transformed into producers of commodities and thus made dependent on the market (288). Pokrovskii apparently considered this pattern of development a by-product of the measures adopted by the state to transform its social base.

When Pokrovskii wrote about capitalism, he did not have in mind present-day indices of industrial civilization: per capita production and consumption, the number of hospital beds per thousand of the population, level of technology, and so on. He meant that the peasant had become dependent on the market and subject to the cycles of world trade. More important, he meant that class warfare was rife in the villages, that the vast majority of the peasants fought or could be led into a fight against capitalism. According to his analysis, by 1905 the rural bourgeoisie, though small in numbers, predominated in the villages. On the other hand, the rural proletariat amounted to half the population in the countryside.

> *Almost three-quarters* of all the peasants were by the end of the nineteenth century drawn into the sphere of commodity production. There remains only one-fourth for the natural economy. What room is there left for speaking of the *predominance of pre-commodity relations*. (288)

Slepkov finally carried the day! Perhaps it would be more accurate to write that Pokrovskii, under the prodding of his students, finally comprehended and assimilated Lenin's analysis of agrarian relations. Pokrovskii's evolution on this point has an ironic twist. In emphasizing the role of merchant capital, he had stressed the backwardness and homogeneity of the peasants. Merchant capital locked the peasants in feudal relationships. They were struggling, under the leadership of the kulaks, for private property and the establishment of capitalism. All this was now reversed when, in stressing the "feudal essence" of Imperial Russia, he brought out the advanced character of social relations among the peasants with the stratification in the villages making them ripe for a revolution *against* capitalism. We might say that Pokrovskii committed himself to a thesis "refuted by life itself." If the peasants had followed an anti-capitalist course, why had Lenin in 1917 found it necessary to place the land of the nobility at their disposal? Why had he not immediately created collective farms?

Let us consider finally Pokrovskii's political theory. In his original synthesis of Russian history he had employed the concept of merchant capital chiefly to demonstrate and reiterate the class character of Russian autocracy. It is in connection with this idea that one can observe how far-reaching were the modifications of Pokrovskii's system as a result of his reconsideration of autocracy in the light of the new perspective on feudalism. In the preface to the final edition of his *Brief History,* he wrote, "I have to confess—it ['polemical heat' concerning merchant capital] tended to obscure the feudal essence of the Russian landlord state" (1, 13). Not only had he assigned power to the wrong class; a more profound principle was at issue:

> Finally, I have to admit that the early version of my conceptions did not sufficiently take into account the fact that the political superstructure may be *relatively independent* of the economic foundation. (284)

The relative independence of the state: Is this anything other than capitulation to what Pokrovskii had dubbed the supraclass theory of the state? It is not quite that, but rather a reformulation of the notion of the class character of the state in a manner that gives considerable ground to Chicherin, Kliuchevskii, and others. Pokrovskii continued:

> Feudalism implies . . . a definite *political system,* a definite state form. My conception of feudalism consequently contains a political component: the close connection of the political power with landowning and a hierarchy of landowners. (285)

Presumably Pokrovskii meant that the feudal monarchy was a weak state circumscribed by the power of landowning magnates. Under feudalism, he wrote, "there was plenty of *arbitrary* rule, but no *absolute* rulers" (289).

The Russian feudal monarchy underwent significant modification in the seventeenth and eighteenth centuries, he continued, quoting Lenin and Engels copiously. Under Peter I a national market came into being linking the feudal monarchy and commodity production. "The modified form assumed by the feudal state under the action of commodity production was the *absolute monarchy* or to be still more precise—the bureaucratic monarchy" (289). Such a state was typical in the period of the "disintegration of the feudal economy." Its three main attributes were a bureaucracy, a standing army, and taxation in money. In other words, the rationalization of the state permitted the monarch to liberate himself, at least in part, from dependence on the magnates. It was commodity production then, citing Lenin, that accounted for "the very great independence of Tsarism and of the bureaucracy—from Nicholas II right down to the last police officer" (290). Even though feudal relations predominated, the state had "become linked through its administrative machine, the bureaucracy, with . . . the rising bourgeois world" (291). The actual link was somewhat obscure. Clearly the state was not the tool of the bourgeois world; it was not simply the executive committee of the bourgeoisie. The state was, however, in some sense dependent on the bourgeois world.

Moreover, "Tsarism . . . had a constant tendency to develop in the direction of a bourgeois monarchy."[18] By this Pokrovskii implied that the state had certain interests of its own—to enhance its independence and enlarge the scope of its activities. This is probably what Pokrovskii meant by his assertion quoted above that "the political superstructure may be *relatively independent* of the economic foundation." The state sought to nurture those social elements that had engendered and could further its relative independence. In short, it cultivated the development of capitalism. If this interpretation of what Pokrovskii meant by the tendency of Tsarism to evolve in the direction of a bourgeois monarchy is correct, then clearly he attributed to the state a creative role in social evolution.

Although one could argue that Pokrovskii's willingness to countenance the relative independence of the state constitutes a reversion to the supraclass theory, this probably would be an overstatement. Yet clearly his final theory contradicts earlier statements about the class-dominated character of the state. He has, to say the least, watered down his earlier conception, and in the light of his final observation, the meaning of "class dominated" is questionable. One is justified in stating that Pokrovskii finally terminated his conflict against the supraclass theory. And one may conclude that he severed the red thread that tied together his interpretation of Russian history. Nothing that was distinctively Pokrovskiian remained.

Capitulation

Why did Pokrovskii change his mind so drastically? Ambition, duty, and fear were among the motives that must be mentioned. In a battle not of his own choosing, he was for himself and against Iaroslavskii. He sought to uphold his reputation as a historian and his legacy as a founder of Soviet historical scholarship. And Pokrovskii was a disciplined party scholar. He took pride in acting in accord with standards he had helped to establish. One cannot escape the feeling, however, that the drastic character of his subservience marked it off from what he had originally meant by service to the cause of the proletariat. As in the closing of RANION's Institute of History, he was allowing himself to be used in a new way. That is why fear ought to be brought into the account. To be sure, an atmosphere of calm prevailed compared with that of 1938. Yet high stakes were evident: he knew that life and death issues were involved. Concern for his good name, for the comfort of his family, the professional status and safety of his associates and students affected him.

In addition to ambition, duty, and fear, respect for evidence and regard for truth motivated Pokrovskii. There is no basis to doubt that research, including work by his own students, on such matters as Russian imperialism and agrarian history persuaded him to change his conclusion. And there can be little doubt that the concept of merchant capital had lost some of its luster in his own eyes. Yet there is a touch of fraud in Pokrovskii's final writings. He responded to his critics differently than he would have if he had not been seeking to appease those who held power over him. His new system, which gave so much ground to or was by implication a capitulation to the supraclass theory of the state, and the theory of cultural revolution he had enunciated in connection with the closing of RANION's Institute of History, seem to contain assertions that he did not believe.

Pokrovskii's behavior was law-governed or logical in the sense that his was not a unique dilemma or merely a personal problem. It was a single instance of a dilemma widespread among old Bolsheviks. Even though he accepted collectivization of agriculture and did not oppose Stalin's rise to power, he had to pause before the discrepancy between the original promise and the emerging definition of socialism. Pokrovskii was responding to the same situation Piatakov found himself in when, taunted by his capitulation to Stalin, he delivered his now famous peroration:

> What was the October revolution, what indeed was the Communist party, but a miracle. . . . The essential characteristic of this party is that it is bounded by no laws, it is always extending the realm of the possible until nothing becomes impossible. Nothing is inadmissible for it, nothing unrealizable. For such a party a true bolshevik will readily cast out from his mind ideas in which he has believed for years. A true bolshevik has submerged his personality in the collectivity, "the party" to such an extent that he can make the necessary effort to break away from his own opinions and convictions, and can honestly agree with the party—that is the test of a true bolshevik.[19]

Pokrovskii's mutilation of his synthesis of Russian history was not identical to Piatakov's response but was akin to it.

Both Pokrovskii and Piatakov's behavior can be thought of as steppingstones to the pathetic if still heroic scene in 1938 when Bukharin stood in the witness box during the Trial of Anti-Soviet Rightists and Trotskyites. Bukharin's allowing himself to be used by Stalin, his persuading himself that his mouthing of Stalinist fictions would provide an occasion to convey the truth about his own destiny and the fate of the Revolution (Katkov, 1962), resembles Pokrovskii's persuading himself that only rhetorical exaggerations were at issue in modifying his system and that in eschewing what he was to call "academicism," he was serving a higher truth. Neither Pokrovskii's nor Bukharin's responses were the only ones possible, however. For example, Lunacharskii, with-holding himself from the cultural revolution, refused to degrade the intel-lectual traditions and national aspirations to which he was committed, even though he thus sacrificed his position as Peoples' Commissar of Enlightenment.

Pokrovskii's health deteriorated sharply in June 1931, and he was frequently hospitalized thereafter. Still he was active, writing and editing documents on the Civil War and on the outbreak of World War I. He interrupted his work one day to reply to an old friend:

> Your letter aroused so many memories about 1906 and 7, when I, no longer a very young man, was a young party member and there was still so much to happen. Now before me stands nothing but the crematorium. But along the road to that establishment, I hope still once more to tweak the respectable imperialists, by publishing the documents of their war. (Lutskii, 1965:368)

Polina Vinogradskaia, a comrade who shared memories with Pokrov-skii of the October days in Moscow, visited him in the hospital: "I sowed dragon seeds" she recalls him saying, "but raised only fleas. And what's more, I'm the only one they bite."[20]

On December 10, Pokrovskii braved the Moscow winter to travel the few blocks from the Kremlin hospital to the Bol'shoi Theater. There he joined the tenth anniversary celebration of the Institute of Red Profes-sors. He had headed the commission that organized the celebration and shared with Iaroslavskii and others the honor of belonging to its presid-ium. This was Pokrovskii's last public appearance, his last address. It was a rambling set of reminiscences about the good old days, about battles won. As an expression of probably both fear and gratitude he praised Stalin throughout. He had lost sight of any part of himself that failed to coincide with the image of an old Bolshevik, militant and faith-ful. Yet there was something of a malcontent in him to the very end. He chided the young historians about excessive specialization, perhaps guessing that he belonged to the last generation that would attempt a personal synthesis of the entire course of Russian history. And in beat-ing the drum of class struggle, he neglected to use the term partiinost'. Perhaps a reflection in a curved mirror brought to his mind his original understanding of revolutionary historiography. "My advice to you is not to follow the academic path as we did, for academicism contains within itself recognition of . . . objective scholarship, which is non-existent" (*Pamiaty*, 1932:67). He contrasted "bourgeois academicism" with the commitment to a high and noble cause and urged the students to eschew the former. But he failed to claim that the nobility of the cause imparted a higher objectivity to one's work.

Were his words heeded? We may doubt the stenographic notation that his speech was received with "prolonged applause" and then followed by the singing of the "International." We can only guess what must have been the noise level in the great theater as he took leave: "Comrades, I have spoken considerably longer than I intended to, and longer it seems than I can hold your attention. Therefore, I finish" (*Pamiaty*, 1932:71). On April 10, 1932, after sending greetings to his friends and even to some former students who had become foes, he died.

Epilogue
Pokrovskii's Double Death

"Pokrovskii died twice" is the phrase used by a prominent German scholar (Mehnert, 1952) to describe the strange career of this historian and to suggest the enigmatic character of Soviet historical writing. Pokrovskii's first death was the outcome of a long struggle with cancer. It is customary in the West to describe his funeral as reported in *Pravda* and to enumerate the honors heaped upon him. Few individuals had received such splendid public tribute. Few historians had the leaders of a great state act as their pallbearers and deliver orations on behalf of them and their craft. It is also customary to describe Pokrovskii's second death—the protracted, ignominious process in which his life's work was discredited and deracinated, and which made a mockery of his first death. Not only were Pokrovskii's views refuted, but the period of his activity was described by the term *pokrovshchina*—era of the wicked deeds of Pokrovskii.

Pokrovskii died twice, but his death has not proved final. His influence has been revived in the Soviet Union. Even though his system is still discredited, he remains a troublesome figure, a stimulus to the thinking of historians trying to fathom the legacy of Stalinism.

In 1932—while still untombed—Pokrovskii became a center of controversy. A subdued controversy, it was attended only by the initiated. The press hailed him as an old-Bolshevik hero, but it is easy to praise a man just dead. Yet even at Pokrovskii's funeral there were signs that he had fallen from the lofty eminence he held in 1928, when his colleagues and public officials had lauded him as a creative historian. At his funeral, they praised him but not so much for how he wrote history as for his militance. He was presented as a model of self-criticism (*Pamiaty*, 1932: 37–38; passim). Pokrovskii's legacy was troublesome. It was so during his lifetime, immediately after his death, and during the late 1930s when it became clear that Stalin was the great Bolshevik historian. During the anti-cosmopolitanism campaign after World War II, and even at the present time, it has been impossible for Soviet historians to assign Pokrovskii a place in the history of their craft without raising a host of interlocking political and ideological problems.

In the first stage of the debate concerning this legacy, up to May 16, 1934, Anna Mikhailovna Pankratova emerged as Pokrovskii's champion. In an article published very shortly after his death, she lauded him as "the greatest universal scholar of our time." She considered him "one of the most talented warrior-historians who educated our party." While she praised and defended Pokrovskii, she drew attention to his "mistakes and exaggerations." His *History of the Revolutionary Movement* more than any other of his works, she conceded, contained "errors, exaggerations, risky assertions and historically incorrect analogies." Pankratova did not conceal the fact that her own assertions about him were controversial: "Very many ironically note the 'ease' with which M.N. Pokrovskii 'today rejects that which he defended yesterday.'" To her this was part of his greatness, his capacity for self-criticism (1932:29, 32, 35).

While Pankratova's article was openly partisan, assertions of others were frequently understated and consisted of innuendoes, some of them extremely subtle. For example, the republication of his works after his death was an event in the debate. They became the victim of tendentious editing. In the posthumous edition of his speech delivered on the occasion of his sixtieth birthday, the statement "I am still not a genuine proletarian historian" was expurgated.[1]

A. Lomakin, who had been a student-critic in Pokrovskii's seminar, spoke up for Iaroslavskii. He found a way to denigrate Pokrovskii with laudatory phrases by applying the concept of the "Leninist stage." Soviet historiography had become truly Leninist only in 1931, as a result of Stalin's letter.[2] Pokrovskii's works, by implication, were pre-Leninist. Pankratova seized upon this interpretation and forcefully rejected it. As if to forestall just this accusation, she treated this matter emphatically in her first article:

> M.N. Pokrovskii considers himself, and was in fact, a pupil of Lenin. It was precisely his service to treat historical scholarship on the basis of Leninist doctrine. Being a historian in the most exact and complete sense of the word, treating questions, not only of the history of the peoples of the USSR, but of world history, M.N. was a brilliant example of the synthesizing historian from the standpoint of the working class. (1932:31)

In the same vein as Lomakin, I. Tokin, a member of the editorial board of *Bor'ba klassov*, criticized Pokrovskii by designating the period since Stalin's letter as the Leninist stage of Soviet historiography. He devoted an article to the virtues of historicism; in contrast, he reviled the evils of schematism, which he considered the worst form of voluntarism. It would be immediately evident to Soviet historians that this constituted an attack on Pokrovskii. To avoid any confusion, Tokin quoted Lenin's famous letter to Pokrovskii written on the occasion of the publication of the *Brief History*. Tokin cited only Lenin's proposal for improving the book by appending tables and made no mention of Lenin's praise. Tokin also commented on the exaggerated emphasis on political history in Soviet historiography (1932:47–48).

Tokin's jibes at Pokrovskii, even though they consisted mainly of veiled allusions and hints, clarify some of the underlying issues of the debate. It is evident that the issues that had earlier occupied Soviet historians had disappeared. First, the rout of the old specialists had been complete. Some of them were brought back into the historical profession, but only to work as Marxists or, at least, to embellish their works with citations from the masters. Second, the theory of growing over had become an assumption of Soviet historiography no longer open to challenge. The debate about Pokrovskii suggests the beginning of a new era. Pokrovskii, nevertheless, remained a revered public figure. Perhaps his highest tribute was the renaming of Moscow State University in his honor.[3]

After Pokrovskii's death problems connected with the teaching of history moved increasingly into the foreground. Historians became preoccupied with the writing of textbooks after the Commissariat of Education in 1931 expressed the intention of replacing courses in social studies (*obshchestvovedenie*) with a systematic history course in the secondary schools.[4] This is the context of Tokin's condemnation of "schematism." Social studies teachers had concerned themselves mainly with the definition, delineation, and comparison of universalized structures such as the proletariat, feudalism, and revolution. Pokrovskii's writings were not schematic in this sense, but his name was associated with the teaching of social studies. Teachers were now urged to talk about events in the lives of particular proletariats, to depict the distinctive qualities of feudalism as manifested in individual nations, and to narrate the causes, processes, and consequences of particular revolutions.

Once again events in the field of history embodied trends in evidence throughout Soviet society—the abandonment of revolutionary innovation in favor of traditional techniques and forms. The shortcomings of the schematic approach in comparison with the sweep of a narrative line were becoming evident to Soviet authorities. Leading historians devoted their energies to textbooks; party leaders underlined their concern by instructing historians at an official Kremlin reception.[5] Their concern became a drive for change on May 16, 1934, with the publication of the famous decree "On the Teaching of Civic History." This directive in the name of the Central Committee and the Council of Peoples' Commissars was a concise condemnation of schematism and a celebration of narrative history. Two more decrees were issued on August 8 and 9 but withheld from the public for the time being.[6] Signed by Stalin, Kirov, and Zhdanov, these were specific directives for the implementation of the May 16 decree. They made adverse judgment about draft textbooks on European history and Russian history prepared under the supervision of Lukin and Vanag. These latter decrees were read and known by word of mouth only to a very small group of historians.[7] Though the decrees did not mention Pokrovskii, it was evident that the party opted for his detractors. This is evident, among other places, in the increasing reticence of Pankratova's praise of Pokrovskii in her perennial summations of Soviet scholarship.[8]

The decrees were published in *Pravda* only on January 27, 1936, in an article that condemned Pokrovskii—the first public repudiation ("Na fronte," 1936). Articles by Bukharin (1936) and Radek (1936) accompanied it. Only in 1937 did the party judge one of the new textbooks prepared in the competition reasonably acceptable for its purposes ("Postanovlenie," 1937). Then in 1938, after the purges and the fall of Postyshev, the Central Committee for the first time carried the denigration of Pokrovskii to its own resolutions ("O Postanovke," 1954). Though under preparation since 1936, it was not until 1939–40 that the great monuments of Stalinist culture, two works of monumental distemper, *Against the Historical Conception of M.N. Pokrovskii* and *Against the Anti-Marxist Conception of M.N. Pokrovskii*, were published (*Protiv:* 1939–40).

Why were seven years required for historians to prepare a satisfactory textbook? First, they had not only to popularize and simplify the existing understanding of the course of Russian history, they had to elaborate it. Second, the national theme in Soviet culture after 1934 must have created emotional obstacles for the leadership that had taught or studied in the IKP. But these answers are unduly general. The Marxist leadership had a wealth of talent to draw upon; the theory of growing over was sufficiently comprehensive to guide the creation of a new synthesis without delay. Moreover, the historians readily acquired the new rhetoric growing up around the term fatherland (*otechestvo*). Those who had been close to Pokrovskii were by this time accustomed to repressing personal feelings for the sake of fulfilling current tasks. A third consideration may clarify the matter further. How were historians expected to treat the Soviet period? How should one treat the Right Opposition at a time when it seems that members of the Central Committee opposed the purging of Bukharin? Only Stalin could answer these questions, which he did both in the purges and in the *Short Course*, his own history of the party, published in 1938.

For whatever reasons, it was decided that the governing historians needed assistance. The former bourgeois professors attained increasing prominence in the profession after 1934. Then after the assassination of Kirov late in 1934 it seems that all party historians were under suspicion. The Communist Academy was closed in 1936 and the Institute of History was amalgamated with the various historical bodies of the Academy of Sciences. Many former non-Marxists, now having been instructed in historical materialism and having mastered at least its terminology, were brought from Leningrad to Moscow. In the years following, the graduates of RANION's Institute of History had easier access to better positions and a higher probability of staying alive (Sidorov, 1964:132).

The revival of the nationalist school and the renunciation of Pokrovskii were presided over by none other than Emelian Iaroslavskii. Beginning in 1935, we find him making major pronouncements about the tasks of historians. Less than ever before these pronouncements state themes of research and resolve pivotal problems of interpretation; more than ever, they indicate the status of individual historians. Zaidel fell in connection with the Leningrad purge following Kirov's assassination (*IM*, 1935, 5–6:201). On the pages of *Istorik-marksist*, Iaroslavskii attacked, among others, Vanag, Fridliand, Nevskii, Prigozhin, and Tomsinskii (Iaroslavskii, 1936:13–14). Pankratova he chided for "rotten liberalism," the toleration of wicked opinions. Then later he denounced Gorin, Tatarov, Knorin, Popov, and Bubnov (*IM*, 1938, 5:5). Finally, in 1938, Lukin fell (*IM*, 1938, 6:200). Iaroslavskii was made a member of the Academy of Sciences, and he became chief editor of *Istorik-marksist*, now titled *Istoricheskii zhurnal*. Sidorov became the academic secretary of the Institute of History. Mints became a corresponding member of the Academy of Sciences; Pankratova, after a brief exile (Druzhinin, 1967:56), returned as a leader and collaborated with Iaroslavskii in preparation of the two volumes dedicated to the denigration of Pokrovskii. The assignment was carried out hand-in-hand with the defamation of Pokrovskii's earlier non-Marxist opponents—Grekov, Bakhrushin, Druzhinin, and others.

Pankratova, who changed sides under pressure, was one of the few of Pokrovskii's followers to outlive Stalin. There is a redeeming irony in the fact that it was Pokrovskii's critics, most of whom were aligned with Iaroslavskii, who initiated Pokrovskii's rehabilitation after Stalin's death. To Mints, Sidorov, Dubrovskii, and Nechkina belongs the honor of raising the issue after 1953. Probably Pankratova deserves mention; she changed sides again just before her death in 1957; she was among those working for the de-Stalinization of Soviet historiography.

It was not the senior historians who opposed Pokrovskii's rehabilitation but younger men who were no doubt scandalized by the entire campaign against Stalin (Enteen, 1969). As early as 1957 they had worked out an interpretation that retained the essential meaning of Stalin's views while employing the rhetoric fashionable after the Twentieth Party Congress. In due course, they revived and refined Lomakin's argument about the Leninist stage, contending that only under Stalin's auspices did the work of Marxist historians become truly Leninist. With the fall of Khrushchev in 1964, a shadow fell across Pokrovskii. The call for objectivity was taken to mean less discussion of the "cult of personality." The editorial of *Voprosy istorii* marking the fiftieth anniversary of the October Revolution not only omitted the conventional censure of the cult, it spoke out against a nihilistic attitude toward the past that had allegedly emerged in the 1950s and early 1960s.

Soviet historians, in the course of and as a result of dispelling the fictions that Pokrovskii was an anti-Marxist historian and that Stalin was a great historian, have solved and posed a vast range of problems in the history of their fatherland. Surely the future historian will have no recourse to the notion of "de-rehabilitation."

Conclusions

At the end of the Civil War, and with the establishment of the New Economic Policy in 1921, the Communist Party caught its breath and then began to tighten its grip on society. But just as it sought to extend its influence, it was stricken with indecision about where to lead society. The indecision within the party resulted from the failure of Bolshevik tradition to provide a concrete program for a revolution confined to an underdeveloped country. This circumstance was the ground for the theory of socialism in one country. In the fall of 1924, at virtually the same time that Stalin put forth this theory, the decision was reached to create the Society of Marxist Historians. The activities of the society reflected both the will to lead and the indecision about where to lead society. It was essentially a vehicle to enhance the influence of Marxism, and it became an instrument for the stifling of opposition within the party.

The theory of socialism in one country was at once a program for the future and an interpretation of the past. In a sense, the SMH was the instrument for working out this theory as it applied to the past. Pokrovskii created the essentials of the theory of growing over by 1927. But it was in the period after 1928, after Stalin's defeat of the Right Opposition, that this theory bulked larger than ever in historical writing, cleansing the slate of all ideologically incompatible interpretations and compelling a reformulation of historical materialism. These are the most difficult years to fathom and Pokrovskii's activities the most elusive. He was at once the champion of the Marxist forces, their victim, their critic, and finally a displaced elder. His roles were so numerous that his career slips out of focus. One of the most arresting aspects at the outset of this period was Pokrovskii's vacillation—his truculent phrases and his civilized reluctance to act upon them—though finally he got in step. It testifies to the cunning of both reason and Stalin that Pokrovskii became the foremost symbol of this period and that its most deleterious characteristics came to be associated with his entire career.

I have sought to clarify the context and consequences of Stalin's intervention in 1931, but the question of why Stalin upheld Pokrovskii cannot be precisely answered. The matter clearly warrants further study. It should not be too great a surprise if someday archives reveal that the letter to *Proletarskaia revoliutsiia*, in the measure that it upheld Pokrovskii's authority, represented a defeat for Stalin. After all, the bare facts are that Pokrovskii's authority gradually disintegrated in the course of Stalin's triumph over his rivals. The letter to *Proletarskaia revoliutsiia* suddenly, if only temporarily, reversed this trend. The trend became evident again as Stalin gained absolute control over the party.

The year 1931 was a turning point, climaxing the previous four years and beginning the great reorientation that would result in the overthrow of Pokrovskii's legacy and the revival of the national school. The ground was cleared of old ideas and the foundation laid for a new synthesis. When the term monolithic was used to describe the new state of affairs, I did not mean to suggest that uniformity of opinion and approach had been achieved, which is not possible in an imperfect world. I meant merely that variety of opinion had lost legitimacy and that a hierarchical structure had been created to strive for unity. That is to say, the arrangements were not monolithic in a literal sense; that merely seems to be the best predicate to approximate the leaders' aspirations as summed up in the notion of partiinost'.

These arrangements were not inevitable; other conditions for Marxist scholars were imaginable. In my view, the existing arrangements derived from Stalin's understanding of socialism. My assumption is that pluralism and rivalry is a natural condition of the intellectual life, and sharp controversy is predictable in Soviet circumstances, where thought had to accommodate the unexpected isolation of the revolution. The subordination of scholarship to immediate political tasks, the mobilization of historians for factional purposes, and the dire personal consequences of controversy resulted from Stalin's intervention. When they realized what had happened, the Marxist scholars, wedded to the idea of ideological conflict, must have greeted with surprise arrangements that prohibited conflict. Yet Pokrovskii himself, by his manners, his attitudes, and in some respects by his words, helped to elaborate the notion of partiinost'.

The disintegration of Pokrovskii's synthesis of Russian history yields a number of conclusions. Pokrovskii revised his understanding of three major problems—the Revolution of 1905, imperialism, and merchant capitalism. The first two problems represented controversial aspects of the theory of growing over, and his revisions made him a conventional adherent of this theory.

Pokrovskii revised his interpretation of Imperial Russia (merchant capitalism) under the influence of this same theory of growing over. The crucial problem here was agrarian relations. Pokrovskii first presented the Russian Revolution as one instance of a universal socialist revolution. Once he accepted the isolation, or temporary isolation of the revolution in Russia, he was at a loss as to how he should explain this on the basis of his analysis of merchant capital. His theory was a muddle that seemed to countenance the view that Russia was moving away from revolution in the years after 1905, and that only World War I made the Revolution possible. Stressing the "feudal essence" of autocracy led Pokrovskii out of the impasse. The following picture emerged. The evolution of feudalism inevitably created the preconditions of a democratic revolution in Russia. Special circumstances existed which made possible the growing over of this democratic revolution into a socialist revolution. In the first place, this was a democratic revolution taking place in the era of imperialism. Second, the mass of impoverished peasants were enmeshed in capitalist relations and ripe for an uprising against capitalism. A radical working class led the revolution; through the Bolshevik party, it was possible to bring the great mass of poor peasants into an alliance with the workers. The moving forces of the revolution were anti-liberal or anti-capitalist. Moreover, the constellation of international circumstances, the fact that imperialism had made the entire world ripe for anti-capitalist revolution, enhanced the possibility of transforming the revolution into a socialist one. Pokrovskii's final depiction of Imperial Russia thus neatly dovetailed with the theory of growing over. He described agrarian relations in a manner that stressed the anti-capitalist character of the peasant revolution and thus supported the Bolshevik claim that it had the support of the vast majority of the people in October 1917.

Contemporary Soviet scholarship tends to judge Pokrovskii's historical writings merely by the degree to which they approximate present-day conclusions. A final evaluation will rest on studies of Pokrovskii's contributions to a variety of particular problems—the Decembrists, Pugachev, and so on. I wish merely to suggest that he enriched a great host of discussions. As concerns populism, he merely increased the clamor. In other discussions, such as the one on the outbreak of World War I, through his writing, editing, and teaching, he deepened and broadened this very important controversy. His final interpretation of the Russian Revolution posed methodological problems about the treatment of Lenin's writings that engage Soviet and Western historians to the present day.

In Chapter 2 I indicated some of the defects of Pokrovskii's synthesis—his sociologism and his application of the concept of merchant capitalism. In conclusion, some of the merits of his approach should be noted. The theory of merchant capital not only calls attention to certain continuities in Russian history, and remains a challenging hypothesis about the origins of autocracy, it brings out important similarities to evolutions elsewhere. By depicting it as a species of plantation life with respect to forces of production and organization of labor Pokrovskii enlarged the understanding of mercantilism, that important stage in the evolution of capitalism. Another virtue of Pokrovskii's work is that it was somehow a steppingstone to a new understanding of feudalism. The new theory was arrived at not just by rejecting Pokrovskii's, but by passing through his school. He was a bridge from Pavlov-Silvanskii to Grekov, Smirnov, and others.

But there lay at the heart of Pokrovsii's system a dogma. It is summed up in his assault on the supraclass theory of the state. He denied a generalization that few historians of Russia have been able to dispense with. In seeking a fresh perspective, he overshot the mark (*peregibal palku*). We can agree with his best critic, Rubinshtein, that he mechanically denied the views of his predecessors instead of mastering their work and transcending them in a higher synthesis.

The discussion of socioeconomic formations yields a definite conclusion. As stated previously, the collaboration of various factors necessitated a reconsideration of historical materialism. The immediate occasion of the debate was the discussion of Petrushevskii's theories and the incipient influence of Alphonse Dopsch, through which Soviet historians directly encountered the teachings of Max Weber. In particular they argued against the concept of the ideal type, which they sought to expose as bourgeois idealism and then to banish. Pokrovskii considered Weber's teaching a degenerate form of Rickertism expressing too great a concern with cultural values, which are subjective. The point is that the debate about socioeconomic formations never completely transcended the discussion of Petrushevskii. The problem of the ideal type remained at the heart of the discussion. This is suggested by the very fact that the term socioeconomic formation dominated the debate. Marx's historical materialism consisted of numerous conceptions including the economic base, the superstructure, social class, economic motivation of groups. Marx's version included the conception of the socioeconomic formation, but he did not emphasize it. In the Soviet version it was the glass through which all the other elements were viewed. It was non-Marxist historiography that posed the central problem of the discussion.

What Soviet Marxists discovered in Weber's thought was *fortuna,* a sense of the intractability and irony of the historical process. And they modernized historical materialism in the course of the discussion of socioeconomic formations by incorporating Western social scientists' concern with unconscious behavior and apparently gratuitous events. Even if history continued to be about how one formation inevitably replaces another, the modernized version stressed the variety of forms that the transition might take in any given society. Human will and fortuitous events inevitably affected historical transformations. In taking note of such categories, the new theory became sensitive to the possible effects of national traditions, the activity of the state, and the acts of exceptional individuals. Historical theory incorporated elements of Bolshevik politics.

Perhaps it is inaccurate to consider the socioeconomic formation a variant of the ideal type. One might just as well write, in view of Weber's lifelong encounter with historical materialism, that the ideal type was a variant of the socioeconomic formation. Perhaps the best formulation is that Weber's teachings and Soviet Marxism represented rival interpretations of classical Marxism. One may conclude at least that Soviet Marxism has been forged in contest with modern Western social theory.

If it was the struggle for leadership among historians that sent Pokrovskii's system out of its trajectory, then it was the theory of growing over that fixed its new course. This theory is a brilliant interpretation of the Russian Revolution even to one dissatisfied with its terminology and unsympathetic to the values implicit in it. It called attention to the interaction of various processes at work in an underdeveloped society under the impact of capitalism and to the various but not unlimited number of possibilities inherent in such a state of affairs. In particular, it stressed the importance both of international affairs and agrarian relations. Finally, it emphasized the role of leadership in such a fluid state of affairs.

But this theory is more than an interpretation of a past event. For one thing it was Lenin's theory of revolution. Lenin envisioned the possibility of a democratic revolution growing over into a socialist one, and he gradually worked out the tactics for achieving power in a backward society. He did not propose in 1917 or before that a communist regime in Russia could hold power indefinitely and build a socialist society. Of course, after the October Revolution, he bent every effort to hold power, while waiting for the revolution to spread westward.

Stalin's theory of growing over twisted Lenin's to fit the circumstance of socialism in one country. According to Stalin, as early as 1905 Lenin had formulated a theory of world revolution that included the provision of the building of socialism in backward Russia, clearly a tendentious and misleading interpretation of Leninism. Yet, following Stalin's lead, Soviet historians depicted the isolation of the revolution as being in conformity with Lenin's original expectation and as a confirmation of Marxism-Leninism. Lying at the heart of communist ideology and Soviet historiography, this theory is one of the most important justifications of Soviet power. As such it has withstood de-Stalinization without ever being in danger.

The fact that the theory of growing over stood behind the disintegration of Pokrovskii's classical synthesis is instructive, and the manner in which it disintegrated suggests further conclusions. That Pokrovskii's final views so remarkably anticipated that synthesis of the revived national school indicated a certain logic or regularity in the evolution of historiography. In 1932, the very year of Pokrovskii's death, B.D. Grekov delivered a historical report containing his famous thesis on Kievan Russia, in which he stressed its feudal essence. Kievan Russia, in his view, was not a slave-owning order, not a social form *sui generis,* but rather an early instance of feudalism.

What is the connection between Grekov's thesis and the ideas embraced by Pokrovskii when he was in the process of liquidating his own system? It would surely be an overstatement to allege that Grekov's thesis was implicit in Pokrovskii's new ideas. Yet both ideas tended in the same direction, and Grekov's thesis constituted a refinement of Pokrovskii's conception of feudalism. This is not to say that Pokrovskii influenced Grekov directly: rather Pokrovskii, following Pavlov-Silvanskii, had always considered appanage Russia feudal, but feudalism had not been a major element in his system. Only with the disintegration of his system in 1931 did it become important in his thinking, and then it was too late to do more than barely state the problem. Grekov's thesis likewise had roots in the pioneering work of Pavlov-Silvanskii, but he developed it in connection with a tradition alien to Pokrovskii. His thesis grew out of the works of non-Marxist, nationalist historians who had been at work on the problem since pre-Revolutionary days. Yet in one sense this theory, *as formulated by Grekov,* derived from a tradition other than the national one. The doctrine of socioeconomic formations affected Grekov's formulation; his theory thereby became wedded to historical materialism and therefore represents something of a synthesis of Marxist and non-Marxist traditions.

This shows continuity between pre-Revolutionary and post-1931 historiography and underlines an important discontinuity. The original rationale or existential base of this theory was probably the fact that Russian society, early in the twentieth century, seemed to be evolving along the same lines as other European societies, and these similarities called to mind earlier ones. Moreover, liberal historians were probably not adversely disposed to interpretations that deemphasized Russian distinctiveness and thereby sapped the ideological base of Tsardom. Grekov's theory had a far different function in Soviet historiography. It served as a vehicle for the glorification of the Russian nation, which experienced the full-blown development of feudalism, and of the Russian people, who therein succeeded in bypassing the slave-owning stage of development. This instance of stage-skipping, posited by the theory, was, of course, in itself instructive and useful.

The point is that Grekov's thesis was ideologically compatible with the theory of growing over; more than that, it was its ideal handmaiden. This precisely is the connection with the outline that emerged amidst the ruins of Pokrovskii's system. Both were sanctioned by the same forces that disrupted Pokrovskii's original synthesis—the theory of growing over.

The disintegration of Pokrovskii's system and the emergence of Grekov's were aspects of the process that Miliukov described as Stalin's affirmation of the dogma of the national origins of the Russian Revolution (1937:379). Socialism in one country is an inherently nationalistic slogan; the confinement of the revolution to one country for an indefinite period of time in itself implied Soviet patriotism—loyalty to the hearth of the revolution. Grekov's thesis broadened the framework of this patriotism. Perhaps the greatest achievement of Soviet historiography has been to provide it with content.

In the Soviet context, national glorification has always been held in check by the doctrine of socioeconomic formations. As transcendingly glorious as Russian history may be, it is pegged to the ground by its normality. It is but one manifestation of a universal pattern. Just as a boy becomes a man, all nations, each in its own way, must arrive at socialism. This is the principal message of Soviet historiography.

Notes

The abbreviations used in the Notes are given in full in the List of Abbreviations preceding the text. For works that appear in the Bibliography, the author's name and date of publication are given in the Notes. If a work is not in the Bibliography, a complete citation appears in the Notes. Most works cited just once in the Notes are not included in the Bibliography.

Introduction

1. J. Robert Oppenheimer is the American whose role most closely resembles Pokrovskii's. The physicist Peter Kapitsa, a successor of Pokrovskii and a Soviet counterpart of Oppenheimer, wrote: "In science, too, as it involves a large-scale collective effort, the director is most necessary. And what demands do we make of him? Our chief demand is that his role be a creative one and not purely administrative. He should comprehend the sense and the goal of scientific research, and he must correctly appraise the creative possibilities of the researchers, so that he can distribute their roles in accordance with their talents, placing them in such a juxtaposition as to have all the facets of the problem at hand develop in harmony with one another. Doubtless, however, we are now entering a period in the development of science when an increasingly important role will be allotted to organizers of science." *Peter Kapitsa on Life and Science,* ed. and trans. Albert Parry (New York and London, 1968), pp. 192–93.

2. Bell and Howell (Cleveland, 1965).

3. Sometimes typed, sometimes mimeographed, it appeared from November 1930 until, it seems, sometime in 1932. Only twelve copies of the first issue appeared; it contained four pages. In 1931, issues appeared six times a month on the average; each contained about thirty pages and was issued in 225 copies. Complete files, it would seem, are available only in archives; as a result of chance, most likely, different libraries hold different issues.

4. The first issue appeared on February 21, 1931. Subsequent issues were scheduled to appear every ten days, but only fourteen appeared all year. At first it was published as the organ of the Party Committee of The Communist Academy as such; later in the year it became the organ of the Institutes of Red Professors that were absorbed into the Communist Academy in the course of the year.

Chapter 1

1. *Pravda*, 16 May 1934.
2. Tsarist police records, scrupulous about social rank, refer to M.N. Pokrovskii as *dvorianin*. See "Neskol'ko dokumentov iz tsarskikh arkhivov o M.N. Pokrovskom," *Krasnyi arkhiv* 3 (1932):10.
3. Komarev, 1932:19.
4. Kizevetter, 1929:287. According to police records published in *Krasnyi arkhiv* (see above, note 2) and in M.A. Tsiavlovskii, ed., *Bol'sheviki: Dokumenty po istorii bol'shevizma s' 1903 po 1916 god'byvsh. moskovsk. okhrannogo otd'eleniia* (Moscow, 1918), p. 223, Pokrovskii did hold the title *privat dotsent* of Moscow University. He received the title automatically, having passed his master's examination. This meant that he had the right to lecture at Moscow University. In fact, he did not do so.
5. He taught in the Ekaterinskii Institute and in the Higher Woman's Course, now the Moscow Pedagogical Institute.
6. Kizevetter, 1929:287. He was also a member of the Society for the Propagation of Technical Knowledge.
7. Sokolov, 1970:50; an almost complete bibliography of Pokrovskii's works can be found in *IM* 1–2 (1932):216–48.
8. For an enumeration of Pokrovskii's articles see *Ocherki istorii istoricheskoi nauki v SSSR*, 1963, 3:219.
9. This is affirmed in all the standard biographies; Dubrovskii (1962:5) cites the archives of the Academy of Science.
10. His first publication in this journal, "Idealizm i zakony istorii," concerned philosophy of history (Feb.–March 1904; reprinted in *Izbrannye proizvedeniia*, 1967, 4:227–65). Ivanova (1968:177) states that Pokrovskii became a member of the Russian Social Democratic Labor Party in 1903. She is well informed and accurate but offers no documentation on this point. Perhaps the problem is that there is no clear definition of what is meant by membership at this early date. Pokrovskii was already in association with Bogdanov, Lunacharskii, Skvortsov-Stepanov, and other Social Democrats by this time. The police reported that he had had associates with bad political profiles since 1902. *Krasnyi arkhiv* 3 (1932):10.
11. Kizevetter, 1929:219–20. Even a sympathetic witness reported that in the late 1890s Pokrovskii stood further from Marxism than many of his contemporaries, including Vinogradov, Petrushevskii, Vipper, and Rozhkov (N.M. Lukin, "Akademik M.N. Pokrovskii," *Izvestiia Akademii Nauk SSSR* [otdel abshchestvennykh nauk] 9 [1932]:774).
12. Kizevetter, 1929:285; according to Richard Pipes, whose information is based on interviews, Pokrovskii was a member of the Historians' section of Group A of the Union of Liberation (*Struve: Liberal on the Left* [Cambridge, 1970], p. 345).
13. Pokrovskii, *1905 god* (Moscow, 1930), p. 31; Lutskii, 1965:343.
14. The Bolshevik Center was the Bureau of the Committee of the Party Majority, a Central Committee set up by Lenin in 1904 to rival the Central Committee elected by the Second Congress of the Russian Social-Democratic Labor Party. It was designated publicly as the Enlarged Editorial Board of *Proletarii*.
15. A typical old Bolshevik, Pokrovskii treasured his memories of the underground: "I bought a ticket and sat down on the Helsinki train. The spies who were all about on the Kuokkala Station did not pay the slightest attention to me since I traveled daily from Teriok where I lived to Kuokkala where headquarters were. Just a few seconds before the train left, on the platform appeared a man in a fur cap pulled down over his eyes and a turned-up collar, who also did not draw much attention to himself; [he] came to my compartment; I gave him the ticket and went out on the platform. Now perhaps the spies took note, but it was too late since the train was already leaving." (Sokolov, 1966:12.)

16. Pokrovskii, under the pseudonym Domov, actively participated in the life of the faction. In addition to lecturing at the Forwardist schools in Capri and Bologna, he participated in an underground trial of a former member of the Moscow Committee. Pokrovskii presented evidence of Leonid's having been a provocateur. (Hoover Institution, Okhrana Archives. XXIVa, folder IA, no. 733, 1910; XVIb[6]a, folder 1, no. 375, 1909.)

17. Sokolov, 1966:15. Suspicion of Taratuta was widespread among the Forwardists. According to an Okhrana report, Bogdanov and Krassin were responsible for the rumor (XVIb[6]a, no. 375, 1909).

18. Ibid., XVIb(2), folder 2, no. 469, 1911.

19. *Vpered*, 1 (1915):2–3.

20. St. Petersburg, Granat Brothers. He also contributed forty-six articles, most very brief, to the Granat *Entsiklopedicheskii slovar'*, 1910–18.

21. *Russkaia istoriia s drevneishikh vremen* (1910–14, with some chapters by N. Nikol'skii and V. Agafonov; 3d through 8th, final, 1933–34, ed. in 4 vols.). The 7th edition (1924–25) is the basic text for the version in *Izbrannye proizvedeniia* (1965–66, 1–2). It has been translated in part by J.D. Clarkson and M.R.G. Griffiths as *History of Russia from the Earliest Times to the Rise of Commercial Capitalism* (New York, 1931). References are to the English version unless otherwise noted, cited as *HR* (*History of Russia*). Reviewed by Samuel H. Cross, *Journal of Modern History* 4 (1932):282–85.

22. For a richly detailed account of Pokrovskii's splendid ordeal see A.I. Gukovskii's two-part article, "Kak sozdalas' 'Russkaia istoriia s drevneishikh vremen' M.N. Pokrovskogo" (1968, 1969).

23. *Ocherki istorii russkoi kul'turi* (Moscow, vol. 1, 1914; vol. 2, 1918). References are to the single-volume 6th ed. (1924f). Cited hereafter as *Outlines of Culture*.

24. He stated this in a letter to a publisher; see Gukovskii, 1965:123.

25. See Pokrovskii, 1958b and "Novye dokumenty V.I. Lenina," *VIKPSS* 4 (1958): 30–33.

26. Lutskii, 1965:348. Trotsky considered Pokrovskii a member of his interdistrict (*mezhraionnaia*) organization, a group that stood close to the Bolsheviks during World War I and then, for the most part, merged with them at the Sixth Bolshevik Congress, August 1917 (*Stalin: An Appraisal of the Man and his Influence*, ed. and trans. Charles Malamuth [New York, 1941], p. 217). Again, membership is difficult to define. Perhaps in this case it means no more than an "ideological tendency" and journalistic collaboration. At any rate, Pokrovskii returned to Russia after the Sixth Congress.

27. Lutskii, 1965:352; Sokolov, 1967:117–20; Kotov, 1966:68. *Entsiklopidecheskii solvar'*, Russkogo bibliograficheskogo instituta Granata (7th ed., Moscow, n.d.), t. XL1–2, col. 119.

28. *Moskovskii*, 1968:34–35. Relations were established with the American and Swedish consuls. Maddir Summers, the American consul, received a pass to the offices of the Military-Revolutionary Committee.

29. According to a well known story, when the Germans first revealed their terms at Brest-Litovsk, Pokrovskii wept: "How can you talk of peace without annexations," he sobbed, "when nearly eighteen provinces are torn from Russia." This story should not, I believe, be credited. Pokrovskii, 1970:215, 236.

30. U.S. Department of State Archives. Record Group 59 Decimal File 861.00/1447. I am grateful to my colleague Robert Maddox for calling my attention to this reference.

31. According to Summers, "There is no doubt that the present regime can no longer count upon support of workmen peasants or bourgeoisie whose sympathies are still with the allies, though it is doubtful whether they can render any further military resistance unless allied aid is sent as a nucleus around which they can rally." Ibid.

32. Ibid., 861.00/2020.

33. In 1924, he wrote about Lenin as follows: "There was above all, his enormous capacity to see the root of things, a capacity which finally awakened in me a sort of superstitious feeling. I frequently had occasion to differ from him on practical questions but I came off badly every time. When this experience had been repeated seven times, I ceased to dispute and submitted to Lenin even if logic told me that one should act otherwise. I was henceforth convinced that he understood things better and was master of a power denied to me, of seeing about ten feet into the earth." (1929b:16, as translated in Wolfe, 1955:363.)

34. A.I. Gukovskii, "Kak ia stal istorikom," *ISSSR* 6(1965):76–99; translation adapted from *Soviet Studies in History* 5 (Fall 1966):14, 12.

35. *Russkaia istoriia v samom szhatom ocherke* was originally a set of lectures to an audience that Pokrovskii felt "had to be hurriedly pumped with Marxism" on its way to the front. Parts 1 and 2 were published in 1920, part 3, which treats the first decade of the twentieth century, appeared in 1923. An English version, *Brief History of Russia,* trans. D.S. Mirsky (London, 1933), is based on the final Russian editions (no. 10 for vol. 1, no. 4 for vol. 2). It is reprinted in *Izbrannye proizvedeniia* 3 (Moscow, 1967), cited hereinafter as *BH (Brief History)*. Unless the edition is indicated, the reference is to the English translation.

36. The letter is included in the English translation. Though long misrepresented, it was read to the Twenty-Second Congress of the CPSU and published in *Pravda,* 26 Oct. 1961.

37. The Communist Academy grew out of an educational committee created under the Moscow Soviet in 1917. Its immediate goal was to instruct workers in connection with the impending elections for the Constituent Assembly. But even at the time its members aspired to make it into a center of proletarian education. Most of its founders, who included Bogdanov and Pokrovskii, had been associated with the Forwardist schools at Capri and Bologna or with Lenin's rival school at Longjumeau. The Comacademy was in a sense then an offspring of Bogdanov's theories of proletarian culture. See St. Krivtsov, "Organizatsiia sotsialisticheckoi nauki," *Rabochii mir'* 16–17 (1918):56–59; cf. I.S. Smirnov, *Lenin i sovetskaia kul'tura* (Moscow, 1960), pp. 297–306, who stresses Lenin's importance in organizing the Communist Academy. Pokrovskii was given a two-week leave to draft the KA charter.

38. See E.H. Carr, *Socialism in One Country* (3 vols., New York, 1958), 1:51. Nevertheless, even later Pokrovskii would recall with nostalgia his earlier associations: "I shall not begin to defend the political line which characterized our party schools in 1910–11, but I must say that those who passed through these schools, although now far removed from their former political position, all the same recall [them] with great warmth." ("A.V. Lunacharskii," *Narodnoe prosveshchenie* 11–12 [1927]: 21–22.) For a history of the Commissariat of Enlightenment that brings Pokrovskii's role clearly into focus and that also illuminates various aspects of cultural policy, including the conflict with Proletcult, see Shiela Fitzpatrick, *The Commissariat of Enlightenment: Soviet Organization of Education and the Arts under Lunacharsky* (Cambridge, 1970).

39. See *Protsess esserov: rechi zashchitnikov i obvinaemykh* (2 vols., Moscow, 1922). Pokrovskii's brochure, *Chto ustanovil protsess tak nazyvaemykh 'sotsialistov-revoliutsionerov'?* (Moscow, 1922).

40. *Ocherki russkogo revoliutsionnogo dvizheniia XIX–XX vv.* (1924b) was originally a set of lectures for regional party secretaries read at Sverdlov Communist University. Cited hereinafter as *HRM (History of the Revolutionary Movement).*

Chapter 2

1. L.V. Cherepnin discussing S.M. Dubrovskii, "Akademik M.N. Pokrovskii i ego roli v razvitii sovetskoi istoricheskoi nauki," *VI* 3(1962):37.

2. "History has more to say about the dead than about the living, but that does not keep it from being the most lively, the most *political* of all the sciences there are." *TP*, 1:XV.

3. For example, see Rubinshtein, 1941:580–82.

4. A sketch of the most salient features of Pokrovskii's system must necessarily exclude the problem of Normanism. In the 1930s and 1940s it became an urgent question for Soviet historians, but for Pokrovskii it was a trivial matter. Late in life, in holding up Soloviev as a model for his students, Pokrovskii pointed out how the nineteenth-century master, in treating the ancient period, had dealt with the problem of clan organization, a matter having wide political ramifications. He praised Soloviev for ignoring the ethnic question, a sterile problem according to Pokrovskii. (*TP*, 1:77–78.) Soviet historians disagree among themselves about whether Pokrovskii was a Normanist. Cf. V.V. Mavrodin, "Sovetskaia istoriografiia drevneirusskogo gosudarstva," *VI* 12 (1967):53–54; and L.V. Danilova, "Stanovelnie marksistskogo napravleniia v sovetskoi istoriografii epokhi feodalizma," *Istoricheskie zapiski* 76 (1965): 82. My understanding is that despite statements that could put him on both sides of the subsequent discussion, he moved from a Normanist to a non- or an a-Normanist position. For a concise discussion, see the editors' footnote in Pokrovskii, 1965–67, 1:97–98.

5. *HR*: 18–19; see Danilova, *Istoricheskie zapiski* 76 (1965):82. Before the twentieth century, the application of the concept of feudalism to Russia by professional historians was largely unsystematic. Even though Pokrovskii built on the findings of Pavlov-Silvanskii, he was himself something of a pioneer. He brought out the "socioeconomic lining" of the juridical traits of feudalism. Ibid., p. 81; for his most complete definition of feudalism see *HR*: 14–15.

6. 5th ed., pp. 165–56; 1965–67, 1:219–20.

7. Merchant capital was the "actual Tsar standing behind the royal throne, in essence the spirit, or, if you wish, the force behind the crowned puppet—[it] was the ruling force that created the Russian Empire and serfdom" (1923a:30).

8. The characteristic enterprise of merchant capital is the plantation, of which the Russian estate is a variation.

9. *BH* (3d ed., 1923), 1:66, 74.

10. Ibid., p. 66.

11. *HR* (4th ed., 1922), 2:201–7.

12. For a brief but comprehensive summary of Pokrovskii's interpretation of the Revolution a few years after the event, see 1922b. Volume 2 of *BH* is mainly a study of the preconditions of the 1917 Revolution. *HRM* contains the final formulation of Pokrovskii's *first* interpretation of the Revolution. This work is treated in detail in Chapter 4. Many of his articles on the Revolution or those with close bearing on his understanding of it were published in a separate volume, *Oktiabr'skaia Revoliutsiia* (1929b).

13. Pokrovskii's most detailed treatment of historiography is *Bor'ba klassov i russkaia istoricheskaia literatura*, which is reprinted in volume 1 of *Istoricheskaia nauka i bor'ba klassov* (1933a) and volume 4 of *Izbrannye proizvedeniia* (1965–67). A brief summary is included in the translation of *HR* and was apparently written especially for it.

14. *BH*, 1:238; see also 1923a:33–37.

15. *BH*, 1:239–40; see also 1923a:37.

16. *BH*, 1:122; see also 1934:63.

17. *BH*, 1:67; see also *HR*:139.

18. *BH*, 1:107, 108; see also 1923b:4.

19. Pokrovskii's preference for basing analysis of foreign relations on the "real economic interest" of ruling groups rather than their own statements about their motives is stated explicitly. Ibid., p. 390.

Chapter 3

1. See p. 25 above.

2. Earlier in 1923, in part 3 of *BH* (vol. 2 of the English edition), Pokrovskii treated the same problem. He brought the account up to 1910 only and ended on an ambiguous note. The Stolypin reform "did produce the illusion of rapid progress along *bourgeois* lines." He denied the reality of such progress, but instead of arguing this point, he suggested that those who held the illusion showed a lack of faith in the peasants who had been fighting the squires since 1605 (p. 302).

3. Nationalization of banks, factories, and land was an "instinctive gesture" by the workers, like disarming an enemy. *Sputnik kommunista* 18 (1922):34.

4. *HRM*:229. "Eight months passed before the conquest of that which had come in hand as early as March, 1917" (1929b:85).

5. It indicates the persistence of his Bogdanovite past. This interpretation of the Revolution was shaped in large measure by the perspective he had maintained in 1907, his expectation of a cataclysmic rising by the workers. See p.18 above.

6. Interview with S.M. Dubrovskii, Moscow, 6 Dec. 1966.

7. 1924c; "Otvet Tomsinskomiu," *VKA* 15 (1926):284–99. Slepkov's (1925) reiteration of his views was followed by a two-part article by Pokrovskii (1925a), in which he outdid even himself in sarcasm. Slepkov confined his reply to a half-page statement consisting mainly of a passage from Lenin's work, which he felt supported his position ("Malenkoe dopolnenie," *Bol'shevik* 9–10 [1925]:124).

8. On one occasion, he seemed to concede to Slepkov that the landlords had become bourgeois ("Predposilki i rezultati revoliutsii 1905 goda," *Pravda*, 18 Dec. 1925). Elsewhere he underlines their feudal characteristics (1925b).

9. On one occasion, Pokrovskii formulated this thesis in the following terms in order to make its meaning evident to all: "Merchant capital even in this period [1906–14] could play the role of master, and industrial capital was, so to speak, the guest, but such as is admitted to his rooms from necessity, and upon whose departure, the servant is summoned to open the *fortochka* [hinged window pane used for ventilation] in order to banish the smell of this unpleasant guest" (1925a, 4:135).

10. There is little doubt that he had Stalin and like-minded party historians in mind when he wrote, "But Lenin himself, there can be no doubt, would have strictly censured the transformation of his thought into a formula suitable for all instances of life, for all times, in all countries" ("O deiatel'nost' Kommunisticheskoi akademii," *VKA* 22 [1927]:6). And even in 1928 he indicated clearly enough that in his view it was only in 1918, during the Brest-Litovsk negotiations, that Lenin first saw the possibility of building socialism in one country (1928c:16).

11. The expurgated version of the letter can be found in *Works* (9:179–91); the deleted portion is in Sokolov (1962:77), who cites Central Party Archives.

Chapter 4

1. See *Organizatsiia nauki v pervye gody Sovetskoi vlasti (1917–1925), sbornik dokumentov* (Leningrad, 1968), p. 46 and passim, for evidence of how deeply this value permeated cultural life.

2. From Central Party Archives as published in Nosov, 1967:59–60.

3. Ibid. From September to November 1920, 175 problems were discussed in Agitprop; 108 of them concerned "academic-organizational" matters.

4. See *Ocherki istorii istoricheskoi nauki v SSSR* 4 (Moscow, 1966), various entries in *Sovetskaia istoricheskaia entsiklopediia*, and Katz (1957).

5. *VKA* 12 (1926):365; the other branches were an Institute of World Economics and World Politics, a section for natural science, a section for Soviet construction (jurisprudence), an agrarian commission, a Society of Marxist Statisticians, a commission for the publication of the *Great Soviet Encyclopedia* (Pokrovskii became head of the socioeconomic department). Within a few years the KA sponsored ten societies. Aside from the SMH, there were societies for philosophy, jurisprudence, biology, medicine, mathematics, orientology, folklore, statistics, and economics. (*Arkhiv Akademii Nauk SSSR,* II, Vyp. 5 [1946], 61.)

6. Miliutin, at one time a Menshevik, had been a member of the Bolshevik Central Committee in 1917 and then the following year a member of the first Council of Peoples' Commissars.

7. Ivanova, 1968:186. On Shestakov, see E.A. Lutskii, "Andrei Vasilievich Shestakov," *ISSSR* 3 (1967):139–41. For details about the founding of the Society and the organization of its journal, *Istorik-marksist,* see the documents presented in Levshin, 1976.

8. *IM* 1 (1926):317; see also pp. 318–21 and Doroshenko, 1966:10–22, which draws upon archival material.

9. *IM* 4(1927):297; Doroshenko (1966:12) compiled the following figures from the archives of the Academy of Sciences:

	Active	Corresponding	Total
June 1925	—	—	29
Jan. 1926	29	11	40
Jan. 1927	90	88	178
Jan. 1928	123	127	250
Jan. 1929	191	208	399

These figures are slightly higher than those published in contemporary chronicles and those cited by some present-day Soviet historians; cf. Naidenov, 1966:34.

10. *IM* 1 (1926):3; translated by Rufus Mathewson in Fritz Stern, ed., *Varieties of History* (New York, 1956), p. 330.

11. *IM* 1 (1926):8–9; Stern, *Varieties of History,* pp. 333–34.

12. For a time he headed the Central-European Secretariat of the Comintern. He was a secretary of Agitprop in the 1920s and then of Kultprop, the Cultural Propaganda Department of the Central Committee, in the early 1930s. From the time of the Fifteenth Party Congress (1927) until his death during the purges, he was a member of the Central Committee. In the 1930s he was on the editorial boards of *Pravda* and *Bol'shevik.* He had a prominent role in the training of specialists in party history, and his own writings were widely known until they were supplanted by Stalin's *Short Course.* Like Iaroslavskii, he came to be associated with Kaganovich. See *Malaia Sovetskaia Entsiklopediia,* 2d ed., V, cols. 596–97; *International Press Correspondence (Inprecor)* (9 March 1933), p. 263; *Pravda,* 3 Sept. 1965; *ISSSR* 2 (1967):105–10; *VIKPSS* 8 (1965):107.

13. He was often referred to as Lukin-Antonov; as noted earlier, Antonov was his revolutionary pseudonym. His most important writings have been republished in three volumes, *Izbrannye trudy* (Moscow, 1960–63); a volume dedicated to his memory, *Evropa v novoe i noveishee vremia* (Moscow, 1966) contains articles about him and a bibliography of works by him and about him. See the appreciation by A.L. Sidorov in *Istoriia i sotsiologiia* (Moscow, 1964), p. 177. He should be the subject of a separate study.

14. Nikolai Leonidovich Rubinshtein was a lecturer at the Higher Party School and specialist in diplomatic history who died in 1952; he should not be confused with the Nikolai Leonidovich Rubinshtein who was a professor at Moscow University, a specialist in historiography and eighteenth-century history, who died around 1964.

15. *IM* 3 (1927):201–2; *PR* 8(1928):208.

16. "Yes, in those years the Marxist elaboration of the history of pre-revolutionary Russia was not the center of attention and if works devoted to that subject appeared, they were for the most part not written by Marxists. This was characteristic of the era." M.V. Nechkina, "Results of the Discussion on the Periodization of the History of Soviet Historical Scholarship," *Soviet Studies in History* 1 (Winter 1962–63):49; first appeared in *ISSSR* 2 (1962):57–79.

17. See note 34, below, and E. Maximovich, "Istoricheskaia nauka v SSSR i marksizm-leninizm," *Sovremennye zapiski* 62 (1936):415.

18. Grekov attended the universities of Warsaw, Moscow, and St. Petersburg, where he studied under D.M. Petrushevskii and M.K. Liubavskii; he also participated in a seminar of A.S. Lappo-Danilevskii. He began publishing as early as 1908. See *Akademiku Borisu Dmitrievichu Grekovu: Ko dnei semi-desiatiletiia* (Moscow, 1952), pp. 5–19, and S.N. Valk, "B.D. Grekov kak deiatel' arkheografii," *Arkheograficheskii ezhegodnik za 1958 god* (Moscow, 1960), p. 223.

19. Formed by the amalgamation of the academy's Permanent Historical Commission, founded in 1903, and the Archeographic Commission of the Ministry of Education, founded in 1834.

20. D.A. Magerovskii, "Rossiiskaia assotsiatsiia nauchno-issledovatel'skikh institutov obshchestvennykh nauk," *NR* 11 (1927):56. For a personal account of the academy that brings out many of the distinctive features of the evolution of historiography in Leningrad, see the essay of S.N. Valk dedicated to I.I. Smirnov in *Krest'ianstvo i klassovaia bor'ba feodal'noi rossii,* Trudy Instituta Istorii Leningradskoe Otdelenie (Leningrad, 1967), 9:5–41.

21. Magerovskii, *NR* 11 (1927):56; the association had 412 members and 311 research associates (p. 53).

22. For a vivid account of RANION's Institute of History, see A.S. Nifontov, "Iz opyta nauchnoi raboty istorika," *ISSSR* 2 (1963):118–40. For additional information, *Ocherki istorii istoricheskoi nauki v SSSR,* 4:233–37, and Ivanova, 1968:84–121 and passim. The institute's own publication, *Uchenie zapiski,* vols. 1–4, 6, 7 (1926–29), is not available in the United States.

23. See Ivanova, 1960:66; *VKA* 26 (1928):257; *IM* 5 (1927):276.

24. Ivanova, 1960:69; see also Vainshtein, 1966.

25. Brochures, journal, encyclopedia, and newspaper articles, reviews, speeches, prefaces, and remarks in public discussions. There are two bibliographies of Pokrovskii's works. The first was assembled for his sixtieth birthday celebration (*IM* 9 [1928]:213–31); the second was published shortly after his death (*IM* 1–2 [1932]:216–48); it excludes mainly unsigned reviews written by Pokrovskii in his early years and posthumous articles and collections.

26. Party Archives have preserved a letter Pokrovskii wrote in response to an inquiry about the positions he held. It is undated but was probably written in 1927. The following version was slightly abridged by O.D. Sokolov.

To the Department of Agitation and Propaganda of the CC. CPSU(b) Comrade A. I. Krinitskii

Dear Alexander Ivanovich,

In accordance with our conversation I am providing you with a list of the posts I hold, and my thoughts about possible "unloading." . . . I group the information under the central agencies among which my work is divided: the People's Commissariat of Education, the USSR Central Executive Committee, and VTsIK. I list only the posts involving some degree of regular work, and omit "titles" that commit me to nothing—thus, I am a member of the Central Council of the VNO [Military-Scientific Society], where I have never been; a member of the council of the Museum of the Revolution, which I attended once; a member of the Commission for Publication of the works of L. Tolstoy, which hardly ever meets, etc. Along the same lines, I do not list the post of Vice-Commissar of Education, which is also a "title": if A.V. Lunacharskii is absent, his place is taken by V.N. Iakovleva, and she also represents the People's Commissariat of Education at the RSFSR Council of People's Commissars. All I do is very rarely chair meetings of the Collegium, which I have to attend in connection with my other duties. However, I do note chairmanship of the Commission on the Chernyshevskii Anniversary, as that does involve some additional work (organizing the collected works, contacts with the Chernyshevskii Museum and other institutions, etc.). First I provide the list, and then some thoughts on reducing the load.

I. People's Commissariat of Education: (1) Chairman of GUS; (2) Chairman of the Science Policy Section of GUS; (3) Chairman of the Subsection on Higher Educational Institutions of that section; (4) Chairman of the Commission on Training Personnel for the Sciences; and (5) Chairman of the Presidium of RANION (an association of twelve institutes in the social sciences).

II. Central Executive Committee of the USSR: (6) Member of the Committee on Guidance to Scientific and Educational Institutions of TsIK; (7) Rector of the Institute of Red Professors (to be transferred to VTsIK as of the next fiscal year); (8) Chairman of the Presidium of the Communist Academy; (9) Chairman of the Section on the History of the Revolutionary Movement of that academy; (10) Chairman of the Society of Marxist Historians, same place; (11) member of the editorial board of the *Vestnik Kommunisticheskoi Akademii* and of the *Istorik-marksist;* (12) member of the Presidium of the *Bol'shaia Sovetskaia Entsiklopediia*, with responsibility for the political line of that work; (13) editor-in-chief of the entire social sciences section of the BSE; (14) an editor of the Russian history section, same work; (15) Chairman of the Commission on the Chernyshevskii Anniversary; (16) member of the Commission for the 10th Anniversary of the October Revolution.

III. VTsIK: (17) Chief, Tsentroarkhiv RSFSR.

IV. Teaching assignments: (18) two seminars at the Institute of Red Professors; (19) one seminar in RANION (All-Russian Association of Scientific Research Institutes of Social Sciences); in addition, perhaps I am still considered a member of the editorial board of *Pod znamenem marksizma,* although I sent my resignation to the press department long ago. Total: 19 or 20 functions involving some degree of actual work. All the teaching and all the work connected with the Communist Academy should be regarded as absolutely not to be interfered with, because of "irreplaceability," or at least that's how people have regarded it until now. I'd be very happy if the view on this has changed. Further, I'm also looked upon as "irreplaceable" by the People's Commissariat of Education with respect to GUS (they have no "name" person; and this is necessary, because GUS governs the destinies of all professors, and it would create difficulties if someone were put at the head of this machinery who did not enjoy sufficient authority in the eyes of the academic community); and it would also be very difficult to find a substitute for me at Tsentroarkhiv (where there is need for a combination of that same academic competence and the presence of a long-time party member) because of the political significance of the archives, which contain many secrets of all sorts, some of them quite pertinent to current matters.

By some strange misunderstanding I am regarded as "irreplaceable" as Rector of the Institute of Red Professors, although there I am not only not "irreplaceable" but simply a poor rector: neither an administrator nor a political leader. For the latter function there can be no question that a member of the Central Committee is needed; it is too important and complex an institution for anyone of lesser party caliber. . . . My "irreplaceability" as Chairman of the Science Policy Section of GUS is also quite arbitrary, although the People's Commissariat of Education takes that stand. . . . Finally, the *Bol'shaia Sovetskaia Entsiklopediia* also falls into the category of dubious "irreplaceabilities." I understand that an undertaking of that kind can't do entirely without me, but if I were to carry out conscientiously all that has been heaped upon me, three weeks compressed into one wouldn't do. I very strongly requested the Politburo to release me at least from political responsibility, which compels me to read 50 percent of all the articles. Comrade Knorin held up that request. I repeat it now, and add to it the request to be released from heading the social sciences section as a whole. This work could be performed splendidly by N.L. Meshcheriakov, whose principal work is presently at the *Encyclopedia*. Were that done, I would still have: (1) participation in its presidium, and (2) direction of the Russian history section; these I do not refuse. Because of the association with the Communist Academy, I have to remain a member of the sciences committee of TsIK. Next comes functions in which I am replaceable—beyond all question: (1) Subsection on Higher Educational Institutions of the Section on Science Policy . . . (2) the Commission for Training Scientific Personnel . . . inasmuch as the commission is under GUS, I will continue to be in overall charge as chairman of the latter, (3) chairmanship of RANION. . . . And so here is my ultimate dream: in the People's Commissariat of Education to remain only Chairman of GUS, and outside it to remain only head of Tsentroarkhiv (which takes four hours a week of my time, as all the organizational work is done by my assistants, Comrades Adoratskii and Maksakov); that my principal work be in the Communist Academy, while that at the *Bol'shaia Sovetskaia Entsiklopediia* be cut to a minimum; and that I be released entirely from (the journal) *Pod znamenem* and all the other things.

With communist greeting,
M. Pokrovskii

VI 6 (1969):41–2; as translated in *Soviet Studies in History* 8, no. 4 (Spring 1970):348–51.

27. *Plan*, 1927:52–55, 83; *Plan*, 1928:79.

28. Pokrovskii was the first chairman of Istpart. Even though he resigned in favor of M.S. Ol'minskii, he continued as one of the editors of *Proletarskaia revoliutsiia* for some time.

29. N.L. Rubinshtein, "O putiakh istoricheskogo issledovanii," *ISSSR* 6 (1962):95–96; *Biulliten' zaochnoi konsyl'tatsii* 4 (1930):38. Rubinshtein writes that an article of his on the Decembrists was accepted by *Katorga i ssylka* because it criticized ideas of Pokrovskii.

30. Pokrovskii's attribution of the supraclass theory to the populists is a premise of his analysis and seems to be the basis of many of his distinctions in *HRM* (see esp. pp. 45–96). He made this judgment explicit somewhat later. "The present interlacing of right and left deviations we meet even among the populists of the 70's, who unanimously affirmed that the then-existing Russian state is a supra-class organization . . . " (1931c:6).

31. *Russkaia istoricheskaia literatura v klassovoi osveshchenii* (2 vols., Moscow, 1927–30); *Ocherki po istorii oktiabr'skoi revoliutsii* (1927a). Though long passed over in silence, in 1957 a Soviet author cited these two volumes as the outstanding work on the Revolution written by 1927. (M.E. Naidenov, "Velikaia Oktiabr'skaia Sotsialisticheskaia Revoliutsiia v osveshchenii (russkoi) istoriografii," in *Iz istorii Velikoi Oktiabr'skoi Sotsialisticheskoi Revoliutsii* [Moscow, 1957], p. 300.) A.I. Gukovskii, a former student of Pokrovskii, has written that one of the works edited by Pokrovskii, *Vosstanie dekabristov* (5 vols., Moscow-Leningrad, 1925–29), is "justifiably considered the best scholarly publication of Tsentroarchiv" ("Spornye voprosy sovetskoi arkheografii," *VI* 5 [1966]:67). According to Academician Nechkina, 2030 works—articles and books—on the history of the revolutionary movement appeared in 1925 alone. Over half of them were devoted to the Revolution of 1905 (*ISSSR* 1 [1960]:87).

32. *Trudy istoriko—arkhivnogo instituta* 25 (1967):57–58. Pokrovskii headed a commission of experts that awarded Lenin Prizes, and he had an important role in selecting scholars who would be permitted to travel abroad. It should be mentioned in this connection that he was the author of a governmental decree of February 19, 1919, which authorized the creation of a special commission of scholars to draw up a list of 100 scholars who would be eligible to receive food and clothes from the stores of the Red Army. In 1921 Pokrovskii also helped form and participated in the work of the Central Committee for the improvement of living conditions for scholars (TsKUBY); see *Organizatsiia nauki v pervye gody Sovetskoi vlasti,* pp. 339–40, 344, 346, 363, 368, 393.

33. *Leninskii sbornik* (Moscow, 1945), 35:231. Lenin replied not earlier than March 4, 1921. Though he expressed doubt and requested more information, he indicated that he would forward the matter to the Politburo for discussion.

34. At the time of the Trial of Socialist Revolutionaries, 71 individuals and their families were expelled (see S.P. Mel'gunov, *Vospominaniia i dnevniki*, Vyp. II[chast' tretiia] [Paris, 1964], pp. 81–82, and M.M. Novikov, *Ot Moskvy do N'iu-Iorka: maia zhizn' v nauke i politike* [New York, 1952], pp. 324–28).

35. *Kommunisticheskaia revoliutsiia* 5 (1927):23. In 1924 Pokrovskii affirmed that non-Marxists "should have . . . a *consultative vote* even at party meetings dedicated to educational matters" (1933d:15). Just a year later, such a suggestion would have been inexpedient.

Chapter 5

1. The following institutions were represented: the Lenin Institute, the Marx-Engels Institute, Istpart, the International Agrarian Scientific Research Institute, RANION, the Ukrainian Institute of Marxism, Sverdlov Communist University, Gosplan, and the Museum of the Revolution of the USSR (*NR* 5–6 [1928]: 117). The summarized protocol was published as "Pervaia vsesoiuznaia konferentsiia marksistsko-leninskikh nauchno-issledovatel'skikh uchrezhdenii," *VKA* 26 (1928):239–94.

2. *Pravda*, 1 Dec. 1931; it is not entirely clear whether supporters of Stalin achieved a majority in the IKP party bureau at this time or only after the July plenum of the Central Committee. Cf. Stephen F. Cohen, *Bukharin and the Bolshevik Revolution: A Political Biography, 1888–1938* (New York, 1973), p. 296.

3. On March 20, in a report to the KA plenum, Pokrovskii had stressed the organization's material shortcomings. The budget for 1927–28 had increased only five percent, but expenditures required an eight percent increase. As a result, the staff had to be reduced just when new sections were being created. ("Obshchee sobranie plenum chlenov Komm. Akademii, 20 Marta 1928," *VKA* 26 [1928]:213.)

4. Ibid., p. 258. The communist nucleus was indeed a compact one; in 1927 only 12 of the 64 research associates and 22 of the 66 graduates in the Institute of History were party members. According to Magerovskii, the situation was worse than the figures show, because some of the party members were so burdened with assignments that they worked only nominally in RANION. (*NR* 11 [1927]:53, 59.)

5. *VKA* 26 (1928):265, 268–69. Just a few months earlier, at the Fifteenth Party Congress in December 1927, Pokrovskii affirmed that "it is fully possible for us to have our own scientific staff, [made up of people] from those social classes bound to the October Revolution" (*XV S'ezd vsesoiuznoi kommunisticheskoi partii* [Moscow-Leningrad, 1925], p. 1017). Such assertions were suitable for what was in some respects a ceremonial occasion, but in professional discussions he reverted to a more conservative position.

6. It included M. I. Iavorskyi, V.V. Adoratskii, a specialist in philosophy and head of the Lenin Institute, E.B. Pashukanis, the leading legal theorist and a member of the higher councils of the KA, I.I. Mints, Pokrovskii's assistant and head of the party unit at the IKP, S.M. Dubrovskii, one of Pokrovskii's most talented students at the IKP, and V.A. Iurinets, a Ukrainian philosopher who had studied under Deborin and Pokrovskii. The non-Marxist component of the delegation consisted of V.I. Picheta, a specialist in the history of the Slavs, S.F. Platonov, a well-known non-Marxist historian and head of the Historico-Philological Department of the Academy of Sciences, M.K. Liubavskii, a former rector of Moscow University, and D.N. Egorov, a specialist on European feudalism. German scientists had prepared a similar reception the previous year for Soviet scientists. (I.I. Mints,

"Marksisty na istoricheskoi nedele v Berline i VI istoricheskom Kongresse istorikov v Norvegii," *IM* 9 [1928]:84–85, 88; E.B. Pashukanis, "Nedelia sovetskikh istorikov v Berline," *VKA* 30 [1929]: 238, 240, 242; see also Shteppa, 1963:43.)

7. Pashukanis, 1929:238–40; Mints, 1928:87.

8. The delegation of thirteen Soviet historians consisted mostly of holdovers from the Berlin week. Platonov, however, had been dropped. There were in fact no members of the Academy of Sciences at the congress. Tarle had been included in the delegation but reportedly fell ill in Paris. M.S. Hrushchevskii, the eminent Ukrainian historian, was also a member of the delegation, and like Tarle he failed to appear. Tarle was scheduled to represent the Academy of Sciences. It may be that he fell ill in Paris or that he, along with Platonov and others, were denied permission to attend. Cf. Pokrovskii, 1929a:236 and Shteppa, 1963:43. There is a curious discrepancy in reports of the composition of the delegation. Mints, who was not a member, but who accompanied it, includes M.I. Iavorskyi, the prominent Ukrainian Marxist historian (*IM* 9 [1928]). According to the O.V. Treskova (1973:53), editor of some recently published documents, Iavorskyi was dropped and A.E. Presniakov, one of the best known non-Marxist historians of Russia, was included.

9. Pokrovskii, 1929a:234; for some of the relevant statements, see also Samuel Harper, "A Communist View of Historical Studies," *Journal of Modern History* 1 (1929):77–86.

10. Ellipses in original.

11. *Ocherki iz ekonomicheskoi istorii srednevekovoi Evropy* (Moscow, 1928). Dmitrii Moiseevich Petrushevskii (1863–1942) was a renowned specialist in European history, whose chief specialty was English feudalism. He graduated from Kiev University and wrote his dissertation under the direction of P.G. Vinogradov in Moscow. He became a professor in the Department of World History of Imperial Moscow University in 1906, and resigned in 1911 to protest policies of the Ministry of Education. For an appreciation, see E.A. Kosminskii, ed., *Srednye Veka* sb. Vyp. II. *Posviaschaetsia pamiati akademika D. M. Petrushevskogo* (Moscow-Leningrad, 1946).

12. Just a year before the campaign now being treated, *IM* (6[1927]:299) reported that a paper on Dopsch had been delivered in Leningrad under the auspices of RANION. L.V. Cherepnin, then a student at the Institute of History, presented Dopsch's hypothesis concerning Charlemagne's *Capitulare de Villis*. The report noted that a lively discussion ensued.

13. See I.M. Kushner's attempt to define the term "socioeconomic formation" and to counterpoise his definition to the concept of the ideal type (*VKA* 8 [1928]:105–6).

14. The remarks were combined with comments on Petrushevskii and published as a lead article in *IM* (Pokrovskii, 1928b).

15. *IM* (1928):108; 1929, 13:235–38, 276. At a discussion in Leningrad, some students defended the book, and then the discussion itself became the subject of a brief controversy at the First All-Union Conference of Marxist Historians. The Leningraders succeeded in convincing the Muscovites that no Marxists had been among Tarle's defenders. See *TP*, 1:49.

16. I.K. Luppol, "Ob otnoshenii sovetskikh uchenykh k uchenym emigratsii," *NR* 12 (1928): 13–22, and the chronicle of the same issue, pp. 111–14. For further information and additional references, see Loren R. Graham, *The Soviet Academy of Sciences and the Communist Party, 1927–1932* (Princeton, 1967), pp. 104–8, and L. Hamilton Rhinelander, "Exiled Russian Scholars in Prague: The Kondakov Seminar and Institute," *Canadian Slavonic Papers/Revue Canadienne des Slavistes* 16, no. 3 (1974):331–52. Zhebelev himself fared well subsequently and continued his work in the Academy of Sciences. During the siege of Leningrad, he had the responsibility of preserving the local buildings of the academy. He perished in the siege.

17. A.M. Pankratova, who was close to Pokrovskii at this time, seems to have understood him in this way. She gently chided him and implied that a solution would have to address itself to the non-Marxists; see the review of volumes 6 and 7 of *IM* in *PR* 8–9 (1928):208.

18. *VKA* 26 (1928):14–15. It is worth noting that Pokrovskii praised Bukharin in the same speech. By this time, Bukharin's supporter Uglanov had already been defeated in the struggle for control of the party bureau of the IKP.

Chapter 6

1. See p. 84 above.

2. An article surveying the journalistic literature appeared in *IM* 10 (1928):262–75.

3. The minutes of the celebration were published in a volume entitled *Na boevom postu marksizma* (Moscow, 1929).

4. Quoted from Central State Archives of the October Revolution in Lutskii, 1965:363.

5. *NBPM*:34. *TP*, 1:303.

6. Fridliand no doubt was being modest when he proposed that only 100–150 delegates had been expected, but the leaders probably were surprised when 600 historians, about 300 delegates and 300 guests, presented themselves. Of the delegates, 123, including 10 women historians, had voting rights, while 273 others had consultative votes. In all, 46 reports were delivered. Other basic data: 82 percent of the 123 voters had published works; 70 percent were between 25 and 35 years old; 15.4 percent were workers, 17.3 percent were peasants, 53.7 percent intelligentsia, 6.5 percent other, and 7.1 percent did not indicate; 87.8 percent were party members and 1.7 percent were candidates; 72.4 percent had received higher education, 8.9 some higher education, 8.1 secondary education, 7.3 other education. Of the total number present, 70 percent were teachers. The absence of a breakdown according to nationality suggests a Great-Russian preponderance. (Ts. Fridliand, "O bor'be za marksistskuiu istoricheskuiu nauku v SSSR," *Pod znamenem marksizma* 2–3 [1929]: 105–6; *TP*, 1:73–74; *Pravda*, 5 Jan. 1929.) Fridliand claimed that 800 historians attended the conference; G.D. Alekseeva, writing long after the event, gives the figure 600 (*OI*, 4:205).

7. *TP*, 1:303. Pankratova interprets this passage to signify that Pokrovskii leaped from economic determinism to subjective fatalism (*Protiv Pokrovskogo*, 1:56–57). My understanding is that the passage represents Pokrovskii's inability, having abandoned economic materialism, to formulate the tenets of historical materialism.

8. As late as 1960, Nechkina, in the course of rehabilitating Pokrovskii, attributed to him a statement at the conference to the effect that a normal person cannot study the middle ages (*ISSSR* 1 [1960]: 87).

9. For a listing in English of the papers and their authors, see Shteppa, 1963:50–53.

10. *TP*, 1:IX, 493; see also *VKA* 32 (1929):215.

11. *TP*, 1:456; see also *Pravda*, 4 Jan. 1929.

12. *TP*, 1:77. Apparently the Ukrainian delegation had opposed this decision at a preliminary conference but had then acceded to it by the time of the final vote (*VKA* 32 [1929]:215).

13. The conference was considered such an extraordinary success that it was decided to hold an International Congress of Marxist Historians in 1930—an unfulfilled plan (*Plan*, 1928:130).

14. *Pravda*, 10 Feb. 1929; *Prapor marksizmu* 2 (1929).

15. For a somewhat different interpretation see Aron, 1963:300; see also F.E. Los, "K

voprosu o periodizatsii istorii sovetskoi istoricheskoi nauki," *ISSSR* 4 (1960):147; N. Po-
lonska-Vasylenko, *Ukrains'ka academiia nauk* (2 vols., Munich, 1955, 1958); George
Luckyj, *Literary Politics in the Soviet Ukraine, 1917–1934* (New York, 1956).
    16. The best standard accounts are Robert V. Daniels, *The Conscience of the Revolu-
tion: Communist Opposition in Soviet Russia* (Cambridge, 1960); Popov, 1934, 2, Moshe
Lewin, *The Russian Peasants and Soviet Power: A Study of Collectivization* (Evanston,
Ill., 1968), and Vaganov, 1969 and 1970.

Chapter 7

    1. *NR* 5–6 (1929):100. A few of the institutes, mostly for work in the natural sci-
ences, evidently lingered on until early 1930. *OI,* 4:237.
    2. Interview with M.E. Naidenov, Moscow, 19 Nov. 1966.
    3. *TP,* 1:24. In a somewhat ceremonious testimonial to Riazanov, Pokrovskii credited
him with first suggesting the creation of a Marxist Institute of History. He stated that he
and Riazanov had disagreed as to under whose auspices it would be formed. (*IM* 15
[1930]:168–69.)
    4. "Vsesoiuznaia konferentsiia istorikov-marksistov," *IM* 11 (1929):6–7; in fact it
was registered in the resolution of the conference (see *IM* 15 [1930]:166 and also Doroshenko, 1966:18); see also P.O. Gorin, *Arkhivnoe Delo* 20 (1929):23.
    5. *VKA* 4–5 (1932):44–61 and *PM* 4–5 (1932):3–13.
    6. *VKA* 31 (1929):239; see also ibid., 39 (1930):15.
    7. *VKA* 33 (1929):282–83; Ivanova, 1968:119; Barber, 1971:91–92; *Sotsialisticheskii
vestnik* 23 (1929):15.
    8. *PM* 4–5 (1932):9–10; cf. *VKA* 4–5 (1932):52. It should be recalled that as late as
August 1928, RANION had been included in an enumeration of party schools in a resolution of the Party Central Committee. See above, p. 73.
    9. As summarized in *VKA* 33 (1929):270.
    10. *Pravda,* 17 March 1929, "O nauchno-issledovatel'skoi rabote istorikov." Preo-
brazhenskii defended himself in the 12 April issue, and in the same number, Pokrovskii
highhandedly dismissed his defense. All three were associated with RANION's Institute of
History. Preobrazhenskii taught ancient history; Veselovskii, a future Academician, taught
Russian history. The following month Druzhinin defended his dissertation at the institute;
it was accepted but declared to be non-Marxist.
    11. The following passages are from *IM* 11 (1929):3–7.
    12. *Pravda,* 25 Jan. 1929; I.K. Luppol, "K vyboram v akademii nauk SSSR," *NR* 11
(1928):3–4; Shteppa, 1963:48.
    13. *Pravda,* 25 Jan. 1929; 1 Feb. 1929; 9 Feb. 1929. For a more complete account of
this event, and its antecedents and consequences, see Loren Graham, *The Soviet Academy
of Sciences and the Communist Party, 1927–1932* (Princeton, 1967); see also Alexander
Vucunich, *The Soviet Academy of Sciences* (Stanford, 1956), pp. 21–41.
    14. *Pravda,* 16 Nov., 19 Nov. 1929; *NR* 1 (1930):97. Ol'denburg had hitherto enjoyed
considerable security. He had known Lenin's brother Alexander, and when Lenin first
arrived in St. Petersburg, he sought out Ol'denburg to discuss with him Alexander's
scientific work. See A.I. Ivanskii, ed., *Molodye gody V. I. Lenina: Po vospominaniam
sovremennikov i dokumentakh* (2d ed., Moscow, 1958), pp. 389–90. I am indebted to my
former student Paul Soifer for this reference.
    15. Shteppa, 1963:49; see also E.F. Maksimovich, "Istoricheskaia nauka v SSSR i
marksizm-leninizm," *Sovremennyia zapiski* 62 (1936):417–18; "The Treatment of Scholars
in the U.S.S.R.," *Slavonic and East European Review* 11 (1933):710–14; *VKA* 32
(1929):229; Naidenov, 1961:92.

16. *Sotsialisticheskii Vestnik* 22 (1931):15; Stuart Thompkins, "Trends in Communist Historical Thought," *Slavonic and East European Review* 13 (1934):308; G. Zaidel and M. Tsvibak, "Vreditel'stvo na istoricheskom fronte. Tarle, Platonov i ikh shkoli," *PM* 3 (1931):96. Soviet historians usually remained silent about the arrests or referred to them obliquely; note the following statement by F. Potemkin, who was, like Tarle, a diplomatic historian: "Not only theoretical differences separate us now from Tarle, but—speaking without metaphor—thick walls with firm bars separate [us]" (*IM* 21 [1931]:53). In March 1930 Pokrovskii referred directly to a purge going on of historians in institutions of higher learning (*IM* 16 [1930]:16).

17. Interview with M. E. Naidenov, Moscow, October 1966.

18. On October 10, 1930, a report was heard and a discussion held at a joint meeting of Sections on Industrial Capitalism of the Institute of History and the SMH, published as "Burzhuaznaia istoriografiia i ideologiia restavratorstva," *IM* 18–19 (1930):157–77. A similar meeting was held in the Methodological Section of the SMH on December 18, 1930, "Burzhuaznaia istoriki Zapada v SSSR (Tarle, Petrushevskii, Kareev, Buzeskul i drugie)," *IM* 21 (1931):44–86. Meetings were held in Leningrad on January 29, February 12 and 16, 1931 (*PM* 3 [1931]:86–120). Other materials are listed in the bibliography.

19. *VKA* 32 (1929):211–12; *Sovetskaia istoricheskaia entsiklopediia* (Moscow, 1965), 7:col. 588. For a more detailed description of the KA than can be found in the standard Soviet encyclopedias, see its *Kratkii otchet o rabote Kommunisticheskoi Akademii za 1928–1929 gg.* (Moscow, 1929), the appendix of which lists its members. The IKP was separated from the KA in 1931.

20. *VKA* 42 (1930):163; *VKA* 37–38 (1930):156. Evidently the institute did not fully share the new prosperity of the KA. Though two floors were added to the building on Volkhanka (presently the Institute of Philosophy of the Academy of Sciences), the Institute of History was confined to three rooms. Presumably, like the members of the SMH, the members of the institute had to do their work on the premises of others.

21. Piontkovskii was an experienced party specialist in Russian history who became academic secretary of the Institute of History. He served there, according to one of the institute's graduates now in the West, as an intemperate watchdog. (Interview with N. Ulianov, New Haven, 20 June 1969.) Savel'ev was an old Bolshevik and in 1918 a Left Communist who became prominent in journalism (on the editorial boards of *Pravda* and *Izvestiia*) and scholarly institutions (in the leadership of the Lenin Institute, the SMH, and the Institute of History; in 1931 a deputy chairman of the KA). He was promoted to candidate member of the Central Committee in 1930. (*Nauka i nauchnye rabotniki* (1934):192, 249; *Teoreticheskii front* 4 [Feb. 1932]; *VKA* 1 [1934]:108–11; *BKA* 7–8 [1931]:3.)

22. *BK* 1 (1931):120. In 1928 Pokrovskii had been appointed to the editorial board of a commission, whose chairman was Iaroslavskii, for the publication of minutes of party conferences and congresses (*ITsK*, 25 May 1928:13).

23. Out of a total of about 500. Most historical work outside the major cities was, at this time, devoted to folklore (Doroshenko, 1966:16).

24. *KA otchet, 1928–1929:*57. A complete listing of reports is given on pp. 57–59. It includes one by the Norwegian Marxist Halvdan Koht, who spoke on the class warfare of the peasantry in the history of Norway.

Chapter 8

1. The amalgamation, which occurred in 1928, also brought the Society of Old Bolsheviks into the Lenin Institute. In 1931, after the dismissal of Riazanov, the Lenin Insti-

tute would be consolidated with the Marx-Engels Institute, which laid the foundation for the present Institute of Marxism-Leninism.

2. See *PR* 4 (1929):230, which, while praising the SMH, calls for strict delimitization of the work of the various institutes.

3. *VKA* 33 (1929):271. Kaganovich, secretary of the Moscow organization, evidently himself signed the resolution making him a member of the KA.

4. Zhdanov, speaking in Stalin's name, repudiated the study of terrorists. See *Istoriia i istoriki*, 1965:257.

5. For an enumeration of the 1928 writings on Chernyshevskii by both Steklov and Pokrovskii and a concise discussion of them, see the observation of M.V. Nechkina in *Ocherki istorii istoricheskoi nauki v SSSR* 4 (1966): 354–56. What is probably one of Pokrovskii's best essays, "N.G. Chernyshevskii as an Historian" is reprinted in his *Iz-brannye proizvedeniia* (1965–67, 4:395–425).

6. Phrase used by Sidorov, 1964:136.

7. O.D. Sokolov, quoting Central Party archives (1962:73).

8. Ivan Adol'fovich Teodorovich, a member of the Polish nobility whose family had lost its estate after the 1863 Uprising, was born in Smolensk. He enrolled in the science faculty of Moscow University and quickly became involved in revolutionary activity. Arrest, imprisonment, and escape followed. In 1905 he was secretary of the Editorial Board of Lenin's *Proletarii*, and thereby a member of the Bolshevik Center. During the revolution that year, he returned to Petrograd. At the Fifth Congress (London), he was elected to the Central Committee. He spent 1908–13 in exile. In 1917, he was a member of the Bolshevik Central Committee, a member of the Central Executive Committee of the First Congress of Soviets, and chairman of the Petrograd City Duma. He was a member of the first Soviet government but resigned when the Bolsheviks refused to form a coalition government. He fought against Kolchak as a member of a partisan unit. In 1920, he became deputy commissar of agriculture. (*Malia Sovetskaia Entsiklopediia* [Moscow, 1932], 8:col. 738–39; *Geroi oktiabria: kniga uchastnikh velikoi Oktiabr'skoi sotsialistiches-koi revoliutsii* [2 vols., Moscow, 1967], 2:470–71; Hoover Institution, Okhrana Archives, XVIb[6]a, No. 375, 1909.)

9. Teodorovich, 1929, reprinted in a book by Teodorovich (1930) in which he assembled his major statements in the dispute, cited hereafter as *Znachenie narodnoi voli*.

10. Published as *Diskussiia o narodnoi vole* (Moscow, 1930); a briefer version appeared in *IM* 15 (1930):86–143.

11. Stenographic notes published as *Voprosy prepodavaniia leninizma, istorii VKP (b), Kominterna* (Moscow, 1930); cited hereafter as *Voprosy prepodavaniia*. This is a valuable source on a variety of questions. As far as I know, the only copy, outside of closed collections in the Soviet Union, is held in the Butler Library of Columbia University.

12. "Tezisy k 50 letiiu Narodnoi voli," *Pravda*, 9 Apr. 1930. A statement drafted by Tatarov, an associate of Pokrovskii, and approved by the SMH formed the basis of the Kultprop theses (*OI*, 4:364). In *Pravda* (22 Nov. 1930) Teodorovich confessed to a variety of political errors, including having opposed the Bolshevik seizure of power in 1917. He refrained from apologizing for a single word about *Narodnaia volia*.

13. Andrei Sergeievich Bubnov, a prominent Bolshevik leader, was elected to the first Politburo in 1917. He supported Trotsky in 1923 but then went over to Stalin after Lenin's death. In 1929 he replaced Lunacharskii as commissar of education and thereby became Pokrovskii's superior. (S.V. Utechin, *Everyman's Concise Encyclopedia of Russian* [London, 1961], pp. 75–76.) N.N. Popov was the author of a widely read history of the party that passed through many editions. He joined the party in 1919 and in 1930 became a candidate member of the Central Committee.

14. Nosov & Zakharikov, 1962:75. The ellipses are probably theirs, not Pokrovskii's. A briefer version can be found in Sokolov, 1962.

15. All quotations in this discussion are from *Voprosy*, 1930: 160–68 passim.

16. Interview with S.M. Dubrovskii, Moscow, December 6, 1966.

17. *Voprosy*, 1930:211. K.A. Popov, who read the controversial report on Leninism at the First Marxist Historical Conference (see Chapter 6 above), is not to be confused with N.N. Popov (see note 13 above). He was Pokrovskii's deputy in GUS and a member of the editorial board of the Lenin Institute. A former Menshevik, he graduated from the IKP. D.Ia. Kin was a graduate of Pokrovskii's IKP seminar and from 1928 to 1931 an editor of *IM*. Like Popov, he was a member of the editorial board of the Lenin Institute. He was deputy director, under Adoratskii, of the Historico-Party Department of the IKP, a position he retained when the department became a separate institute in 1930.

18. See note 12 above.

19. *VKA* 39 (1930):14–90. Page numbers appearing in parentheses in the text refer to this source.

20. Gorin, 1933:106–7. Later in 1930 it seems that Pokrovskii lost his majority in the bureau of the KA presidium. An unknown economics teacher named O.P. Dzenis was suddenly elevated into the KA leadership. That Kaganovich had promulgated the resolution making himself a member of the KA leadership, and that he seemed to be the only major party leader involved directly in the activities of the KA at this time, and the fact that Dzenis adhered to the line of Pashukanis and Ostrovitianov all suggest that he was an associate of Kaganovich. See *Za povorot na fronte estestvoznaniia. Diskussiia na zasedaniiakh Presidiuma Komakademii 23/XII 1930 g.—6/I 1931 g.* (Moscow-Leningrad, 1931), pp. 64–70 and passim.

21. For an excellent discussion of the concept of partiinost', see David Joravsky, *Soviet Marxism and Natural Science, 1917–1932* (New York, 1961), ch. 2 and passim. Partiinost' "represents an effort to blur the distinction between two assertions. First, Soviet historians assert that the mind of the investigator, shaped by its vantage point in society affects his findings. Thus, very much in the spirit of the new history, they deny the contrary notion, that the investigator faithfully reproduces the past as it was. They equate this first assertion with what is actually a second and separate assertion that all historians serve some vested interest and that they themselves serve the interest of the proletariat. They employ arguments for the first easily demonstrable and almost universally accepted insight to justify the second statement, which is essentially an exhortation." George Enteen, "Two Books on Soviet Historiography," *World Politics* 20 (Jan. 1968):349–51.

22. See Chapter 2 above.

23. *Protokoly pervogo s'ezda arkhivnykh deiatelei RSFSR* (Moscow, 1926), p. 277; emphasis added.

24. See Chapter 6 above; see also his rejoinder to Gorin at the First Conference of Marxist-Leninist Research Institutions in 1928 in *VKA* 26 (1928):267. This matter provides an excellent illustration of the treatment of Pokrovskii's writing during his posthumous denigration. Compare Pokrovskii's plea to student archivists for the study of pre-nineteenth-century history, "Politicheskoe znachenie arkhivov," *Arkhivnoe delo* 2 (1925):3, with the view attributed to him on the pages of the same journal fourteen years later. (A.' Mukhin, "Reshitel'no i do kontsa likvidirovat' oshibki 'shkoli' M. N. Pokrovskogo v oblasti Arkhivnogo Dela," *Arkhivnoe delo* 2 [1939]:6–14).

25. From the resolution of the general meeting of the SMH, March 19, 1930 (*IM* 15 [1930]:165).

26. See Chapter 6 above.

27. *VKA* 39 (1930):27; page numbers appearing in parentheses in the text refer to this source.

Chapter 9

1. F. Litvinov in a discussion published in *IM* 22 (1931):113.
2. See David Joravsky, *Soviet Marxism and Natural Science, 1917–1932* (New York, 1961), ch. 14, 16.
3. See Gorin's remarks in *VKA* 42 (1930):62–65.
4. Sokolov, 1962:77, citing Central Party Archives. Ellipses are most likely by Sokolov. Both sides bombarded the Central Committee and Kultprop with such notes. Doroshenko, 1966:21.
5. Nosov & Zakharikov, 1962:88; Sokolov, 1962:77.
6. Iaroslavskii became a party secretary in 1921, a year before Stalin did. He became a member of the Siberian Bureau of the party the following year, probably owing to his familiarity with the area. He had been born in Chita, the offspring of an exiled family. That he was not banished to Siberia by Stalin is suggested by the fact that the following year he became a secretary of the Central Control Commission. All the standard biographical sources have accounts of Iaroslavskii; perhaps the most useful is the *Malaia entsiklopediia* (2d ed., Moscow, 1947), 11:cols. 1170–71. For a popular biography of this important figure neglected by Western historiography see D. Grigor'ev & E. Kut'ev, *Boets i letopisets revoliutsii* (Moscow, 1960).
7. Sokolov, 1962:77; the following, in addition to Pokrovskii and Kaganovich, were members of the presidium: Miliutin, Kerzhentsev, Pashukanis, Ostrovitianov, Bubnov, Varga, Gaister, Deborin, Kritsman, Krzhizhanovskii, Lukin, Ronin, Riazanov, Savel'ev, Stetskii, Schmidt (*VKA* 39 [1930]:88). With some confidence one can guess that two members of the troika were Pashukanis and Ostrovitianov; with less confidence one can guess that the third was either Varga, Riazanov, or Bubnov. Perhaps it was Dzenis (see Chapter 8, note 20).
8. The archives contain five separate drafts of the letter. Though one of them is signed by Kaganovich and Molotov, for some reason there is a disagreement among Soviet specialists as to which is the final draft. (Interviews with A.P. Nosov, Moscow, 14 Dec. 1966.) It seems that Pokrovskii denounced his opponents by name and that some drafts contain more names than others. Passages from the letter or summaries of it have appeared in six recent works: Nosov & Zakharikov, 1962:87–88; Sokolov, 1962:75–78; Sokolov, 1966:67; Sidorov, 1964:63; Lutskii, 1965:364; Ivanova, 1968:180. Early in 1931 Pokrovskii published "O russkom feodalizme, proizkhozhdenii i kharaktere absolutizma v Rossii" (1931b), translated and included as an appendix in *BH*, which, I think, contains the gist of the historical portions of the letter. It is discussed in Chapter 10.
9. Ivanova, 1968: 180. The ending *shchina* means era of the wicked deeds of; the term *pokrovshchina* may be understood as the pernicious influence of Pokrovskii. *Rubinshchina* refers to a body of economic theory, allegedly Menshevik, that had recently been discredited in that sector of the intellectual life; *deborinshchina* refers to similar discussions among philosophers. I.I. Rubin, a distinguished marxologist, had been a lecturer at the IKP.
10. "No etomu pis'mu ne bylo dano khodu." Nosov & Zhakharikov, 1962:88.
11. Sokolov, 1970:100–101; ellipses by Sokolov.
12. Ibid., p. 100. In this context editing should be understood as something far removed from copy-editing and much closer to ideological supervision.
13. Interview with V.A. Doroshenko, Moscow, November 1966.
14. *BKA* 7–8 (1931):3; *VKA* 5–6 (1931): 126.
15. *BK* 1 (1931):108; *IM* 21 (1931):136.
16. See Chapter 8.
17. "Tezucy k 25 letnemu iubileiu revoliutsii 1905 g." Signed by Kultprop and the Lenin Institute. Sokolov (1966:31) contends that the dispute ended in a victory for Pokrov-

skii. See also *PR* 2–3 (1931):218. I.I. Mints (interview, State College, Pa., November 1964) contends that his side won.

18. *Istoriia VKP(b)* (1926–30). These volumes are the chief manifestation of Iaroslavskii's school. The contributors (with the exception of Piontkovskii) make up the nucleus of the faction. The contributors to volume 1 (1926): T. Kramol'nikov, N. El'vov, O. Riimskii; volume 2 (1930): T. Kramol'nikov, I. Mints, I. Nikitin, O. Riimskii, A. Roos, N. El'vov; volume 3 (1929): D. Baevskii, A. Vaks, A. Sidorov; volume 4 (1929): D. Kin, I. Mints, S. Piontkovskii. A second edition of volume 3 appeared in 1931. I have not seen it, but it appears to have been more sharply adverse to Pokrovskii, especially his theory of imperialism, than any of the others.

19. Small-scale landowners predominating as a result of the expropriation of the gentry.

20. *Bol'shevik* 7 (1931):87–88; 9 (1931):71.

21. Gorin, 1933:113. Gorin, a Belorussian, had a faulty command of Russian, which was not overlooked by his critics. To the extent that his health permitted, Pokrovskii participated publicly in the controversy. On the pages of *Bol'shevik:* "How is it possible that one can hear even now that Lenin did not pose the question of the growing over of the bourgeois revolution into a socialist [revolution] in 1905; how is it possible to hear even now that our Revolution of 1905 was for the Bolsheviks only a *peasant* revolution, that such an evaluation distinguished Leninism from Trotskyism, which ignored the peasants" (1965–67, 4:217).

22. See *Biulleten' oppozitsii* 3–4 (1929); 6 (1929); 17–18 (1930).

23. Pokrovskii stood above public criticism, but Kritsman, whom Pokrovskii had cited in support of his theory of imperialism, was censured in an editorial in *IM* (21 [1931]:12). In the same issue, Iaroslavskii's supporter Kin wrote, "Comrade Kritsman's views of our Revolution are based on the untrue, in essence, Trotskyite theory that Russia before October was a colony of foreign finance capital." ("O proletarskoi revoliutsii, burzhuaznykh restavratorakh, i melkoburzhuaznom likvidtorchestve," p. 32.)

24. From Sokolov, 1969:43, as translated in *Soviet Studies in History* 8 (Spring 1970):341–42.

25. For an interpretation of Slutskii's article that comprehends it as an attack on Stalin's leadership, see G.A. Tokaev, *Betrayal of an Ideal* (Bloomington, Ind., 1955), p. 146. Though I think Tokaev's conclusion about Slutskii's intentions is unwarranted, it is understandable that many of those who, following Rakovskii, equated Centrism with Stalin's position understood the article this way. There is, however, another sense in which the article may have been a criticism of one of Stalin's policies. One can read the article as a gentle reproach by the author to Lenin for his failure to support Rosa Luxemburg, "the healthy core" of German Social Democracy, against the Center. And this could be taken as disapproval of the communists' opposition to Social Democracy in Weimar Germany and elsewhere and as disapproval of the theory of Social Fascism, which pronounced the SD's, not the Nazis, as the main enemy. This was perhaps hinted at by Kaganovich: Karl Radek "developed the theory that Rosa Luxemburg was a bridge by which the better type of Social Democratic workers could cross over to our Party and that therefore she should not be severely criticized. First of all, his theory is incorrect: it is not necessary for the workers to cross over to us by means of the Luxemburg bridge. Secondly, the workers who are still connected with the bridge must know the mistakes of the Left Social-Democrats in order to learn from these mistakes and become true Bolsheviks. If they do not, if the mistakes of Rosa Luxemburg are slurred over, this bridge will be a bridge to Social-Democracy and not to Communism. Exposing the mistakes of Rosa Luxemburg in a Bolshevik manner is in itself a bridge for the workers, leading from Social-Democratic mistakes to Bolshevism." (See *The Communist* 12 [1932]:175.) But it is difficult to reconcile this interpretation of Slutskii's intentions with the fact that Iaroslavskii

supported him in any measure. (See below, note 26.) Perhaps the mere fact that the article lent itself to conjectures about current policies was sufficient reason for Stalin to use it to break the stalemate on the historical front.

26. Em. Iaroslavskii, "V redaktsiu *Bol'shevika*," *Bol'shevik* 21 (1931):68; see also *PM* 8–9 (1931):14.

Chapter 10

1. "O nekotorykh voprosakh istorii bol'shevizma," *PR* 6 (1931), also published in a multitude of other journals; translated in *Problems of Leninism* (1953:483–97). According to A. Avtorkhanov, the letter was the result of an initiative by Sergei Ingulov, chairman of the Central Committee's Press Bureau (*Stalin and the Communist Party: A Study in the Technology of Power* [Institute for the Study of the USSR; New York, 1959], p. 186).

2. Remarks of I.I. Mints, *Vsesoiuznoe soveshchanie istorikov* (Moscow, 1964), p. 75.

3. According to Avtorkhanov, all fields felt the impact of the letter—science, literature, painting, theater, music, movies, and even the circus. Not only suspicious books but stenographic reports of congresses, old speeches of Stalin, Kaganovich, and Molotov were withdrawn from party libraries for editing. (*Stalin and the Soviet Communist Party*, p. 187.)

4. See Mints' public recantation in which, among other things, he confessed the error of voting for an incorrect resolution on November 10, which interfered with the mobilization of historians (*Bol'shevik* 23–24 [1931]:135). It was reported in *VKA* 1–2 (1932):42 that during the first half-hour of the meeting, the discussion was at too low a political level. Since the session lasted for three days, and the opposition proposed a resolution, the controversy probably lasted considerably longer.

5. *Bol'shevik* 22 (1931):5. Isaac Deutscher, who was in Moscow at the time, recalled that "such was the dismay caused even among Stalin's henchmen that soon his [Iaroslavskii's] disgrace had to be lifted" (*The Prophet Outcast: Trotsky, 1929–1940* [London, 1963], p. 164). Iaroslavskii addressed a Central Committee plenum on February 10, 1932: "I should state here about myself—repeat what I have already written in *Pravda*. In this connection I erred in [my] slipshod selection of collaborators and in the fact that I myself was neglectful of the duty that I took upon myself when I undertook to be Editor-in-Chief of such a serious work as a four volume 'History of the Party' " (Nosov & Zakharikov, 1962:100–101, quoting Central Party Archives).

6. Remark by A.L. Sidorov, *VI* 3 (1962):35.

7. It should be remembered that most IKP students were not youngsters but experienced party officials.

8. A phrase of I.I. Mints. Interview, Ithaca, New York, November 1964.

9. Ibid.

10. Almost all the commentaries decried Mints' "theoretical error"; for example, see Kaganovich's sarcasm (note 26, below) about Mints' "feeble talk" about "objectivity" and "political expedience."

11. *Sovetskaia istoricheskaia entsiklopediia* 7:col. 717.

12. As translated in *The Communist* 12 (1932):171. Not only the current periodical literature, but a major textbook stressed the same point: "These contrabandists denied that the Bolsheviks, headed by Lenin, even before 1905 had propounded the theory that the bourgeois-democratic revolution would grow into a socialist revolution and that they had carried out this theory in practice at the time of the revolutions of 1905 and 1917" (Knorin, 1935:459). An editorial in *IM* stated the same idea as follows: "There can be no doubt that the study of the problem of the growing over of the bourgeois-democratic

revolution into a socialist [revolution], the study of the October Revolution should be at the center of attention of the entire historical front'' (23–24 [1932]:10).

13. *IM*, 1932, 26–27:357. Vanag had capitulated orally even earlier; see p. 155 above.

14. The following account is based on I.V. Frolov's report to the presidium of the KA, published as "O rabote Instituta istorii za pervoe polgodie 1932 g.," *VKA* 7–8 (1932):199–207.

15. V.A. Doroshenko, interview, Moscow, 25 Oct. 1966.

16. *VKA* 9–10 (1932):179–80; 11–12 (1932):196.

17. *IM* 30 (1933):186, and perhaps in a similar celebration held elsewhere (*IM* 29 [1933]:149).

18. *Arkhiv AN*, fund 234, p. 69. I am grateful to Professor Marin Pundeff for informing me of this reference. G.D. Alekseeva reports that the SMH was closed only in 1936 (*Sovetskaia istoricheskaia entsiklopediia*, 10: col. 411). It seems that an unpublished Central Committee resolution was circulated at this time.

19. IKP Brigade Tolstukhina and Miller, "O rabotakh t. Piontkovskogo," *IM* 23–24 (1932):192–200, the same issue that eulogized Pokrovskii.

20. O.D. Sokolov, interview, Moscow, 12 Nov. 1966.

21. This Rubinshtein is Pokrovskii's former student, not the author of *Russkaia istoriografiia*. Sidorov was expelled from the party in 1936. To avoid the almost certain fatal consequence, he immediately transported himself from Khabarovsk to Moscow. Thanks to Iaroslavskii, the secretariat of the Central Control Commission reviewed his case. "I left the meeting again a party member. In Kuibyshev, on the street where I walked, everyone greeted me with smiles of springtime" (K.N. Tarnovskii, "Put' uchenogo," *Istoricheskie zapiski* 80 [1967]:223).

22. He was arrested in the Leningrad roundup that followed Kirov's assassination (N. Ulianov, interview, New Haven, 20 June 1969). He was arrested again after World War II. After Stalin's death he became a professor at the Institute of History.

23. For details about his sad fate, see Evgeniia Ginzburg, *Journey in the Whirlwind* (New York, 1964), part 1. Her work also contains a vivid portrait of Iaroslavskii (pp. 32–34).

24. *VKA* 7–8 (1932):205; 1 (1934):117; *IM* 23–24 (1932):11; *Pervaia oblastnaia konferentsiia Ts. Ch. O.*, p. 49.

25. "Za bol'shevitskoe izuchenie istorii partii," *Pravda*, 12 Dec. 1931; republished in a score of journals. As translated in *The Communist* 12 (1932):159–78.

26. *Teoreticheskii front* 2 (1932). On January 23, in a report to the Moscow regional and city committee of the party, Kaganovich again complained about the continued existence of "rotten liberalism." He repudiated instances where "people have been mechanically expelled" from the party. "But there were others who consciously began to evolve a definite theory of a 'milder, more liberal attitude.' " He then outlined a theory of capitalist encirclement and cited it as justification for greated terror. (L.M. Kaganovich, *The Moscow Bolsheviks in the Struggle for Victory of the Five-Year Plan* [Moscow, 1932], pp. 121–23.)

27. See Mariagin 1965:209, 215–17, 221, 229–30, 231–35, 298, and passim. A major theme of the work is that Postyshev pursued a policy of not letting collectivization outstrip technical preparation, which in the context of the book means no all-out collectivization in a region where the Machine Tractor Stations had not yet been built. A Central Committee commission arrived in Kharkov to investigate alleged mistakes with regard to the tempo of collectivization and charges of political deviation that grew out of a stated criticism by Postyshev of an article in *Pravda*. The article in question seems to have been Stalin's speech to party agrarian specialists, in which he called for all-out collectivization and the elimination of the kulaks as a class. Ordzhonikidze, chairman of the commission, cleared

Postyshev and his associates in the Kharkov party committee of the charges. This occurred in February 1930, just a few months before Postyshev's transfer to Moscow.

Chapter 11

1. Interview with I.I. Mints, Ithaca, New York, November 1964.
2. Nevertheless, in August he became a corresponding member of the KA.
3. As quoted by Pokrovskii, *IM* 16 (1930):15.
4. *Protiv mekhanisticheskoi teorii v istoricheskoi literature* (Moscow, 1930). An abbreviated version of the report but not the discussion is available in *Biulleten' zaochnoi kontsul'tatsii* 4 (1930):16–23, at the Lenin Library.
5. *Spornye voprosy metodologii istorii* (Leningrad, 1930); *Diskussiia ob aziatskom sposobe proizvodstva po dokladu M. Godesa* (Leningrad, 1931). See also Karl A. Wittfogel, *Oriental Despotism* (New Haven, 1957), p. 404.
6. Danilova, *Istoricheskie zapiski* 76 (1965):103. She had in mind his report "Slavery and Feudalism in Ancient Russia," which was published in *Izvestiia GAIMK*, no. 86.
7. *Karl Marks i problema sotsial'no-ekonomicheskikh formatsiei* (Leningrad, 1933). The purpose here is not to describe all sides of this profound and learned debate, which might be considered one of the finest flowers of Soviet historical scholarship, but merely to describe the facet that constitutes a commentary on Pokrovskii's system and affected its standing. The discussion has been the subject of a number of excellent studies: Leo Yaresh, "The Problem of Periodization," in C.E. Black, ed., *Rewriting Russian History: Soviet Interpretations of Russia's Past* (New York, 1956); Danilova, *Istoricheskie zapiski* 76 (1965) and her chapter in *OI* 4 (1966): 732–44. For interesting details, see the essay by S.N. Valk cited in Chapter 4, note 20, and for an evaluation that differs from my own, see the remarks of M.V. Nechkina, *Istoriia i sotsiologiia* (Moscow, 1964), pp. 228–34. For the political ramifications of the theory of the Asiatic mode of production, see the remarks at the Fifteenth Party Congress, which includes a debate between Lominadze and Bukharin (*XV s'ezd vsesoiuznoi kommunisticheskoi partii* [*b*] [Moscow, 1961], 1:732–42, 801–11, 839–41). The debate warrants further study both for its own sake as a component of Russian culture and as an important context of recent discussions of historical materialism.
8. *IM* 16 (1930):126; further references to this source appear in parentheses in the text.
9. *Karl Marks i problema sotsial'no-ekonomicheskikh formatsiei* (1933:15); further reference to this source appear in parentheses in the text.
10. Prigozhin thus tacitly admitted that his work did not wholly conform to Marx's theories. He noted explicitly that Lenin's explication of Marxism put an end to any skepticism, any denial that the theory can be found in Marx's writings (15).
11. Prigozhin could cite neither Marx nor Lenin to support the assertion that there are only three antagonistic formations. By limiting the number to three, he banished the Asian means of production (see esp. pp. 78–80).
12. It should be recalled that at the time Pokrovskii had argued with Lenin about this very point. See above, p. 18.
13. *BH*, 2:328; also p. 321. In the article "1905 goda," Pokrovskii noted that for the intelligentsia the Constituent Assembly had value in its own right, but this was not so for the Bolsheviks, for theirs was a "program of struggle for socialism" (*Bol'shevik* 1 [1931]:48–49). It is noteworthy that the portion of the speech quoted in the text was not included in the version published in Russian. See 1930e:19.
14. 1931c, translated by Rufus Mathewson in Stern, *Varieties of History*, pp. 335–41. Pokrovskii still commanded deference all the same; some of the younger historians had the same ambivalent feelings toward him as he to them, but they expressed their diffidence

with greater subtlety. When his health had begun to fail, he received the following note from some of the staff and students at the IKP: "It seems to us that now, when the period of intensive organizational work has been passed, part of the work can be transferred to the shoulders of students trained by you. You should organize your work so that at least three days a week are wholly set aside by you for rest and theoretical work. And the Peoples' Commissariat of Education, and the Comacademy, and Central Archives, and even more so the Institute of Red Professors will willingly accommodate you by holding their sessions either at the beginning or at the end of the week, avoiding the three days that you keep for yourself." From the personal archives of Academician I.I. Mints, as published in Sokolov, 1969:42.

15. 1931b, translated as an appendix in *BH*, 1:281–95. The article was based on Pokrovskii's concluding remarks to his IKP seminar, November-December 1930 and February 1931. Because its content and purpose correspond closely to his February 5 letter to the Central Committee, it is likely that the article and the letter contain many identical passages.

16. *BK* 4 (1932):37. Earlier he had stressed the capitalist component of Russian historiography (see Chapter 2 above).

17. *BH*, 1:289. Page numbers in parentheses in the text refer to this volume.

18. Pokrovskii quoting Lenin (293).

19. See N. Valentinov [N.V. Vol'skii], "Sut' bol'shevizma v izobrazhenii Iu. Piatakov," *Novyi zhurnal* 52 (1958):151–53. The passage quoted is from Leonard Shapiro's summary, which is based on this article and on Shapiro's conversations with its author, *The Communist Party of the Soviet Union* (New York, 1960), p. 381.

20. Polina Vinogradskaia, *Sobitiia i pamiatnye vstrechi* (Moscow, 1968), p. 127. Pokrovskii quoting Lenin, who was quoting Marx's paraphrase of Heine.

Epilogue

1. Cf. Pokrovskii, 1933a, 1:300 and *Na boevom*, 1929:34.

2. "Leninskii etap istoricheskoi nauki," *IM* 1 (1934):3–4. An editorial note in the next issue dissociated the editor's thesis from Lomakin's (2[1934]:167).

3. *Front nauki i tekhniki* 2 (1935):131; *VKA* 3 (1935):51. For an enumeration of the other posthumous honors to Pokrovskii, see *VKA* 4–5 (1932):92.

4. See *BK* 5–6 (1934):2, and Bushchik, 1961:248–58.

5. A.I. Gukovskii, "Kak ia stal istorikum," *ISSSR* 6 (1965):96–97. This memoir contains much useful information on the preparation of textbooks.

6. "Zamechaniia po povodu konspekta uchebnika po istorii SSSR" (Stalin, Zhdanov, Kirov) and "Zamechaniia o konspekte uchebnika novoi istorii" (Stalin, Kirov, Zhdanov) were both published for the first time in *Pravda* (27 Jan. 1936). The second decree is translated in *International Literature* 9 (1937):53–55. The most important decrees on the teaching of history have been collected in *K uzucheniu istorii* (Moscow, 1938). St. Krasnikov indicates that Kirov's part in drafting the "Remarks" was slight and that he was indisposed to intervening in the writing of history. In *Sergei Mironovich Kirov: zhizn' i deiatel'nost'* (Moscow, 1964), p. 196, he reports that Kirov visited Stalin and Zhdanov in Sochi while they were preparing their observations on the history textbooks. They invited him to spend a few days and work with them. Kirov became embarrassed: " 'Well, Joseph Vissarionovich, what kind of historian am I?'

" 'No matter, sit down and listen.' "

7. For an informative discussion of the decrees see M.V. Nechkina, *ISSSR* 2 (1962):73–74.

8. For example, see "Za Bol'shevitskoe prepodavanie istorii," *BK* 1 (1935):19–36; see also the editorial in *BK* 4 (1934):3–4.

Bibliography

Alatortseva, A.I. 1972. "Struktura i osnovnye napravleniia deiatel'nosti zhurnala 'Istorik-marksist' (1926–1941gg.)." *Istoriia i istoriki: Istoriograficheskii ezhegodnik*. Moscow.

——, and G.D. Alekseeva. 1971. *50 let sovetskoi istoricheskoi nauki: Khronika nauchnoi zhizni 1917–1967*. Moscow.

Alekseeva, G.D. 1968. *Oktiabr'skaia revoliutsiia i istoricheskaia nauka v Rossii (1917–1923)*. Moscow.

"Aperçu sur l'évolution de la conception de l'histoire en Union Soviétique." 1957. *Notes et études documentaires*. 22, 23 Oct.

Aron, Paul. 1950. "Diversity and Uniformity in Soviet Historiography." Paper presented at the Russian Research Center, Harvard University.

——. 1963. "M.N. Pokrovskii and the Impact of the First Five-Year Plan on Soviet Historiography." In *Essays in Russian and Soviet History in Honor of Geroid Tanquary Robinson*. New York.

Asher, Harvey. 1972. "The Rise, Fall, and Resurrection of M.N. Pokrovskii." *The Russian Review*, vol. 31, pp. 49–63.

Avtorkhanov, A.A. 1951. "Polozhenie istoricheskoi nauki v SSSR." *Materialy Konferentsii Nauchnykh Rabotnikov (emigrantov)*. Munich.

Barber, John Douglas. 1971. *The Bolshevization of Soviet Historiography, 1928–1932*. Dissertation submitted for the degree of Doctor of Philosophy, University of Cambridge, Jesus College.

Black, Cyril E. 1962. *Rewriting Russian History*, 2d ed. New York.

Bogdanov, A. 1923. *A Short Course of Economic Science*. London.

Bol'shaia sovetskaia entsiklopediia, 1st ed. 1926–47. Moscow.

Bukharin, N.I. 1928. "Professor s pikoi." *Pravda*, 25 Oct.

——. 1936. "Nuzhna li nam marksistskaia istoricheskaia nauka." *Izvestiia*, 27 Jan.

Bushchik, L.P. 1961. *Ocherk razvitiia shkol'nogo istoricheskogo obrazovaniia v SSSR*. Moscow.

Carson, George Barr, Jr. 1965. "Natural Rights: The Soviet and the 'Bourgeois' Diderot." In *Ideas in History: Essays Presented to Louis Gattchalk by His Former Students*. Durham, N.C.

Chernykh, A.G. 1969. *V.I. Lenin—istorik proletarskoi revoliutsii*. Moscow.

Daniels, Robert V. 1956. "Soviet Thought in the Nineteen-Thirties: An Interpretive Sketch." In Michael Ginzburg and Joseph T. Shaw, eds., *Indiana Slavic Studies*. Bloomington.

Diskussiia ob aziatskom sposobe proizvodstva po dokladu N. Godesa. 1931. Leningrad.

"Diskussiia o germanskoi sotsial-demokratii." 1930a. *IM*, vols. 18–19, pp. 83–156.

"Diskussia o sotsial'no-ekonomicheskikh formatsakh." 1930b. *IM*, vol. 16, pp. 104–60.

"Disput o knige D.M. Petrushevskogo." 1928. *IM*, vol. 8, pp. 79–129.

Doroshenko, V.A. 1966. "Obrazovanie i osnovnye etapy deiatel'nosti obshchestva istorikov-marksistov (1925–1932)." *Vestnik MGU*, Seriia IX Istoriia, vol. 3, pp. 10–22.

Dorotich, D. 1966. "Disgrace and Rehabilitation of M.N. Pokrovsky." *Canadian Slavonic Papers (Revue canadienne de Slavists)*, vol. 8, pp. 169–81.

Druzhinin, N.M. 1967. *Vospominaniia i mysli istorika*. Moscow.

Dubrovskii, S.M. 1929. *K voprosu o sushnosti "aziatskogo" sposoba proizvodstva, feodalizma, krepostnichestva i torgovskogo kapitala*. Moscow.

———. 1962. "Akademik M. N. Pokrovskii i ego rol' v razvitii sovetskoi istoricheskoi nauki." *VI*, vol. 3, pp. 3–30.

———, and D. V. Romanovskii, eds. 1958. "K istorii instituta krasnoi professury." *Istoricheskie arkhivy*, vol. 6, pp. 73–90.

Dunaevskii, V.A. 1966. "Bol'sheviki i germanskie levye na mezhdunarodnoi arene (nekotorye aspekty temy v osveshchenii sovetskoi istoriografii kontsa 20-kh-nachala 30-kh godov." In *Evropa v novoe i noveishee vremia*. Moscow.

Dvadsat' piat' let istoricheskoi nauki v SSSR. 1942. Moscow.

Eissenstat, Bernard W. 1969. "M.N. Pokrovsky and Soviet Historiography: Some Reconsiderations." *Slavic Review*, vol. 28, no. 4, pp. 604–18.

Enteen, George. 1969. "Soviet Historians Review Their Own Past: The Rehabilitation of M. N. Pokrovskii." *Soviet Studies*, vol. 20, pp. 306–20.

Fridliand, Ts. 1928a. "Dva shaga nazad." *Pod znamenem marksiz'ma*, vol. 2, pp. 147–61.

———. 1928b. "Ob ideologicheskoi bor'be na istoricheskom fronte." *Kommunisticheskaia revoliutsiia*, vols. 23–24, pp. 22–33.

Gorin, P.O. 1930. "K voprosu o kharactere revoliutsii 1905 g." *IM*, vol. 20, pp. 164–73.

———, ed. 1933. *M.N. Pokrovskii, bol'shevik-istorik*. Minsk.

Gorodetskii, E.N. 1964. "V.I. Lenin i sozdanie tsentrov istoriko-partiinoi nauki." *VIKPSS*, vol. 8, pp. 17–28.

Gukovskii, A.I. 1968. "Kak sozdalas' 'Russkaia istoriia s drevneishikh vremen' M.N. Pokrovskogo." *VI*, vol. 8, pp. 122–32; 1969, vol. 9, pp. 130–42.

Horak, Stephen M. 1968. "Michael Hrushevsky: Portrait of an Historian." *Canadian Slavonic Papers (Revue canadienne de Slavists)*, vol. 10, no. 3, pp. 341–56.

Iaroslavski, E.M. 1926–30. *Istoriia VKP(b)*. Moscow, 4 vols.

———. 1930. "Nedorazumie li." *Bol'shevik*, vols. 3–4, pp. 121–26.

———. 1931. "O revoliutsii 1905 goda." *IM*, vol. 21, pp. 143–60.

———. 1933. *Bolshevik Verification and Purging of the Party Ranks*. Moscow-Leningrad.

———. 1936. "Itogi protsessa trotsistsko-zinov'evskogo terroristicheskogo kontrrevoliutsionnogo tsentra i istoricheskii front." *IM*, vol. 4, pp. 3–20.

Ivanova, L.V. 1960. "Podgotovka kadrov sovetskikh istorikov (1921–1929)." *ISSSR*, vol. 6, pp. 57–70.

———. 1968. *U istokov sovetskoi istoricheskoi nauki: podgotovka kadrov istorikov-marksistov 1917–1929*. Moscow.

Iz istorii Velkoi oktiabr'skoi sotsialisticheskoi revoliutsii i sotsialisticheskogo stroitel'stva v SSSR. 1967. Leningrad.

Jurij, Boris. 1972. "Who Ruled the Soviet Ukraine in Stalin's Time? (1917–1939)." *Canadian Slavonic Papers (Revue canadienne de Slavists)*, vol. 14, pp. 213–34.

Kabanov, V.V. 1961. "Nekstorye voprosy istochn'ikovedeniia v trudakh M.N. Pokrovskogo (po rabotam 1917–1923 gg.)" In *Trudy Moskovskogo istoriko-arkhivnogo instituta*, vol. 16. Moscow.

Katkov, George. 1962. *The Trial of Bukharin*. London.

Katz, Zev. 1957. *Party Political Education in Soviet Russia*. Ph.D. Thesis, University of London.

Keep, John. 1972. "The Rehabilitation of M.N. Pokrovskii." Alexander Rabinowitch, Janet Rabinowitch, and Ladis Kristof, eds. In *Revolution and Politics, Essays in Memory of B.I. Nicolaevskii*. Bloomington, Ind., pp. 293–313.

Kizevetter, A.A. 1929. *Na rubezhe dvukh stoletii.* Prague.
Knorin, V. G., ed. 1935. *Communist Party of the Soviet Union.* Moscow.
Komarev, A. 1932. *M.N. Pokrovskii.* Voronezh.
Kotov, V.N. 1966. *Istoriografiia istorii SSSR, 1917–1934 gg.* Kiev.
Krasnov, Iu.K. 1967. "M.N. Pokrovskii o nekotorykh voprosakh vneshnei politiki Rossii Kontsa XIX veka." *Voprosy istoriografii i istochnikovedeniia.* Kazan.
Krasso, Nicholas. 1967. "Trotsky's Leninism." *New Left Review,* vol. 44, pp. 64–86.
Kratkaia istoriia SSSR; ot velikoi oktiabr'skoi sotsialisticheskoi revoliutsii do nashikh dnei. 1964. Moscow-Leningrad.
Kratkii otchet o rabote Kommunisticheskoi Akademii za 1928–1929 gg. 1929. Moscow.
Kritsman, L. 1925. *Geroicheskoi period nashei revoliutsii.* Moscow.
"Letter of an Old Bolshevik." 1965. In Boris Nicolaevsky, *Power and the Soviet Elite.* New York-London.
Levshin, B.L., ed. 1976. "U istokov zhurnala 'Istorik marksist.' " *VI,* vol. 6, pp. 97–107.
Lichtheim, George. 1961. *Marxism: An Historical Interpretation.* London.
———. 1963. "Marx and the Asiatic Mode of Production." *St. Antony's Papers,* vol. 14 (Far Eastern Affairs, 3), pp. 86–112.
Lilge, Frederick. 1948. "The Political Control of History Texts in the Soviet Union." *School and Society,* vol. 67, pp. 393–97.
Lukin, N.M. 1931. "Za bol'shevitskuiu partiinost' v istoricheskoi nauke." *IM,* vol. 22, pp. 3–10.
Lunacharskii, A. 1928. "K iubileiu M. N. Pokrovskogo." *VKA,* vol. 29, pp. 9–12.
Lutskii, E.A. 1965. "Razvitie istoricheskoi kontseptsii M.N. Pokrovskogo." In M.V. Nechkina, ed., *Istoriia i istoriki.* Moscow.
Mamet, L., and A. Shestakov. 1927. Review of *Uchenie zapiski Instituta Istorii,* vol. 2 (1927). In *IM,* vol. 5, pp. 210–17.
Mariagin, D.A. 1965. *Postyshev.* Moscow.
Marko, Kurt. 1965. "History and Historians." *Survey,* vol. 56, p. 71–82.
Marksizm v shkole. 1925. Moscow-Leningrad.
Mazour, Anatole G. 1958. *Modern Russian Historiography.* New York.
———. 1971. *The Writing of History in the Soviet Union.* Stanford.
Mehnert, Klaus. 1952. *Stalin versus Marx.* Trans. from German. London.
Mekhlis, L. 1932. "Za likvidatsiiu otstavaniia istoricheskogo fronta." *Bol'shevik,* vols. 5–6, pp. 10–17.
Miliukov, P.N. 1937. "Velichie i padenie M.N. Pokrovskogo." *Sovremennye zapiski,* vol. 65, pp. 368–87.
Mints, I.I. 1944. "Emelian Mikhailovich Iaroslavskii (1878–1943)." *Izvestiia akademii nauk,* seriia istoriia i philosofii, vol. 1, pp. 16–25.
Moskovskii Voenno-Revoliustionnyi komitet: oktiabr'-noiabr' 1917 goda. 1968. Moscow.
Na boevom postu: K shestidesiatiletiiu D.B. Riazanova. 1930. Moscow.
Na boevom postu marksizma. 1929. Moscow.
"Na fronte istoricheskoi nauki." 1936. *Pravda,* 27 Jan.
Naidenov, M.E. 1961. "Problemy periodizatsii sovetskoi istoricheskoi nauki." *ISSSR,* vol. 1, pp. 81–96.
———. 1966. "O leninskom etape v istoricheskom nauke." *VI,* vol. 2, pp. 21–37.
———, ed. 1967. *Ocherki po istoriografii sovetskogo obshchestva.* Moscow.
Nauka i nauchnye rabotniki SSSR. 1925–34. Leningrad. 4 vols.
"Nauka russkoi istorii." 1928. In V.P. Volgin et al., eds., *Obshchestvennye nauki SSSR, 1917–1927.* Moscow.
Nicolaevsky, B. 1954. "Iz istorii ezhevshchiny: padenie Postysheva." Review of H. Kostiuk, *The Fall of Postyshev.* In *Sotsialisticheskii vestnik,* vol. 12, pp. 237–40.

————. 1965. *Power and the Soviet Elite*. Janet Zagoria, ed. New York.

Nosov, A.P. 1967. "Leninskie printsipi vospitaniia kadrov istorikov-marksistov." *Trudy Moskovskogo Gosudarstvennogo istoriko-arkhivnogo instituta*, vol. 25, pp. 31–61.

————, and A.N. Zakharikov. 1962. *Nekotorye voprosy bor'by KPSS za marksistskoe osveshchenie istorii bol'shevizma (1928–1932)*. Moscow.

Novinskii, N. 1933. "Bol'nye voprosy nauchnoi obshchestvennosti." *Front nauki i tekhniki*, vols. 10–11, pp. 27–32.

Ob aziatckom sposobe proizvodstva. 1930. Tiflis.

Obshchestvennye nauki SSSR, 1917–1927. 1928. Moscow.

Obsuzhdenie stat'i S.M. Dubrovskogo "Akademik M.N. Pokrovskii i ego rol' v razvitii sovetskii istoricheskoi nauki." 1962. *VI*, vol. 3, pp. 31–40.

Ocherki istorii istoricheskoi nauki v SSSR. 1955–66. Moscow, 4 vols.

Ocherki po istorii sovetskoi nauki i kul'tury. 1968. Moscow.

"O meropriatiakh po ukrepleniu nauchnoi raboty v sviazy s itogami 2-i vsesoiuznoi konferentsii marksistsko-leninskikh nauchno-issledovatel'-akikh uchrezhdenii." 1929. *Pravda*, 13 July.

"O postanovke partiinoi propagandy v sviazi s vypuskom Kratkogo Kursa istorii VKP(b)." 1954. In *KPSS v rezoliutsiiakh i resheniiakh s'ezdov, konferentsii i plenumov Ts. K*, vol. 3, pp. 316–32.

"O prepodavanii grazhdanskoi istorii v shkolakh SSSR." 1934. *Pravda*, 16 May.

Pamiaty M.N. Pokrovskogo. 1932. Moscow.

Pankratova, A.M. 1932. "M.N. Pokrovskii, bol'shevik-istorik." *BK*, vol. 4, pp. 20–35.

————. 1934. "Novye problemy istoricheskoi nauki v SSSR." *VKA*, vol. 4, pp. 64–77.

Pervaia oblastnaia konferentsiia istorikov-marksistov, Ts. Ch. O. 1934. Voronezh.

"Pervaia vsesiouznaia konferentsiia marksistsko-leninskikh nauchno-issledovatel'skikh uchrezhdenni." 1928. *VKA*, vol. 26, pp. 239–94.

Plan rabot Kommunisticheskoi akademii na 1927–1928 god. 1927. Moscow.

Plan rabot Kommunisticheskoi akademii na 1928–1929 god. 1928. Moscow.

Plan rabot Kommunisticheskoi akademii na 1929–1930 god. 1930. Moscow.

Platonov, S.F. 1927. "Istoriia." In *Akademiia nauk SSSR za 10 let, 1917–1927*. Leningrad.

Pokrovskii, M.N., ed. 1903. "Miestnoe samoupravlenie v drevnei Rusi." In *Melkaia zemskaia edinitsa v 1902–1903 gg.*, 2d ed. St. Petersburg, pp. 202–32.

————. 1907. Preface to K. Levin, *Politicheskaia partii v Rossii*. Moscow.

————. 1910–14. *Russkaia istoriia s drevneishikh vremen*. Moscow, 5 vols. English translation: 1931. *History of Russia from the Earliest Times to the Rise of Commercial Capitalism*. New York.

————. 1917. "Evropa i Vtoraia revoliutsiia." *Izvestiia soveta rabochikh Deputatov*, no. 199, 28 Oct.

————. 1920. *Ekonomicheskii materializm*. Petrograd.

————. 1920a. "Zadachi vyshei shkoly v nastoiashchii moment (pis'mo s'ezdu Kommunisticheskogo studenchestva)." *Narodnoe prosveshchenie*, vols. 18–19–20, pp. 3–9.

————. 1920–23. *Russkaia istoriia v samom szhatom ocherke*. Moscow, 3 vols. English translation: 1933. *Brief History of Russia*. London, 2 vols.

————. 1922a. "Otkuda vzialas' vneklassovaia teoriia razvitiia samoderzhaviia?" *Vestnik sotsialisticheskoi akademii*, vol. 1, pp. 40–54.

————. 1922b. "Piataia godovshchina Oktiabr'skoi revoliutsii i chetvertii kongress Kominterna." *Sputnik kommunista*, vol. 18, pp. 17–45.

————. 1922c. "Pravda li, shto v Rossii absolutizm 'sushchestvoval naperekor obshchestvennomu razvitiiu'?" *Krasnaia nov'*, vol. 3, pp. 144–51.

————. 1923a. *Bor'ba Klassov i russkaia istoricheskaia literatura*. Petrograd.

————. 1923b. *Diplomatiia i voina tsarskoi Rossii v XIX stoletii*. Moscow.

————. 1924a. "Kak voznikla Sovestskaia vlast v Moskve." *Pravda*, 6–7 Nov.

————. 1924b. *Ocherki russkogo revoliutsionnogo dvizheniia XIX-XX* vv. Moscow.

————. 1924c. "O pol'ze kritiki, ob absolutizme, imperializme, muzhitskom kapitalizme i o prochem." *Pod znamenem marksizma*, vol. 12, pp. 250–59.

————. 1924d. "Po povodu stat'i tovarishcha Rubinshteina." *Pod znamenem marksizma*, vols. 10–11, pp. 209–12.

————. 1924e. Letter to the editor of *Proletarskaia revoliutsiia*. *PR*, vol. 7, p. 286.

————. 1924f. *Ocherki istorii russkoi kul'turi*, 6th ed. Moscow.

————. 1925a. "K voprosu ob osobennostiakh istoricheskogo razvitiia Rossii." *Pod znamenem marksizma*, vol. 4, pp. 123–41, vol. 5, pp. 89–109.

————. 1925b. "K voprosu o znachenii revoliutsii 1905 goda." *Pechat' i revoliutsiia*, vol. 8, pp. 1–13.

————. 1925c. "Predposylki i rezul'taty revoliutsii 1905g." *Pravda*, 18 Dec.

————, ed. 1926. "Iaponskaia voina." In *1905: Istoriia revoliutsionnogo dvizheniia v otdel'nikh ocherkakh*. Moscow-Leningrad.

————, ed. 1927a. *Ocherki po istorii oktiabr'skoi revoliutsii*. Moscow, 2 vols.

————. 1927b. "Oktiabr'skaia revoliutsiia v izobrazheniiakh sovremennikov." *IM*, vol. 5, pp. 3–35.

————. 1928a. "Klassovaia bor'ba i ideologicheskii front." *Pravda*, 7 Nov.

————. 1928b. "Novye techeniia v russkoi istoricheskoi literature." *IM*, vol. 7, pp. 3–17.

————. 1928c. "Obshchestvennye nauki v SSSR za desiat' let." *VKA*, vol. 26, pp. 3–30.

————. 1929a. "O poezdke v Oslo." *VKA*, vol. 30, pp. 231–37.

————. 1929b. *Oktiabr'skaia revoliutsiia*. Moscow.

————. 1930a. "Ob odnom opyte avtobiografii." *Bol'shevik*, vols. 7–8, pp. 129–45. Abridged translation in *Labour Monthly*, vol. 9, 1930, pp. 569–73.

————. 1930b. "Ocherednye zadachi istorikov-marksistov." *IM*, vol. 16, pp. 3–19.

————. 1930c. "Vozniknovenie moskovskogo gosudarstva i Veliko-russkaia narodnost." *IM*, vol. 28–29, pp. 14–28.

————. 1930d. "Rol' istoricheskoi nauki v usloviiakh sotsialisticheskogo stroitel'stva." *Biulleten' zaochnoi konsul'tatsii IKP*, vol. 4, pp. 6–9.

————. 1930e. "Rol' rabochego klassa v revoliutsii 1905g." *VKA*, vol. 42, pp. 3–19.

————. 1931a. "Lenin i istoriia." *BK*, vol. 1, pp. 1–7.

————. 1931b. "O russkom feodalizme, proizkhozhdenii i kharaktere absolutizma v Rossii." *BK*, vol. 2, pp. 78–98.

————. 1931c. "O zadachakh marksistskoi istoricheskoi nauki v rekonstruktivnyi period." *IM*, vol. 21, pp. 3–7.

————. 1932. "Po povodu nekotoroi putantsy." *IM*, vols. 2–3, pp. 13–25.

————. 1933a. *Istoricheskaia nauka i bor'ba klassov*. Moscow, 2 vols.

————. 1933b. "Neopublikovannye zakliuchitel'nye slova na seminarakh v IKP istorii." *IM*, vol. 3, pp. 73–78.

————. 1933c. "Rechi M.N. Pokrovskogo v obshchestve istorikov-marksistov." *BK*, vol. 5, pp. 68–76.

————. 1933d. *O Lenine*. Moscow.

————. 1934. *Imperialisticheskaia voina*. Moscow.

————. 1935. *Ob Ukraine: sbornik statei i materialov*. Edited by N.N. Popov. Kiev.

————. 1958a. "Dokladnaia zapiska rektora IKP M.N. Pokrovskogo v Sekretariat Ts. K. VKP(b) ob itogakh raboty instituta za 1921–1928 gg." In *Istoricheskii arkhiv*, vol. 6, pp. 84–90.

————. 1958b. "Kak rozhdalsia Imperializm." *Komsomolskaia pravda*, 22 April.

————. 1965–67. *Izbrannye proizvedeniia*. Moscow, 4 vols.

————. 1968. "Pis'mo M.N. Pokrovskogo S.P. Mel'gunovu." *Sovetskie arkhivy*, vol. 3.

——. 1969. "Lenin i vysshaia shkola." In *Nash Il'ich: Moskvichi O Lenine*. Moscow.
——. 1970. *Russia in World History: Selected Essays*. Roman Szporluk, ed. and trans. Ann Arbor.
Pol', K. 1931. "Bol'shevikii dovoennyi II Internatsional." *PR*, vols. 2–3, pp. 22–58; 4–5, pp. 35–79.
Popov, N.N. 1934. *Outline History of the Communist Party of the Soviet Union*, 2 vols. Moscow-Leningrad.
"Postanovlenie Ts. K. VKP(b) ot 15 Marta 1931 po dokladu presidiuma Kommunisticheskoi Akademii." 1931. *Pravda*, 20 March.
"Postanovlenie zhiuri Pravitel'stvennoi komissi po Konkursu na luchii uchebnik dlia 3 i 4 klassov srednei shkoly po istorii SSSR." 1937. *Pravda*, 22 Aug.
Prigozhin, A.G. 1933. *Karl Marks i problema sotsial'no-ekonomicheskikh formatsii*. Leningrad.
Protiv istoricheskoi kontseptsii M.N. Pokrovskogo; Protiv antimarksistskikh kontseptsii M.N. Pokrovskogo. 1939–40. Moscow-Leningrad.
Protiv mekhanisticheskoi teorii v istoricheskoi literature. 1930. Moscow.
Protokoly pervogo s'ezda arkhivnykh deiatelei RSFSR. 1926. Moscow.
Pundeff, Marin, ed. 1967. *History in the U.S.S.R.: Selected Readings*. San Francisco.
Radek, K. 1936. "Znachenie istorii dlia revoliutsionnogo proletariata." *Pravda*, 27 Jan.
"Rezoliutsiia fraktsii obshchestva istorikov-marksistov po dokladu T. Knorina." 1932. *Teoreticheskii front*, vol. 3, no. 17.
"Rezoliutsiia obshchego sobraniia iacheiki Istoricheskogo Instituta Krasnoi Professory po dokladu o politicheskikh itogakh obsuzhdeniia pis'ma T. Stalina." 1931. *Teoreticheskii front*, vol. 2, no. 14.
"Rezoliutsiia Prezidiuma Komakademii o polozhenii i zadachakh na fronte istorii zapada." *VKA*, vols. 8–9.
"Rol' istoricheskoi nauki v usloviiakh sotsialisticheskogo stroitel'stva." 1930. *Biulletin' zaochnoi konsul'tatsii IKP*, vol. 4.
Rubinshtein, N.L. 1941. *Russkaia istoriografiia*. Moscow.
Sauer, Marian. 1977. "The Concept of the Asiatic Mode of Production and Contemporary Marxism." In Shlomo Avineri, ed., *Varieties of Marxism*. The Hague, pp. 333–72.
Serebriakov, G. 1963. "Mikhail Nikolaevich Pokrovskii." *Literaturnaia Rossia*, 28 June.
"Sergei Ivanovich Mitskevich." 1967. *ISSSR*, vol. 2, pp. 111–18.
Shapiro, A.L. 1962. *Russkaia istoriografiia v period imperializma*. Leningrad.
Shestakov, A. 1929. "Na istoricheskom fronte." *Novyi mir*, vol. 2, pp. 236–42.
Shteppa, Konstantin F. 1963. *Russian Historians and the Soviet State*. New Brunswick, N.J.
Sidorenko, A.A. 1969. "Osveshenie vneshnei politiki tsarizma v rabotakh M.N. Pokrovskogo, 1907–1917gg." *Uchenie zapiski moskovskogo gosvdar'stvennogo pedagogicheskogo instituta*, vol. 309, pp. 18–51.
Sidorov, A.L. 1964. "Nekotorye razmyshleniia o trude i opyte istorika." *ISSSR*, vol. 3, pp. 118–38.
——. 1971. *Istoricheskie predposylki oktiabr'skoi Sotsialisticheskoi revoliutsii*. Moscow.
Slepkov, A.N. 1924a. Review of Pokrovskii's *Ocherki russkogo revoliutsionnogo dvizheniia XIX-XX vv. Bol'shevik*, vol. 14, pp. 113–21.
——. 1924b. Review of "Stalin: O Lenine i Leninizme." *Bol'shevik*, vol. 9, pp. 102–5.
——. 1925. "Ne soglasnyi." *Bol'shevik*, vols. 5–6, pp. 65–73.
——. 1926. "K voprosu evoliutsii samoderzhaviia." *Bol'shevik*, vol. 5, pp. 88–97.
Slutskii, A. 1930. "Bol'sheviki o germanskoi sotsial-demokratii v periodr ee predvoennogo krizisa." *PR*, vol. 6, pp. 38–72.
Sokolov, O.D. 1962. "Ob istoricheskikh vzgliadov M.N. Pokrovskogo." *Kommunist*, vol. 4, pp. 69–79.

————. 1963. Lenin i formirovanie bol'shevitskikh vzgliadov M.N. Pokrovskogo." *VI*, vol. 8, pp. 30–41.

————. 1964. "Revoliutsioner, uchenyi, gosudarstvennyi deiatel." *Voprosy istorii KPSS*, vol. 5, pp. 81–85.

————. 1966. Preface to Pokrovskii's *Izbrannye proizvedeniia*, vol. 1. Moscow.

————. 1967. "Mikhail Nikolaevich Pokrovskii." *ISSSR*, vol. 1, pp. 117–22.

————. 1969. "M.N. Pokrovskii: vydaiushchiisia organizator nauchno—issledovatel'skoi raboti." *VI*, vol. 6, pp. 30–45.

————. 1969a. "Bor'ba M.N. Pokrovskogo protiv dvoriansko-burzhuaznoi istoriografii." *ISSSR*, vol. 5, pp. 33–47.

————. 1970. *M.N. Pokrovskii i Sovetskaia istoricheskaia nauka.* Moscow.

Spornye voprosy metodologii istorii. 1930. Leningrad.

Stalin, J. 1953. *Problems of Leninism.* Moscow.

————. 1954. *Works,* vol. 7. Moscow.

Starikov, N.V., compiler. n.d. *M.N. Pokrovskii—Vydaiushchisia deiatel' sovetskoi Kul'turi i prosvescheniia (k stoletiiu s dnia rozhdeniia 29/VIII 1868 g—29/VIII 1968 g.) Materialy k nauchnoi bibliografii* 61 pp. Unpublished mss. in Lenin Library.

Storozhev, V.N., ed. 1898. *Russkaia istoriia s drevneishikh vremen do smutnogo vremeni.* Moscow.

Szporluk, Roman. 1964. "Pokrovsky and Russian History." *Survey*, vol. 53, pp. 107–18.

————. 1967. "Pokrovskii's View of the Russian Revolution." *Slavic Review*, vol. 1, pp. 70–85.

————. 1971. "Pokrovsky's *Selected Works.*" *Slavic Review*, vol. 30, pp. 649–55.

Tarle, E.V. 1927. *Evropa v epokhu imperializma.* Moscow.

————. 1928. "K voprosu o nachale voiny." *IM*, vol. 9, pp. 101–7.

————, et al., eds. 1943. *Iubeleinaia sessiia AN SSSR.* Moscow-Leningrad.

Tarnovskii, K.N. 1964. *Sovetskaia istoriografiia rossiiskogo imperializma.* Moscow.

Tchernavin, V.V. 1935. *I Speak for the Silent Prisoners of the Soviets.* Boston and New York. Appendix, "The Academic Case," pp. 359–68.

Teodorovich, A.I. 1929. "Istoricheskoe znachenie partii narodnoi voli." *Katorga i ssylka,* vols. 57–58, pp. 7–44.

————. 1930. *Istoricheskoe znachenie partii narodnoi voli.* Moscow.

"Tezisy k 50 letiiu Narodnoi voli." 1930. *Pravda,* 9 April.

Tillet, Lowell. 1969. *The Great Friendship: Soviet Historians on the Non-Russian Nationalities.* Chapel Hill, N.C.

Tokin, I. 1932. "O Bol'shevitskoi partiinosti: istoricheskoi nauki." *BK*, vols. 9–10, pp. 38–70.

Tomsinskii. S.G. 1926. "K voprosu o sotsial'noi prirode russkogo samoderzhaviia." *VKA,* vol. 15, pp. 255–84.

"Traurnyi vecher Pamiati M.N. Pokrovskogo." 1932. *VKA,* vols. 4–5, pp. 31–63.

Treskova, O.V., ed. 1973. "Dokumenty ob uchastii sovetskikh uehenykh v VI mezhdunaradnom kongresse istoricheskikh nauk." *Sovetskie arkhivy,* vol. 6, pp. 50–55.

Trotsky, L.D. 1937. *The Stalin School of Falsification.* New York.

Trudy pervoi vsesoiuznoi konferentsii istorikov-marksistov. 1930. Moscow, 2 vols.

Urban, Pavel. 1958. "Re-Stalinization of Soviet Historical Science." Institute for the Study of the U.S.S.R. *Bulletin,* vol. 5, pp. 45–52.

Utechin, S.V. 1958. "Bolsheviks and Their Allies after 1917: The Ideological Pattern." *Soviet Studies,* vol. 10, pp. 113–35.

————. 1964. *Russian Political Thought: A Concise History.* New York.

Vaganov, F.M. 1969. *Moskovskie bol'sheviki v bor'be s pravym i "levym" opportunizmom.* Moscow.

————. 1970. *Pravyi uklon i ego razgrom.* Moscow.

Vainshtein, O.L. 1966. "Stanovlenie sovetskoi istoricheskoi nauki (20-e gody)." *VI*, vol. 7, pp. 32–47.

———. 1968. *Istoriia sovetskoi medievistiki, 1917–1966*. Leningrad.

"V chem delo, kak podgotovliaetsia nauchnaia smena (za kulisami RANIONa)." 1928. *Vecherniaia moskva*, 6 Feb.

Voprosy prepodavaniia istoricheskikh distsiplin. 1926. Moscow.

Voprosy prepodavaniia leninizma, istorii VKP(b), kominterna. 1930. Moscow.

Vsesoiuznoe soveshchanie istorikov. 1964. Moscow.

Wolfe, Bertram. 1955. *Three Who Made a Revolution*. New York.

"Za boevuiu perestroiku istoricheskogo fronta." 1932. *BK*, vols. 2–3, pp. 8–16.

"Zadachi marksistskoe-leninskoi nauki po istorii zapada." 1931. *Bol'shevik*, vol. 11, pp. 68–79.

Zaidel, G. 1932. "M.N. Pokrovskii, istorik-bol'shevik." *PM*, vols. 1–2, pp. 3–23.

"Zamechaniia o konspekte uchebnika novoi istorii." 1936. *Pravda*, 27 Jan. Signed by Stalin, Kirov, and Zhdanov, 9 Aug. 1934.

"Zamechaniia po povodu konspekta uchebnika po istorii SSSR." 1936. *Pravda*, 27 Jan. Signed by Stalin, Zhdanov, and Kirov, 8 Aug. 1934.

"Zapadno-istoricheskaia nauka na povorote (k itogam diskussi na zapadno-istoricheskom fronte)." 1931. *Biulleten' zaochnoi konsul'tatsii*, vol. 7, pp. 8–14.

"Za povorot k boevym zadacham kominterna." 1931. *PR*, vols. 4–5, pp. 3–34.

Za povorot na fronte estestvoznaniia: Diskussiia na zasedaniiakh Presidiuma Komakademii 23/XII 1930g.–6 II 1931 g. 1931. Moscow-Leningrad.

"Za reshitel'nuiu perestroiku istoricheskogo fronta." 1932. *IM*, vols. 23–24.

Index